D1720148

Vierteljahrshefte zur Wirtschaftsforschung 4.2018

European banking landscape between diversity, competition and concentration

Duncker & Humblot · Berlin

DIW Berlin – Deutsches Institut
für Wirtschaftsforschung e. V.

Mohrenstraße 58, 10117 Berlin
Tel. +49-30-8 97 89-0
Fax +49-30-8 97 89-200
www.diw.de

PUBLISHERS
Prof. Marcel Fratzscher, Ph. D, Präsident des DIW Berlin
Prof. Dr. Martin Gornig, stellvertretender Leiter der Abteilung Unternehmen und Märkte am DIW Berlin
Prof. Dr. Claudia Kemfert, Leiterin der Abteilung Energie, Verkehr, Umwelt am DIW Berlin
Prof. Dr. Alexander Kritikos, Leiter der Forschungsgruppe Entrepeneurship am DIW Berlin
Prof. Dr. Stefan Liebig, Direktor der Längsschnittstudie Sozio-oekonomisches Panel (SOEP) am DIW Berlin
Prof. Dr. Lukas Menkhoff, Leiter der Abteilung Weltwirtschaft am DIW Berlin
Dr. Claus Michelsen, Leiter der Abteilung Konjunkturpolitik am DIW Berlin
Prof. Dr. Dorothea Schäfer, Forschungsdirektorin Finanzmärkte am DIW Berlin (Editor in chief)

Prof. Dr. Bernhard Emunds, Philosophisch-Theologische Hochschule Sankt Georgen
Prof. Thomas Gehrig, Ph. D., Universität Wien, Österreich
Prof. Dr. Horst Gischer, Universität Magdeburg
Prof. Hans-Helmut Kotz, Sustainable Architecture for Finance in Europe (SAFE)
Prof. Dr. Doris Neuberger, Universität Rostock
Prof. Dr. Andreas Pfingsten, Universität Münster
Prof. Andreas Stephan, Ph. D., Universität Jönköping, Schweden

Responsible for the current issue
Prof. Hans-Helmut Kotz
Prof. Dr. Dorothea Schäfer

SALE AND DISTRIBUTION
VERLAG DUNCKER & HUMBLOT GMBH
Carl-Heinrich-Becker-Weg 9
12165 Berlin

Copyright
© 2019 Duncker & Humblot GmbH

DESIGN
Edenspiekermann

LAYOUT AND COMPOSITION
Alfred Gutzler
Ellen Müller-Gödtel

PRINT
2019 bei CPI buchbücher.de gmbh, Birkach

Printed in Germany
Printed on FSC-certified paper

ISSN 0340-1707 (Print) / 1861-1559 (Online)
ISBN 978-3-428-15852-2

European banking landscape between diversity, competition and concentration

HANS-HELMUT KOTZ AND DOROTHEA SCHÄFER

Hans-Helmut Kotz, Center for European Studies, Harvard University, Cambridge, MA, SAFE Policy Center, Goethe-Universität, Frankfurt a. M., e-mail: kotz@fas.harvard.edu
Dorothea Schäfer, German Institute for Economic Research DIW Berlin, CeFEO at Jönköping International Business School and CERBE Center for Relationship Banking and Economics, Rom, e-mail: dschaefer@diw.de

The consequences of diversity over a number of pertinent dimensions is often not adequately acknowledged in economics. As Reinhard H. Schmidt (in this issue) states: "*One could easily cite important recent research contributions with no traces of institutions and institutional differences of any kind and instead just one 'representative agent' living and operating in an institution-free idealized economic environment, an environment without any diversity.*" In reality, however, institutional variety, via its impact on incentives and cost of transactions, obviously has a defining bearing on economic outcomes. This perspective has been stressed by the new institutional economics. The relevance of institutional variety has also been acknowledged in finance (Allen and Gale 2000, Levine et al. 1999), this always held true for economic historians, here Gerschenkron is one of the best-known examples. In the "purer" domains of economics, however, for a long time, research revolved largely around the rather simplistic and binary comparison between bank-based versus market-based financial systems. The Great Financial Crisis has relaunched interest in the debate on the comparative efficiency of financial institutions (intermediaries as well as markets). Interestingly, whereas institutions betting on newfangled instruments fared badly, "boring" banks performed rather well. Of course, they could not escape second-round effects. But they have proven to be more resilient. This also held true at a systemic level. Here, institutional variety has apparently proven beneficial. Given this background, it is somehow surprising that, although the interest in the importance of institutional diversity for the functionality of financial systems has increased, research is still scarce and work on the topic is still pioneering. Therefore, the aim of this issue is to motivate and pave the way for more research on institutional diversity in banking and finance.

The volume starts with "Diversity in finance: An overview" on the different dimensions of institutional diversity. *Reinhard H. Schmidt* finds a decreasing within-country diversity in most countries of Western Europe as large, publicly owned and shareholder value-oriented banks have gained in importance at the expense of banks pursuing a broader, stakeholder value-oriented perspective. The between-country diversity has also declined as national banking systems have become more similar over time. Only in Germany and Austria within-country diversity has remained high. Schmidt identifies also substantial differences in Western European countries' financial systems despite a common trend towards a stronger capital market orientation. On a world-wide scale, between-regions diversity of financial systems is high and almost stable. Schmidt concedes that an overall assessment of dangers and merits of diversity is difficult to establish since we know too little about how differences in institutional diversity affect economic outcomes. However, he emphasizes that *"preserving diversity now is a protection against the risk of later not having something that one might later need even though one does not know now that one will later need it"*.

Giovanni Ferri and *Doris Neuberger* explore the relationship between banking sector diversity and the two most important EU-wide regulatory frameworks for European financial sectors. In their work "How does banking diversity fit in the general vision inspiring the joint process of Banking Union and Capital Markets Union?" they identify the Global Financial Crisis of 2008/2009 and the Euro sovereign debt crisis of 2010/2012 as important drivers for EU-wide institution building. The authors claim, however, that experience made with both efforts calls for a reassessment and reform. In particular, Ferri und Neuberger discuss two unintended side-effects: the tendency of CMU to push financial systems toward market-based systems and the tendency of BU to weaken institutional diversity in the banking sector. They conclude that even if CMU and BU were economically successful, more effort is needed to align both frameworks with social and cultural goals that are an essential part of EU treaties.

Horst Gischer and *Christian Ilchmann* examine in their paper "Banking sector diversity and socioeconomic structure—criteria for matching pairs" whether and how the fit (or lack thereof) of the banking sector and the socioeconomic structure of a country are conducive to economic prospects. By applying a cluster analysis, the authors develop a coherent system of geographic, social and economic characteristics of real economies and assess to what extend EU banking sectors and real economies are "matching pairs".

Andreas Bley studies in his contribution "Limited diversity—business models of German cooperative banks" the degree of diversity within the German cooperative banking pillar. His empirical findings reveal a limited variety in business models applied across institutions. Almost all cooperative banks concentrate on the lending and deposit-taking business with customers. However, some degree of diversity is identifiable. Lending is the dominant item on the balance sheets of one group while in the other group deposits dominate. Bley stresses the importance of the proportionality principle in banking regulation and supervision in order to avoid further disadvantages for smaller institutions.

Franz Flögel and *Stefan Gärtner* present a study on diversity of the UK banking sector. In the work "Lost diversity—business lending in the centralized banking system of the UK", the authors classify the distance between lenders and SMEs in credit decisions for different types of lenders. They find that short distance lenders, such as local banks, have almost completely disappeared in the UK. This loss of proximity comes with costs in terms of access to funds. Therefore, they suggest restoring short distance lending in the country but concede that the running of regional banks is challenging in times of low interest rates and tightened bank regulation.

Karl-Peter Schackmann-Fallis and *Mirko Weiß* remind the reader in their work "Post-financial crisis times: Only a short phase of re-intermediation and re-direction to boring banking business models? Regulatory burden, fintech competition and concentration processes" that some legislators expressed their will to restore the "boring" business model of deposit-based lending when the crisis peaked. The authors assess to what extent legislators have met this objective. They argue that the post-crisis regulation has increased the minimum bank size required for doing business in the banking sector and has initiated a wave of mergers, in particular among small institutions. In addition, policymakers rehabilitated loan securitization without providing an appropriate framework to avoid the inherent incentive to primarily securitize the more vulnerably and risky cash-flows. The authors conclude that the European Union's regulatory framework has so far turned out ineffective in allowing for or even fostering heterogeneous and small-scale market structures and in fostering business models focusing on deposit-based lending.

Mechthild Schrooten examines in "Finance and growth—shortly reconsidered" whether the paradigm of the 1980s and 90s, i. e. that financial development is a major determinant of economic growth and productivity in a country, still holds. This question is important given that the international crisis 2007/8 has clearly revealed the dark side of financial development and credit booms. In her empirical analysis, Schrooten focusses on post-crisis developments and finds that the finance-growth nexus has widely disappeared in the years after the crisis 2007/8.

Axel Bertuch-Samuels' work "Why we should embrace institutional diversity in banking" emphasizes the importance of institutionally diversified financial sectors for sustainable growth and financial stability. The author examines the factors which contributed to the successful evolution of the German savings banks and credit cooperatives over a period of more than 200 years. These factors of success are *"the concentration of their banking activities on a limited geographical region while working as a network of cooperating autonomous institutions, the prioritization of savings mobilization, a mandate to serve the economic and social well-being of the local region, while remaining profitable and financially viable over the long run rather than narrowly focusing on profit maximization"*. The author emphasizes that those factors are crucial also for successful financial institution building and promotion of locally oriented microfinance and banking institutions in developing economies.

Lorenzo Bini Smaghi's article "What future for the European banking system?" provides a contrasting view on the question of what institutional structure the European banking sector(s) needs/ (need). He explores the main factors underlying the decreasing profitability of European banks. Bini Smaghi emphasizes the disadvantage of European banks vis-à-vis US-based banks in terms of interest rate environment, concentration of banking markets, differences in regulation and supervision as well as the existence of a deep and liquid capital market. The author infers from his analysis that true pan-European banks and a true capital markets union are required to strengthen the European banking system.

The volume closes with a note by *Hans-Helmut Kotz* and *Dorothea Schäfer*: "Diversity across EU banking sectors: Poorly researched and underappreciated". The authors take empirically stock of the across country diversity of banking sectors in the European Union before and after the financial crisis. Subsequently, they assess diversity across a number of dimensions (competition/efficiency, stability and business models) and highlight key issues and open questions for a future research agenda for evaluating the importance of diversity in the banking and the financial sectors of the European Union. Given the substantial complementarity between finance and other societal sub-systems, they emphasize the topic's pertinence far beyond the financial realm. Therefore, this is also a debate with high relevance for a general public.

References

— Allen, F., and D. Gale (2000): Comparing financial systems. Cambridge, MIT Press.
— Gerschenkron, A. (1962): Economic backwardness in historical perspective. A book of essays. Cambridge, MA, Harvard UP.
— Levine, R. (2005): Finance and growth: Theory and evidence. In: P. Aghion and S. Durlauf (eds.): Handbook of Economic Growth. Volume 1A. Amsterdam, Elsevier, 865–934.

Diversity in finance: An overview

REINHARD H. SCHMIDT

Reinhard H. Schmidt, Goethe-Universität Frankfurt, e-mail: schmidt@finance.uni-frankfurt.de

Summary: This paper aspires to provide an overview of the issue of diversity of banking and financial systems and its development over time from a positive and a normative perspective. In other word: how different are banks within a given country and how much do banking systems and entire financial systems differ between countries and regions, and do in-country diversity and between-country diversity change over time, as one would be inclined to expect as a consequence of globalization and increasingly global standards of regulation? The general answer to these questions is that there is still today a surprisingly high level of diversity in finance. This raises the two questions addressed in the second part of the paper: How can the persistence of diversity be explained, and how can it be assessed? In contrast to prevailing views, the author argues that persistent diversity should be regarded as valuable in a context in which there is no clear answer to the question of which structures of banking and financial systems are optimal from an economic perspective.

Zusammenfassung: Der Beitrag behandelt die Unterschiedlichkeit – oder Diversität – von Bank- und Finanzsystemen in Deutschland, der Europäischen Union und weltweit und deren Veränderungen im Zeitablauf. Damit wird zugleich die Frage angesprochen, ob sich die Bank- und Finanzsysteme im Zeitablauf aneinander angleichen. Allgemein wird vermutet, dass unter dem Einfluss der Globalisierung und der zunehmend international werdenden Regulierung Unterschiede immer mehr verschwinden und dass dies wirtschaftspolitisch wünschenswert ist. Der empirische Befund ist allerdings, dass das Ausmaß der Diversität in den letzten Jahren erstaunlich wenig abgenommen hat. Dies wirft die zwei Fragen auf, denen der zweite Teil des Beitrags gewidmet ist: Wie ist es zu erklären, dass sich eine höhere Diversität erhalten hat, als weithin vermutet wird, und wie ist Diversität im Finanzsektor zu bewerten? Dazu argumentiert der Verfasser, dass es angesichts der Tatsache, dass man nicht weiß und nicht wissen kann, welche Strukturen im Finanzsektor optimal sind, Diversität ökonomisch als vorteilhaft und damit als erhaltenswert einzustufen ist.

→ JEL classification: F02, F39 und G16
→ Keywords: Financial systems, diversity, convergence

I Introduction

I.I Diversity as a largely neglected topic in economics

One can hardly overlook that these days diversity is a hot topic—though not in economics. The outcome of the recent mid-term elections for the US Congress that seems to have attracted more attention than any other one is an "increase in diversity": The share of members in both houses of the US Congress who are not elderly white men is now higher than it has ever been. It is also widely discussed among experts and in the general public that there has recently been a loss of diversity in nature, due among other things to the use of powerful pesticides and other agricultural inputs.

It is so evident what diversity means in these contexts that it does not even require a definition, let alone a well-defined measure, of diversity. Moreover, most references to diversity in this broad sense do not only mention facts but also include value judgements: more women in Congress or in corporate boards and more different species of plants and animals on a given area of land are simply good.

It would go too far to say that diversity is completely ignored in economics. However, in itself diversity in that sphere of reality economics deals with rarely attracts attention among economists. The more respect formal and abstract models and the statistical significance of econometric findings are gaining, the more economists seem to lose sight of the fact that countries, firms, states and human actors differ in many respects. One could easily cite important recent research contributions with no traces of institutions and institutional differences of any kind and instead just one "representative agent" living and operating in an institution-free idealized economic environment, an environment without any diversity.[1]

Of course, microeconomics and the theories of international trade, competition policy and distribution cannot address their topics without accepting the fact that countries, firms and human beings differ. However, even there diversity is not per se an interesting issue but rather only one among other starting points of the analysis.

This neglect of heterogeneity/differences/diversity in today's economic discourse stands in a marked contrast to other social sciences that have always laid much more focus on how different countries and their institutional features, firms and their structures and strategies and human actors and their endowments, expectations and aspirations are. For instance, within jurisprudence there is a well-established sub-discipline called comparative law with its own journals, chairs and conferences. Equally, the presumed fact that there are different "varieties of capitalism" and its implications for economic development and welfare have for many years held a top position among research topics in sociology and political science.[2] In contrast, works on comparative economics are rare exceptions and therefore diversity per se hardly has a place within the universe of economic science.

---

1   This critical remark mainly refers to the so-called new macroeconomics. However, Binder et al. (2017) show that this line of research is no longer state of the art and therefore the critique does no longer fully apply.

2   Standard sources include Hall and Soskice (2001) and Amable (2003).

1.2   Diversity in finance

There is one field of economics to which the above assessment that diversity hardly matters does no longer apply, namely finance. The modern debate[3] started with the empirical work of King and Levine (1993) on the relationship between finance and development and growth in the early 1990s and the theoretically oriented landmark book "Comparing Financial Systems" by Allen and Gale from 2000. Together with various coauthors, Levine and Allen have since that time continued to investigate financial systems and their diversity in empirical as well as theoretical studies. Boot and Thakor (e.g. 1997) have made important theoretical contributions to our understanding of "financial system architecture". Corbett and Jenkinson (1997) have analyzed "how investment is financed" in the major economies. Hackethal et al. (2002) have investigated whether the financial systems of different EU countries have become more similar as a consequence of globalization and European economic integration. And ten years after Allen and Gale, two monographs explicitly addressed the "diversity of banking systems in Europe"[4].

The interest in comparative finance has been stimulated by the advances achieved in the so-called new institutional economics, a field which emphasizes the importance of information and incentives for economic cooperation and the role that institutions play in mitigating the negative consequences of asymmetrically distributed information and distorted incentives. This branch of economic theory provides the conceptual basis for taking institutions and institutional diversity seriously and in doing so permits to go beyond mere descriptions. Thus, it does not come as a surprise that even the recent editions of the well-known corporate finance textbook of Richard Brealey and Stewart Myers, in which Franklin Allen is now a coauthor (e.g. Brealey et al. 2019), has incorporated sections on financial systems and corporate governance from comparative perspective and that Jean Tirole's "Theory of Corporate Finance" (2006) starts out with more than one hundred pages which describe the diversity of financial and governance systems in different parts of the world. As these authors evidently see it, institutions matter more than most economists had acknowledged before; institutional frameworks differ more between countries than was known before; and understanding these differences is more important for anyone who is working in different financial systems or is involved in designing regulation for finance in different countries and regions than economists had believed and acknowledged for a long time.

1.3   Diversity, comparisons, development and convergence

What exactly is diversity and to what exactly does diversity in finance refer? Trying to answer these questions in some detail here serves to structure the debate at the upcoming DIW-conference in June and the analysis in the present paper. The concept of diversity relates to the fact that not all elements that belong to a given set are similar under certain aspects. As far as finance is concerned, it can relate to banking systems, financial sectors and even to entire financial systems or parts or elements of financial systems such as firms' financing patterns or corporate governance regimes. Moreover, one can look at diversity within a given country or region—henceforth called "in-country diversity"—and to different countries at the same time, labeled as "between-country diversity".

---

3   Of course there were precursors such as Goldsmith or Gurley and Shaw.

4   See Ayadi et al. (2009 and 2010). "Diversity" is also a part of the title of Michie (2011).

As a first level of analysis, one can for instance use the concept of in-country diversity to study how much the banks in a given country differ with respect to their business models, their sizes and complexity and their legal forms. Between-country diversity is almost by definition addressed when countries and their financial systems or some parts or aspects of these systems are compared. Do the predominant financing patterns of large corporations or their corporate governance regimes or even the type of the entire financial systems differ between countries?[5]

Interestingly, one can also combine in-country diversity and between country diversity in order to find out whether countries differ in terms of how diverse their banking systems are, as I will do in Section 2 of this paper.

It would be more than surprising if financial systems and their main elements did not change over time. The concept of diversity also lends itself to describing and analyzing financial system developments including the development of their diversity over time. For instance, one can analyze if the banks or the financing patterns or the corporate governance regimes of large corporations in a given country become more or less similar. And finally, and perhaps most importantly, one can also combine the comparison between countries and that over time to check if the diversity of the entire financial systems of different countries increases, decreases or stays the same. The concept of diversity thus offers a possibility to address the interesting issue of financial system convergence.

This conceptual basis shapes the structure of what is to follow in the remainder of the present article. In the next section I address the development of banking systems and of entire financial systems. The section starts with a look at banking systems and in-country diversity as well as between-country diversity and their respective developments and then turns to between-country diversity of financial systems and its development. As that section leads to the conclusion that there is a certain trend in the direction of convergence but that this trend is much weaker than one might expect, Section 3 discusses possible reasons for the surprising degree of persistence of a remarkable degree of diversity. Section 4 is dedicated to the assessment of (persistent) diversity both within and between countries and summarizes the main conclusions.

---

5   On financing patterns see Corbett and Jenkinson (1997), who argue that there are no systematic differences between countries, and Hackethal and Schmidt (2005), who show that, and why, this view is probably wrong. On national corporate governance regimes, see various articles in Gordon and Roe (2004), notably the reprint of the influential paper of Hansmann and Kraakman from 2000, in which the authors argue that national differences are no longer relevant, and the critique by Bebchuk and Roe. On types of financial systems see Rajan and Zingales (2003), who show that in the past the type of a country's financial systems is not constant over time, and Fohlin (2000) who in contrast identifies permanent patterns.

2 The development and diversity of banking and financial systems[6]

2.1 Banking systems

As is well known, the German banking system rests on three pillars, or, in more prosaic words, it consists of three groups of banks that differ with respect to the legal and ownership structure of a typical bank belonging to each of the groups.[7]

The first "pillar or group" comprises the private commercial banks. Roughly speaking, the entire group holds about 40 percent of all bank assets in Germany, and it can be subdivided into two parts, the small group of so-called big banks (*Großbanken*) and the large and rather heterogeneous group of "other" private credit institutions. In terms of bank assets, the two subgroups are about equally large. The big banks are true universal banks with relatively large branch networks throughout Germany and with a substantial presence in other countries in Europe and worldwide. As far as their legal and ownership structure are concerned, they are corporations subject to the German Corporate Code (*Aktiengesetz*). Their shares are listed and publicly traded and held by the general public and German and foreign institutional investors. By law and by now also in practice, these big banks are essentially managed in the interests of their shareholders, they are "shareholder value banks".[8]

The second "pillar" consists of the public banks that jointly form the savings bank group. Their combined total assets are more or less similar to those of the private commercial banks. The group of public banks can also be subdivided into two subgroups of about equal size in terms of assets. One subgroup comprises the local municipal savings banks, and the other one the public regional banks, called *Landesbanken*. Almost all savings banks are public law institutions, and the regional banks are either also public law institutions or corporations whose shares are held by the savings banks of their respective region and by the respective states (*Bundesländer*). Thus they all do not have private owners. By law and also in practice the public banks have a dual mandate. They are required to be successful as financial institutions and to support the respective local and regional economy. Thus they can be classified as "stakeholder value banks".

The third "pillar" or banking group is formed by the cooperative banks and their central financial and non-financial institutions. Their combined total assets are about half of those of the other two groups. Cooperatives must be successful as institutions and at the same time support the economic undertakings of their owners/members. Thus, like the savings banks, they are "stakeholder value banks".

With its three pillar structure the German banking system displays a high degree of diversity as far as legal forms, ownership structure and business objectives are concerned. Interestingly, the three-pillar structure has a long tradition. Savings banks came into existence in the early years of the 19th century, the first cooperative banks were created some 50 years later, and the group of

---

6   This section builds on Schmidt (2018).

7   As the wording suggests there are a few exceptions within each of the three groups.

8   This has not always been the case, as Kotz and Schmidt (2016) show. About 20 years ago, also big banks were more or less managed with an orientation to the public interest.

private big banks emerged after the first German unification in 1870/71. Thus the diversity of the German banking system has been largely the same since the late 19th century.[9]

How is the situation in other countries of Western Europe? Only 30 years ago, almost all countries of continental Western Europe had a three pillar banking structure that largely resembled that of Germany. Thus in-country diversity had been more or less equally high and also stable throughout the entire 20th century. This implies that as far as in-country diversity of banking systems is concerned, the between-country diversity was at a low level.

However, this is now a thing of the past. With the exception of Germany and Austria, all other countries have experienced fundamental changes in their respective banking systems. A common denominator is a substantial gain of importance of big private shareholder value-oriented banks at the expense of stakeholder value-oriented banks.[10] What does this mean for diversity? First of all, in-country diversity has decreased in a majority of countries. As far as between-country diversity is concerned the parallels in the direction and the timing of change suggest that the diversity between those countries in which fundamental changes occurred, has not changed. However, if one extends the comparison to those countries which have retained their three pillar systems one finds a gradual increase in between-country diversity.

How is the situation outside of Western Europe? Of course, countries differ greatly with respect to their national banking structures including the degree of in-country diversity. In the United States, we now find several very large strictly shareholder value-oriented commercial banks. One type of cooperative banks, the Savings and Loan Associations, had lost much of their former role after the crisis of the 1980s, and after the demise of the Glass-Steagall Act in 1999 the importance of small local private banks also declined. Thus in-country diversity has gone down. In the so-called third world countries, state-owned banks had played a strong role in the past. This is why they used to have substantial in-country diversity, and at least in this respect they were somewhat similar; that is, between-country diversity was relatively low so that about 25 years ago it was still possible to talk meaningfully about the "typical" developing country banking system.

But this has also changed in recent decades. Especially in former colonies and in countries with strong ties to the United States or their former colonial masters, a reform process like that in most of Western Europe has reshaped banking structures. Large private commercial banks have gained in size, market share and power, and other types or groups of banks, notably government-owned banks, have lost ground. As a consequence, in-country diversity has gone down in most countries. But since this process took effect in parallel in many parts of the world, between-country diversity may have also decreased. The common trend of making banking systems more similar to those of Anglo-Saxon industrialized countries gained momentum after the end of the East-West divide and the demise of the Soviet Union. However, there is a remarkable exception to this general trend: Still today, state-owned banks play an important or even dominant role in the so-called BRIC countries. Therefore, a general statement that national banking systems have become more similar, would go much too far.

---

9   For more detail see Schmidt et al. (2014) and Kotz and Schmidt (2016).

10   For details, see the two volumes by Ayadi et al. on savings banks (2009) and cooperative banks (2010) in Europe and the summaries and updates in Bülbül et al. (2013).

2.2   Financial systems

For a deeper understanding of diversity in the financial sphere, it is not enough to look at how diverse banking systems are, how they develop and possibly become more similar in a cross-country comparison. This is why I now broaden the perspective and look at entire financial systems.

I use the term "financial sector" for the totality of financial institutions, which comprise banks, other financial intermediaries and markets. These institutions provide all sorts of financial services to the other parts of an economy. Thus the financial sector constitutes the supply side of the market for financial services. The concept of the financial system is broader than that of the financial sector in that it adds the demand side. The demand for financial services comes mainly from households which typically accumulate savings and transfer income into the future, and firms that need outside financing in order to fund their investments. But not all financial transactions of households and firms involve the financial sector. Therefore, a full picture of the financial system also requires seeing to what extent households and firms make use of the supply from the financial sector or instead rely on their own means for solving financial problems as for instance in the case of internal financing. How firms finance their investments and how households accumulate and transfer wealth over time, and even how the control of capital is organized, i.e. corporate governance, are therefore core elements of any financial system.

For a long time, financial systems have been classified as being either bank-based or capital-market-based.[11] Even though is not possible in my view to claim that one of the two types is better than the other, the classical two-way classification can be used for assessing between-country diversity: Diversity is lower if all or at least most of the countries have a financial system of one and the same type. In addition, countries can differ with respect to the extent that their financial systems are consistent, as I will explain below.

Now look at real financial systems. For a long time, the German financial system was the model case of a bank-based system. This was due to five features: (1) Banks were by far the most important players in the financial sector. (2) Bank loans were the most important source of external funding of non-financial firms. (3) The former three big banks (*Deutsche Bank, Dresdner Bank und Commerzbank*) used to play the central role in the governance of large non-financial corporations. (4) There used to be close relationships, so called house-bank relationships, between large corporations and one among its banks, and house-banks did indeed behave differently from other banks if their partner firms experienced difficulties. Finally, (5) organized capital markets were relatively unimportant as a source of enterprise financing and as an instrument of corporate governance. These five features of the German financial system fitted together well, so that the German financial system was also consistent.

This was the situation about 20 years ago. At that time most other national financial systems on the European continent were equally of the bank-based type. In this respect between-country diversity was limited. However, the British financial system and to a certain extent also that of Ireland were not bank-based but rather capital market-based. Including them into a pan-European picture shifts the balance in the direction of more diversity.

---

11   On the limitations of this two-way classification and the ambiguity of the terms bank-based and capital market-based see Fohlin (2000).

In the meantime financial systems have changed in most countries. As a general rule one can say that the importance of banks has declined and that of capital markets has grown, even though only the French system has been fundamentally transformed from being a strongly bank-based system to a clearly capital market-based system. In most other cases only the extent to which they were bank-based has declined. In so far, diversity on the European continent may have slightly increased.

Germany is a particularly interesting case for assessing the changes that have occurred. At times it appeared as if the German financial system were on its way towards becoming another capital market-based system. However, this may not be the appropriate diagnosis. After all, Germany has retained its three pillar banking system with a preponderance of a stakeholder orientation and the mandatory codetermination and its dual board structure as main characteristics of a bank-based financial system. Instead, the numerous institutional changes that have indeed taken place in Germany around the turn of the century and in particular the transformation of the big banks and their interaction with German companies make me think that instead of a fundamental transformation what did occur in the German financial system was a loss of consistency (Hackethal et al. 2005).

An important change in recent years concerns bank lending policies. Especially large banks in the advanced economies no longer refinance their lending operations mainly with customer deposits but rather by borrowing in the interbank markets, and their lending rates have come to reflect the terms at which they can obtain funds from the interbank market rather than from their client deposits. Thus they now more and more follow a strategy which Hardie and Howarth (2013) call "market based banking". Moreover, the former widely adopted stakeholder value orientation of many European banks, including most large private banks, has given way to a stronger shareholder value orientation.

All in all, there seems to be a general and common trend in the development of most financial systems in *Western Europe*: they seem to lose their former bank orientation and adopt more elements of a capital market orientation. As this is a common trend, diversity has somewhat declined over the past two decades. But this decline is weaker and between-country differences are still today stronger than had been anticipated when European financial and monetary integration began to have a high place on the EU's political agenda.

On a *worldwide* scale, financial systems differ more than in Europe and these differences are surprisingly stable, as Allen et al. (2004) have demonstrated by comparing total bank assets to the aggregate market values of listed stocks and outstanding public and private bonds (expressed as a percentage of GDP) in the large economic regions of the world for the years 1994 and 2004. One can extend this comparison with more recent data (as in Schmidt 2018) and supplement them with comparative data on the financing patterns of non-financial firms and corporate governance regimes around the world only to find a high and largely stable level of financial system diversity.[12]

---

[12] On the "heterogeneity" of banking systems see Kind (2018), on that of firms' financing patterns see Hackethal and Schmidt (2005) and on corporate governance systems in different regions see Goergen (2007).

2.3 Summing up

Since the concepts underlying the arguments in this section are rather complicated, I conclude this section with a brief summary.

As far as banking systems are concerned, the big picture can be summarized as follows:

- In-country diversity in most of Western Europe has declined as large private share-holder value-oriented banks have gained in importance at the expense of stakeholder value oriented banks.

- In many respects national banking systems have become more similar over time even though there are still many differences which I have not discussed for space reasons. Thus overall between-country diversity may have declined.

- However, as far as differences between European countries in terms of their respective in-country diversity are concerned, one cannot see a change as formerly most banking systems were three pillar systems representing similarly high levels of in-country diversity, while now large banks dominate in most countries, which represents similarly lower levels of in-country diversity.

- Germany and Austria are the exceptions to this general rule. In these countries in-country diversity has remained high and as a consequence their banking systems are now less similar to those of most other European countries.

- On a world-wide scale, banking systems differ greatly, not least with respect to their in-country diversity, and in spite of some common developments there is still a high level of between-country (or between-region) diversity.

As far as financial systems are concerned, the big picture can be summarized as follows:

- Still today the differences between the structures of the financial systems of Western European countries are substantial in spite of a common trend towards a stronger capital market orientation. Thus between-country diversity is still high but somewhat declining.

- On a world-wide level, the differences between financial systems of large economic regions are even more pronounced and also somewhat declining, though less than in Europe. Thus between-regions diversity is high and almost stable.

3 Explaining persistent diversity

As stated in the introduction, it seems highly plausible that financial systems in Europe and even world-wide become more similar over time. In other words, one would expect a decrease of diversity or a more or less gradual convergence. Three drivers of a possible convergence could play a role here.

The first one is common and generally applicable regulation issued by international or supranational organizations such as the Basel Committee, the OECD, the IMF and in particular the EU. It leads to convergence because it forces national decision makers to make their country's financial sector conform better to the common rules. This driver of convergence can be expected to be most effective within the EU.

The second one is pressure from a dominating economy, such as England in the 19th century or the United States after the end of the East-West divide, or from international organizations such as the IMF or the World Bank—or even a combination of both.[13] It is likely to be most effective in countries with strong ties to, or dependence on, an economically and politically dominant power and its allies in the international organizations.

The third possible driver of convergence is one that economists are most prone to think of: competition in combination with globalization. The argument goes like this: The quality of its financial system is a determinant of the economic success of a country. Provided that there is one financial systems design that is widely regarded as being the best one for economic success, one can expect that under the pressure of increasing international competition and trade all countries will end up adopting this financial systems design, just as under international competition all countries that produce steel are likely to sooner or later adopt the best steel-making technology.

However, in reality we observe much less convergence—and even a stubborn persistence of diversity—than the three arguments might suggest. How can this be explained? The roles of international regulation and of hegemonic powers may be weaker than one might think. More importantly, the seemingly plausible analogy between steel making technology and financial systems is misleading. While there probably is just one single and generally acknowledged optimal steel making technology it cannot be taken for granted that there is also just one optimal financial system design. In the years before the turn of the millennium the Anglo-Saxon type of a capital market oriented financial system was widely regarded as the best one and the one that many countries would try to implement. However, from today's perspective, this claim would be hard to substantiate. A number of theoretical papers have shown that under certain conditions and according to certain criteria capital market-based systems are superior to bank-based systems. However, the conditions are rather restrictive, and the assessment standards are quite special. Moreover, other authors have produced models that show the exact opposite. But they equally invoke rather special conditions and standards for assessing financial systems. The outcome of empirical studies of financial systems quality and the finance and growth nexus is similarly ambiguous. Therefore, at least as of today one cannot use the type of a financial system—bank-based or capital market-based—as an indicator of quality.[14]

Moreover, the formerly wide-spread conviction that capital market-based financial systems are superior to bank-based systems has lost most of its former plausibility as a consequence of the great

---

13   A combination of both was certainly behind what is called "the Washington consensus" that emerged in the 1990s. Its effects on financial systems in all parts of the world are well known and clearly favored convergence according to the American model. This powerful de facto alliance was even reinforced by prominent academics such as La Porta and his coauthors. See La Porta et al. (1998) and, with a very critical view on what constitutes an important element of diversity in banking, La Porta et al. (2002). A carefully articulated dissenting view can be found in a series of papers by Olivier Butzbach and Kurt von Mettenheim, e.g. those collected in Part 1 of Butzbach and von Mettenheim (2014).

14   For an overview of the theoretical work see Allen et al. (2014) and for the (earlier) empirical work Levine (2000).

financial crisis. After all, the crisis had started in a country with a clearly capital market-based system, and it has started for reasons that are rooted in the strong market orientation of that system.[15]

In my view, both bank-based and capital market-based systems can be economically valuable. Whether a given financial system is good does therefore not depend on its degree of bank- or market-orientation but rather on other factors. One such factor is whether a financial system is "consistent". Both bank-based and capital market-based financial systems can be more or less consistent and therefore good or not so good.

What does the term consistency mean? A genuine system has an important property called complementarity. Complementarity means that the elements of a (financial) systems have the potential to fit together well in the sense that their positive effects reinforce each other mutually and their negative effects mutually mitigate each other. Financial systems are complementary systems in this sense. Consistency means that the elements of a given (financial) system take on such values that the potential inherent in the complementarity of the system is unlocked. Therefore, the degree of consistency is a good indicator of the quality of a (financial) system.[16]

In a context in which complementarity and consistency play an important role one can rather expect path-dependence and diversity than convergence, and this is even more so the case the stronger the pressure from international competition and globalization is.

4   Assessing diversity

Diversity can be assessed very differently. Persistent diversity can indicate a lack of efficiency or of pressure to adopt the best legal form, size or business model of the banks in a country or region and the optimal structure of a financial systems with respect to the roles of financial intermediaries and financial markets, the financing patterns of non-financial firms and their corporate governance regimes. Diversity can also be understood as a consequence of entrenched interests standing in the way of an economically reasonable modernization of banking and financial systems (Rajan and Zingales 2004). If these are the main causes of diversity, then diversity is simply undesirable.

Diversity is also not positive from the perspective of regulators and supervisors. It makes their job difficult as it stands in the way of developing and using a unified approach to regulation and supervision; and if a unified approach were nevertheless chosen it might not do justice to the differences in financial sectors and systems that exist for good or not so good reasons. Moreover, in-country diversity as well as between-country diversity may be difficult to reconcile with the aim of establishing a level playing field that would make competition in the financial sector effective. And finally a high level of diversity might be incompatible with monetary integration.[17] Thus, there are a number of reasons why diversity may not be desirable.

---

15   See Kotz and Schmidt (2016) and Meyer (2018, chapter 5), who make this point in almost identical words.

16   For more detail, including the theoretical background, see Hackethal and Tyrell (1999) and Hackethal and Schmidt (2000).

17   For details and additional references see Kotz et al. (2017).

On the other hand, diversity of financial systems and their main elements between countries and regions can be understood as a rational response to different requirements that financial institutions are supposed to meet and different legal, economic, social and political environments in which they are embedded. It seems highly plausible that diversity in the financial sphere has the additional advantage of making the financial sector itself and the supply of financial services to the non-financial parts of the economy more stable and shock-resistant.[18]

An overall assessment of the dangers and the merits of diversity is difficult. We do not know enough about how strong the different effects taken one by one are, how important they are, how they interact and how they can be integrated and weighted in order to arrive at a general assessment. Clearly, more research in this area is called for.

However, there is one additional aspect of diversity which in my view speaks strongly in favor of diversity and thus against attempts to aspire or foster convergence through political means:[19] Nobody can really tell to which challenges banking systems and financial sectors will be exposed in the future and to which requirements they will have to respond. Neither researchers nor policymakers know, and in fact nobody can claim to know, which structure of the banking system, the financial sector and the entire financial system will turn out to be best in the future. In this respect, we are in a situation of genuine or structural uncertainty. At the latest, the great financial crisis has demonstrated that one cannot consider a banking system dominated by large shareholder-oriented banks and a capital market-based financial system as being generally superior. The following argument shows why this situation calls for preserving diversity.

Imagine that the type of a banking system and of a financial sector and a financial system that some decision makers and so-called experts currently regard as the best one today would have been implemented everywhere. This would imply that all other relevant institutional forms and thus also diversity would have disappeared. In this situation, the accumulated knowledge about how other types of banks, other banking systems and other financial systems function and can be used by society might very soon be lost. This knowledge is not trivial; it is an essential part of human and social capital.[20] If one could be absolutely certain which institutional structures are optimal this loss of knowledge would not matter. However, nobody can know this for sure. It could well be that in some 50 years people and even a majority of decision makers come to the conclusion that under the circumstances prevailing then it would be better to have those structures in the financial sphere in place that had once been abolished or superseded. Recreating, reviving and implementing them might be simply impossible or at least extremely difficult.

Therefore, preserving diversity *now* is a protection against the risk of *later* not having something that one might *later* need even though one does not know *now* that one will *later* need it. This is the standard argument that biologists or ecologists invoke when they argue for protecting endangered species: We cannot know today how valuable some plants or animals, which are now endangered,

---

18   In particular British authors such as Charles Goodhart or Andy Haldane from the Bank of England emphasize this aspect. See the references in Michie and Oughton (2013).

19   This argument has, according to my information, been first developed in Ayadi et al. (2009) and (2010) and taken up and extended by Michie (2011) and Michie and Oughton (2013).

20   Note that the German concept of a cooperative bank is on the United Nations' list of the World Immaterial Cultural Heritage since a few years.

might be in the future for fighting diseases which may come up in the future and are therefore completely unknown today. This argument can be transferred almost one to one from biology to finance and it leads to the two main normative conclusions of this paper:

1. It should be regarded as unambiguously positive that in spite of globalization and European integration the level of diversity in the German banking system has remained high and that on a global scale the diversity of banking and financial systems has also remained rather high in recent years.

2. Preserving diversity in the financial sector should have a high political priority on the national, European and global level. Its long-term benefits probably outweigh by far the short-term disadvantages that too much diversity may seem to have.

References

— Allen, F., and D. Gale (2001): Comparing Financial Systems. Cambridge, Cambridge University Press.
— Allen, F., E. Carletti and F. Gu (2014): The Roles of Banks in Financial Systems. In: A. Berger, P. Molyneux and J. Wilson (eds.): Oxford Handbook of Banking. 2nd ed. Oxford University Press, 27–46.
— Allen, F., F. Chui and A. Maddaloni (2004): Financial Systems in Europe, the USA and Asia. Oxford Review of Economic Policy, 20, 490–508.
— Amable, B. (2003): The Diversity of Modern Capitalism. Oxford, Oxford University Press.
— Ayadi, R., D. T. Llewllyn, R. H. Schmidt, E. Arbak and W. P. de Groen (2010): Investigating Diversity in the Banking Sector in Europe: Key Developments, Performance and Role of Cooperative Banks. CEPS, Brussels.
— Ayadi, R., R. H. Schmidt and S. Carbó Valverde (2009): Investigating Diversity in the Banking Sector in Europe: The Performance and Role of Savings Banks. CEPS, Brussels.
— Binder, M., P. Lieberknecht, J. Quintana and V. Wieland (2017): Model Uncertainty in Macroecconomics: On the Implications of Financial Frictions. Working Paper 114, IMFS, Goethe University, Frankfurt (forthcoming in D. Mayes et al., eds., Oxford Handbook on the Economics of Central Banking. Oxford, Oxford University Press).
— Booth, A., and A. Thakor (1997): Financial System Architecture. Review of Financial Studies, 10, 693–733.
— Brealey, R., St. Myers and F. Allen (2019): Principles of Corporate Finance. 13th ed. New York, McGraw-Hill.
— Bülbül, D., R. H. Schmidt and U. Schüwer (2013): Caisses d'épargne et banques cooperatives en Europe. Revue d'Èconomie Financière, 111, 159–187 (english version „Saving Banks and Cooperative Banks in Europe" published as SAFE White Paper Series No. 5, Frankfurt 2013).
— Butzbach, O., and K. von Mettenheim (eds.) (2014): Alternative Banks and Financial Crisis. London, Chatto and Pickering.
— Corbett, J., and T. Jenkinson (1997): How is Investment Financed? A Study of Germany, Japan, The United Kingdom and the United States. The Manchester School Supplement, 69–93.

— Fohlin, C. (2000): Economic, Political and Legal Factors in Financial Systems Development: International Patterns in Historical Perspective. Working Paper. California Institute for Technology.
— Goergen, M. (2007): What Do we Know about Corporate Governance Systems? ecgi working paper 163, Brussels.
— Gordon, J., and M. Roe (eds.) (2004): Convergence and Persistence in Corporate Governance. Cambridge, Cambridge University Press.
— Hackethal, A., and R. H. Schmidt (2000): Finanzsystem und Komplementarität, Kredit und Kapital. Beiheft 15 „Finanzmärkte im Umbruch". Berlin, 53–102.
— Hackethal, A., and R. H. Schmidt (2005): Financing Patterns: Measurement Concepts and Empirical Results. Working Paper Series: Finance and Accounting, No. 125. Goethe-Universität Frankfurt.
— Hackethal, A., R. H. Schmidt and M. Tyrell (2002): The Convergence of Financial Systems in Europe. German Financial Markets and Institutions: Selected Studies, Special Issue 1-02 of Schmalenbach Business Review, 7–53.
— Hackethal, A., R. H. Schmidt and M. Tyrell (2005): Banks and Corporate Governance in Germany: On the Way to a Market-Based System? Corporate Governance: An International Journal, 13, 397–407.
— Hackethal, A., and M. Tyrell (1999): Complementarity and Financial Systems. Working Paper Series: Finance and Accounting, No. 10. Goethe-Universität Frankfurt.
— Haldane, A. (2009) Rethinking the Financial Network, Bank of England, mimeo.
— Hall, P., and D. Soskice, (eds.) (2001): Varieties of Capitalism: The Institutional Foundations of Comparative Advantage, Oxford, Oxford University Press.
— Hansmann, H., and R. Kraakman (2000): The End of History for Corporate Law. Georgetown Law Journal, 89, 439–468.
— Hardie, I., and D. Howarth (2003): Market-Based Banking and the International Financial Crisis. Oxford, Oxford University Press.
— Kind, A. (2018): National and International Banking Heterogeneity. Zeitschrift für vergleichende Rechtswissenschaft, 117, 440–454.
— King, R. G., and R. Levine (1993): Finance and Growth: Schumpeter Might be Right. Quarterly Journal of Economics, 108, 717–738.
— Kotz, H.-H., and R. H. Schmidt (2016): The Corporate Governance of Banks: A German Alternative to the Standard Model. Zeitschrift für Bankrecht und Bankwirtschaft, 28, 427–444.
— Kotz, H.-H., W. Semmler and I. Tahri (2017): Capital Markets Union and monetary policy performance: Comes financial market variety at a cost?, Vierterljahrshefte zur Wirtschaftsforschung, 86 (2), 41–59.
— La Porta, R., F. Lopez-de-Silanes and A. Shleifer (2002): Government Ownership of Banks. Journal of Finance, 57, 265–301.
— La Porta, R., F. Lopez-de-Silanes, A. Shleifer and R. Vishny (1998): Law and Finance. Journal of Political Economy, 106, 1113–1156.
— Meyer, C. (2018): Prosperity. Oxfrd, Oxford University Press.
— Mitchie, J. (2011): Promoting Corporate Diversity in the Financial Services Sector. Policy Studies, 32, 309–323.
— Mitchie, J., and C. Oughton (2013): Measuring Diversity: A Diversity Index. Working Paper 113. Centre for Financial and Management Studies, Oxford.
— Rajan, R., and L. Zingales (2003): The Great Reversals: The Politics of Financial Development in the Twentieth Century. Journal of Financial Economics, 69, 5–50.

— Rajan, R. and L. Zingales, (2004): Saving Capitalism from the Capitalists. Princeton, Princeton University Press.
— Schmidt, R. H. (2018): Entwicklung und Vielfalt von Bank- und Finanzsystemen. Zeitschrift für vergleichende Rechtswissenschaft, 117, 429–439.
— Schmidt, R. H., D. Bülbül and U. Schüwer (2014): The Persistence of the German Three-Pillar-System. In: O. Butzbach and K. von Mettenheim (eds.): Alternative Banking and Financial Crisis. London, Chatto and Pickering, 101–122.
— Tirole, J. (2006): The Theory of Corporate Finance. Princeton, Princeton University Press.

How does banking diversity fit in the general vision inspiring the joint process of Banking Union and Capital Markets Union?

GIOVANNI FERRI AND DORIS NEUBERGER

Giovanni Ferri, Lumsa University, Rome, Center for Relationship Banking & Economics (CERBE), Rome, e-mail: g.ferri@lumsa.it
Doris Neuberger, University of Rostock, Center for Relationship Banking & Economics (CERBE), Rome, German Institute for Economic Research (DIW), e-mail: doris.neuberger@uni-rostock.de

Summary: The Global Financial Crisis (GFC: 2008–2009) and the Euro Sovereign Crisis (ESC: 2010–2012) seem a process of creative destruction for the European Union (EU). The huge damage provoked by the GFC and ESC was, in fact, followed by important institutional building steps as the Banking Union (BU) and Capital Markets Union (CMU). Their swift introduction suggests that BU and CMU arrived as emergency solutions. With hindsight we may now reassess them. We posit that two unintended side-effects materialised: 1) CMU twisted the balance against banking and in favour of financial markets; 2) BU is, de facto, weakening banking diversity. Thus, even if CMU and BU were successful at reaching EU's economic goals, their side-effects impair the social and cultural goals equally enshrined in EU treaties. We argue that CMU and BU should be revised to limit the damage to social and cultural goals or, else, other EU policies should be devised to restore the balance.

Zusammenfassung: Die globale Finanzkrise (GFC: 2008–2009) und die Euro-Staatsschuldenkrise (ESC: 2010–2012) scheinen ein Prozess der kreativen Zerstörung für die Europäische Union (EU) zu sein. Den enormen Schäden, die durch die GFC und ESC verursacht wurden, folgten in der Tat wichtige institutionelle Aufbauschritte wie die Bankenunion (BU) und die Kapitalmarktunion (CMU). Ihre schnelle Einführung deutet darauf hin, dass BU und CMU als Notfalllösungen zum Einsatz kamen. Im Nachhinein können wir sie nun neu bewerten. Wir gehen davon aus, dass zwei unbeabsichtigte Nebeneffekte eingetreten sind: 1) Die CMU hat das Gleichgewicht gegen das Bankwesen und zugunsten der Finanzmärkte verschoben; 2) die BU schwächt de facto die Bankenvielfalt. Selbst wenn es CMU und BU gelungen ist, die wirtschaftlichen Ziele der EU zu erreichen, beeinträchtigen ihre Nebenwirkungen die sozialen und kulturellen Ziele, die gleichermaßen in den EU-Verträgen verankert sind. Wir argumentieren, dass CMU und BU überarbeitet werden sollten, um den Schaden für soziale und kulturelle Ziele zu begrenzen, oder dass andere EU-Politiken entwickelt werden sollten, um das Gleichgewicht wiederherzustellen.

→ JEL classification: F36, G15, G18, G21, G28
→ Keywords: Banking diversity, Capital Markets Union, Banking Union, relationship banking, shareholder banks, stakeholder banks

1   Introduction

Banking sector diversity has many dimensions: ownership and corporate diversity reflecting the range of different corporate types, business model diversity indicating different business objectives, balance sheet structures and resilience, and geographic diversity reflecting different geographic spread or distance to customers (Michie and Oughton 2013). While there is a large literature showing the influence of such diversity on economic outcomes such as access to credit, financial stability and competition, there has been little discussion so far as to whether banking diversity corresponds to the political goals of the European Union. Following the Global Financial Crisis (GFC: 2008–2009) and the Euro Sovereign Crisis (ESC: 2010–2012), these goals have been revised among others by the projects of the Capital Markets Union (CMU) and the Banking Union (BU). Whether the CMU action plan sets the appropriate priorities and can ultimately deliver is, however, doubtful (Kotz and Schäfer 2017a, 2017b).

This paper discusses the role of banking diversity within the joint process of CMU and BU and the contributions of this process to the overarching goals of the European Union. It is organised along the following lines. In section 2, we review the objectives of the EU as written down in the EU treaties, differentiating between economic, social and cultural goals (without further political goals). Preserving national diversity belongs to the cultural goal of safeguarding cultural heritage. Within this framework, section 3 reviews the goals of CMU and BU. We argue that CMU and BU are biased towards economic goals and conflict with cultural goals, because they are likely to reduce diversity of financial systems and banks. The composite vision of CMU and BU is that we need more financial market depth, which is a good objective per se but should not be sought, as it seems it has happened, by placing relatively higher burdens on: i) banks vs financial markets and ii) traditional intermediation vs banks engaged in doing finance. The disfavour against banks damages financial system diversity (bias towards market-based systems), and the disfavour against traditional banks damages banking diversity (bias towards transaction banks/shareholder banks vs relationship banks/stakeholder banks). In section 4, we argue that banking diversity contributes to all three goals: the economic goals of allocative efficiency, the social goals of financial inclusion and social responsibility and the cultural goals of safeguarding European values. This is supported by literature and statistics. Section 5 summarizes and concludes.

2   Economic, social and cultural objectives of the EU treaties

The Lisbon Agenda launched by the European Council in 2000 set the goal to make the EU "the most competitive and dynamic knowledge-based economy in the world, capable of sustainable economic growth with more and better jobs and greater social cohesion". An overall strategy to reach this goal aims at economic as well as social goals. The economic goals are in particular completing the internal market, improving policies for the information society, R&D, competitiveness and innovation, and sustaining economic growth. The social goals comprise "modernising the European social model, investing in people and combating social exclusion" (Lisbon European Council 2000). In 2005, the Lisbon strategy was relaunched with the goal "for growth and employment [...] to modernize our economy in order to secure our unique social model" (EU Commission 2005a: 2).

The uniqueness of the European model has been defined by the European Commission as "unity and diversity", meaning that "national economic and social policies are built on shared values such as solidarity and cohesion, equal opportunities and the fight against all forms of discrimination, [...] in favour of a social market economy. They are reflected in the EU treaties, its action and legislation, as well as in the European Convention of Human Rights and our Charter of fundamental rights. [...] a strong "European dimension" reinforces national systems" (EU Commission 2005b: 4–5). Diversity is considered as a strength of Europe in international competition and is explicitly protected by the EU Treaty. According to Art. 295 of the EU Treaty, EU integration policy must by no means undermine the legal and economic norms, by which ownership is governed in the different member states (Ayadi et al. 2010: 110). A resolution of the European Parliament in 2008 states that "the diversity of legal models and business objectives of financial entities in the retail banking sector (banks, savings banks, cooperatives, etc) is a fundamental asset to the EU's economy which enriches the sector, corresponds to the pluralist structure of the market and helps to increase competition in the internal market" (EU Parliament 2008).

According to the Lisbon Treaty of 2007, amending the Treaty on European Union and the Treaty establishing the European Community, the objectives of the EU are, among others: creation of an internal market, sustainable development, a highly competitive social market economy, aiming at full employment and social progress, combatting social exclusion and discrimination, promoting social justice and protection, a high level of protection of the environment, promotion of economic, social and territorial cohesion, and solidarity among Member States. Beyond these economic and social goals, the Lisbon Treaty includes the cultural goal to respect Europe's "rich cultural and linguistic diversity", and to "ensure that Europe's cultural heritage is safeguarded and enhanced" (EU Commission 2007). To reach these aims, the Lisbon Treaty has set the principles of subsidiarity and proportionality. The principle of subsidiarity states that, "in areas which do not fall within its exclusive competence, the Union shall act only if and insofar as the objectives of the proposed action cannot be sufficiently achieved by the Member States, either at central level or at regional and local level, but can rather, by reason of the scale or effects of the proposed action, be better achieved at Union level." According to the principle of proportionality, "the content and form of Union action shall not exceed what is necessary to achieve the objectives of the Treaties" (EU Commission 2007).

The diversity principle allows a variety of types of capitalism within the EU. They may be categorized as Central European, Anglo-Saxon, South European and Nordic European models, which differ with respect to key institutional areas, including financial intermediation and corporate governance. For example, the Central European and Nordic models of capitalism are characterized by a bank-based financial system with relatively low sophistication of financial services, in contrast to the Anglo-Saxon model with market-based finance, sophistication of financial services, financial innovation and strong influence of shareholders (Amable 2003, Rodrigues 2009).

Hall and Soskice (2001) differentiate between liberal market economies and coordinated market economies. Each type of capitalism has particular complementarities between key institutional areas, which lead to different types of competitive advantages. For example, in coordinated market economies, "the existence of durable relationships, and of proximity between banks and firms, enhances the implementation of long-term investment projects, and this in return facilitates the establishment of stable compromises in the labour market" (Amable, 2003: 61). They have a comparative advantage in industries where competitiveness stems from company-specific skills, cumulative build-up of knowledge and incremental innovation. Liberal market economies, in contrast, have the edge in industries where competitiveness is based on fast adaptation to changing market conditions and radical innovation (Amable, 2003: 78–79).

3   Objectives of CMU and BU and relationships with banking diversity

The CMU project aims at the economic goal of strengthening employment and growth by deepening capital markets. The main objectives are: (1) improving access to finance for all businesses, in particular SMEs, and investment projects such as infrastructure, (2) developing and diversifying the supply of funding by boosting the flow of institutional and retail investment into capital markets, (3) making markets work more effectively and efficiently to improve allocation of risk and capital across the EU. Social goals are not mentioned, except the goal of developing markets for environmental, social and corporate governance investments and promoting the provision of risk capital to start-ups and social business (EU Commission 2015).

In the CMU green paper, capital markets are assumed as a complement rather than a substitute to intermediation by banks, whose diversity is considered as an advantage: "While capital markets can complement the role of bank lending for SMEs, their diversity and scant credit information is often better suited to relationship based lending. Alternative funding sources can, however, play an important role, in particular for start-ups and small but rapidly growing firms in innovative industries" (EU Commission 2015: 13). The view that banks and markets should complement each other to perform functions of allocation and risk sharing is supported by theoretical and empirical literature (Allen and Gale 2000).

However, being focused on institutions rather than functions, the CMU project is not institution-neutral. Starting from the diagnosis of over-banking, it aims at strengthening capital markets with a "high quality securitisation market relying on simple, transparent and standardized securitisation instruments" (EU Commission 2015: 10). Its measures to improve market effectiveness, such as the single rulebook, supervisory convergence, strengthening securities law and investor protection through MIFID II and other regulations install a bias in favour of more market-based finance and nonbank intermediation. CMU is based on the theory of finance which hinges on the assumption of market efficiency and postulates the availability and exclusive use of public information. It disregards the role of banks in overcoming asymmetric information problems, in particular for financing SMEs, as explained by the theory of banking intermediation. Since SME loans are highly opaque and idiosyncratic, they are not easily transferable or marketable (Ferri and Neuberger 2014, Kotz and Schäfer 2017a).

Likewise, the BU project has fallen prey to 'market fundamentalism', aiming at a more transparent, unified and safer market for banks. This shall be achieved by the single rulebook, i.e. common rules and administrative standards to regulate, supervise and govern the financial sector in all EU countries (ECB 2018, EU Commission 2012). The EU banking regulation approach has been one-size-fits-all (each bank has to follow the same rules, irrespective of its ownership structure and mission), contrary to the US tiered approach, where commercial banks follow a set of rules different from community banks and yet other rules apply to credit unions. The result of the one-size-fits-all EU approach is that all banks are pushed to behave in the same manner, as if they were all profit maximisers. In turn, this violates the principles of proportionality and subsidiarity and provokes the dilution of social responsibility even for those bank types whose DNA is oriented to serve their stakeholders—rather than pursue profit maximisation—such as the cooperative banks and the savings banks. Moreover, the fixed component of the increased regulatory compliance costs has induced economies of scale at the disadvantage of small banks (Ferri and Pesce 2012, Ferri and Kalmi 2014, Ferri 2017). In that, EU regulators/policy makers' one-size-fits-all approach disregards (if not despises) the specificities of stakeholder-oriented banks. We even have the paradox that Credit Unions and Community Banks—local parallel of the EU stakeholder banks—receive a differential treatment in the US, where peoples' majority values are not so keen to the solidarity mechanisms activated by stakeholder banks.[1]

By focussing on the economic goal of market efficiency, CMU and BU conflict not only with the cultural goal of preserving diversity, but also with social or socioeconomic goals, such as financial inclusion and responsible finance. Financial inclusion means that "individuals and firms are not denied access to basic financial services based on motivations other than efficiency criteria" (Amidžić et al. 2014: 5). It encompasses outreach, usage, and quality of financial services (Amidžić et al. 2014: 8). Beyond that, the goal of responsible finance aims at more transparent, inclusive, and equitable financial markets balanced in favor of all income groups (BMZ/IFC/CGAP 2011: 1).

A trend driven by CMU is to set common standards for all financial services, such as standardized pre-contractual information, product explanation, extended liability of the provider in case of mis-selling, and the duty of intermediaries to have liability insurance. This helps consumers by increasing transparency and closing gaps in unregulated capital markets, for example. However, a drawback of these regulations is that they focus on the sale of financial services, that is, the time before and during the agreed contract period, while duties during the users' entire lifetime, such as access, exploitation, cancellation, usury, debt enforcement, adaptation, and continuity, are neglected (Reifner, 2018, Nogler and Reifner 2014: 41). To ensure responsible finance, capital users must be protected from irresponsible lending in long-term credit contracts.[2]

The same logic of making banking more efficient by increasing competition in the sector seems to have presided the approach to PSD2. In it, obligations were introduced for banks to disclose to qualified third parties information on their customers that were up to then proprietary information. Once more, this approach is not neutral. By forcing banks to release previously proprietary information, PSD2 is debasing the value of customer relationships and implicitly favoring the adoption of a transaction banking model over a relationship banking model.

---

1   Differently from the US (and, in part, the UK), where the majority of citizens believe that each individual gets what he/she deserves, European peoples—irrespectively of their religious faith and/or of latitude and longitude—believe that in general it isn't true that each individual gets what he/she deserves. Rather, Europeans view an individual's income and wealth to depend on factors largely outside his/her control: the percentage of Eurozone citizens agreeing with this view is a majority above 60 percent, as against minorities of 44 percent in the UK and 41 percent in the US (Pew Research Center 2014—due to data availability, the Eurozone is approximated by the population weighted average of France and Germany).

2   See the European Social Contract Declaration (www.eusoco.eu/), the European Coalition for Responsible Credit (www.responsible-credit.net/index.php?id=2516) and the anti-usury initiative StopWucher (http://stopwucher.de/) in Germany. The EU Mortgage Credit Directive 2014 goes in the right direction by calling for a more comprehensive regulation of the principle of responsible lending, which should not be limited to credit scoring. However, these demands have not yet been implemented through legislation in the current implementation. It is up to national legislators to implement them.

4   Contributions of banking diversity to the objectives of the EU treaties

Banking diversity contributes to the economic, social and cultural goals of the EU treaties. It directly addresses the goal of safeguarding the cultural heritage of different financial systems. Literature shows that it fosters access to finance, regional and sustainable development, competition, financial stability and financial inclusion (e.g. Ayadi et al. 2010, Prieg and Greenham 2012).

As evidenced by the EU Commission (2018), the deployment of an appropriate financial system is indispensable to reach the goal of sustainable development as subscribed by the EU. While an important role in this respect will be played by green and responsible market finance (e.g., Green bonds/ Cool bonds, Social bonds, Sustainable bonds/ Social and Development Impact Bonds, and other possibly hybrid securities featuring a sustainable footprint) there is another, complementary, role to be played by Alternative Banks. Alternative banks (ABs) can take various forms: ethical banks, social banks, cooperative banks and savings banks. In any case their focus is not on maximizing profits but on maximizing value for the wide audience of stakeholders rather than simply the shareholders. Thus, often they are called Stakeholder value banks (STVBs). Indeed, ABs are key actors in: i) small business development (by investing in a relationship banking business model and so, overcoming asymmetric information, contributing to less credit rationing, lower loan rates[3]); ii) dampening the cyclicality of credit finance (e.g., ABs are particularly critical in a Credit Crunch as they exhibit less quantity credit rationing, practice lower increase in loan rates at times of stress, are more stable during financial stress); iii) helping financial inclusion/ fighting financial exclusion (ABs' ownership/governance promotes democratic representation and is conducive to the relationship banking business model). If we cast our reasoning in terms of the ESG (Environmental, Social, Governance) indicators—which are increasingly used in the business sustainability evaluation—ABs score definitely well on "S", probably score well also on "E", and they score well on "G", too. In fact, the governance structures of ABs are less conducive to short-termism.

Regarding geographic diversity, decentralized banking systems with short operational and functional distance[4] and embeddedness in supportive regional bank associations improve access to finance for SMEs (Flögel and Gärtner 2018). Small, regional banks have a comparative advantage in relationship lending (Agarwal and Hauswald 2010), which cannot be substituted by transactional lending technologies in SME lending (Bartoli et al. 2013). They are also more effective in promoting local economic growth than big interregional banks, in particular in a financially integrated market (Hakenes et al. 2015). Market integration through CMU and BU therefore even increases the necessity of safeguarding small regional banks.

The aim of CMU to improve market effectiveness through digital finance implies that physical access to bank branches can be substituted by online access. However, the substitutability between both distribution channels depends on the kind of financial service offered, and is lowest for SME finance. Evidence for Germany shows that in particular inhabitants of sparsely populated rural regions have both a relatively poor physical and digital access (Conrad et al. 2018). Rural regions

---

3   Bharath et al. (2011) find that the observed reduction in the cost of borrowing due to relationship lending increases with the information opacity of the borrower, but that there are significant benefits of relationship lending even for publicly traded firms.

4   Operational distance is the distance between customers and their customer advisors, while functional distance is the distance between customer advisors and head offices (Alessandrini et al. 2009).

are more affected by branch closures than urban ones. In the period 2010–2015, the percentage decline in the number of branches was higher for private credit banks (14.0 percent) than for cooperative banks (8.9 percent) and savings banks (11.7 percent) (Schwartz et al. 2017: 2, own calculations).

To gain an idea of whether the negative attitude evidenced above—by both general policies as well as by regulators/supervisors—with respect to the value of banking diversity had visible consequences on the situation on the ground throughout Europe, we used detailed bank data to obtain an indication. Specifically, drawing on the micro data used in Ayadi et al. (2018), we could distinguish the ownership type for each European bank. Namely, we classified banks as: i) commercial banks; ii) nationalized banks; iii) cooperative banks; iv) savings banks. Then we considered 11 EU countries—Austria, Finland, France, Germany, Greece, Ireland, Italy, Netherlands, Portugal, Spain, and the UK—and calculated for each country a simple index of banking diversity given by the share of total assets of the national banking system held by cooperative banks plus savings banks, i.e. the market share of alternative or stakeholder-oriented banks. This was done positing that nationalized banks were bound to be returned to the commercial banking part of the banking system and, as such, belonged to the shareholder-oriented banks.

The results are reported in Table 1. They show that the value of the index exhibits wide variation across the 11 countries, ranging from the minimum of 0.0 percent in Ireland and the UK to the maximum of around 85 percent in Finland, accompanied by almost 80 percent in Austria and by high values about 50 percent in both France and Germany. In terms of dynamics, we chose to look at the difference between December 2010 and December 2015 considering that some of the first important changes in regulation were introduced through the single rulebook and other measures by the EBA, which was established at the beginning of 2011, followed by the gradual phasing in of the Single Supervisory Mechanism between 2012 and 2014 and by the slower inception of the Single Resolution Mechanism, whose measures started to be felt in 2015. If we consider the 11 countries all together, the index drops marginally from 42.1 percent in 2010 to 41.0 percent in 2015. However, the relative stability of the index is the result of two rather diverse trends across Europe. Namely, if we distinguish the countries suffering a sovereign crisis—the so called GIPSI (Greece, Ireland, Portugal, Spain and Italy, in the order of occurrence of the crisis)—from the other euro countries (Austria, Finland, France, Germany, Netherlands) we clearly see two different dynamics. The index drops on average from 28.6 to 23.0 percent for the GIPSI countries whereas it marginally increases from 47.9 to 48.9 percent for the other euro countries. It should be noticed that the GIPSI average is strongly affected by the Spanish case—the index drops from 30.6 to 17.0 percent in Spain—owing to the deep crisis of the savings banks in that country. Nevertheless, we can also see that banking diversity is reduced also in the other GIPSI countries: from 47.8 to 42.2 percent in Portugal; from 32.9 to 31.5 percent in Italy and from 0.9 to 0.6 percent in Greece (Ireland had no banking diversity to start with). At the same time, we may observe that the marginal increase in banking diversity in the other euro countries descends from the increase from 47.7 to 50.7 percent in Germany, and that from 84.1 to 85.6 percent in Finland, and that in France (from 50.3 to 50.6 percent), while the index drops in the Netherlands (from 29.6 to 28.6 percent) and in Austria (from 78.9 to 78.6 percent).

The question we may ask is whether we may draw any inference from the fact that it was the weaker countries—i.e. the GIPSI—to suffer a loss in banking diversity. The possibility should be considered that those countries were in a sense more vulnerable to be enforced the new paradigm shaped by CMU and BU. In a way, it is likely that relationship lenders found themselves engulfed

Table 1

Index of banking diversity
2010–2015, 11 EU member states

Country	Index of Banking Diversity*	
	2010	2015
AT	78.9	78.6
DE	47.7	50.7
ES	30.6	17.0
FI	84.1	85.6
FR	50.3	50.6
GR	0.9	0.6
IE	0.0	0.0
IT	32.9	31.5
NL	29.6	28.6
PT	47.8	42.2
UK	0.0	0.0
Total 11	42.1	41.0
GIPSI	28.6	23.0
Other Euro	47.9	48.9

AT = Austria, DE = Germany, ES = Spain, FI = Finland, FR = France, GR = Greece, IE = Ireland, IT = Italy,
NL = Netherlands, PT = Portugal, UK = United Kingdom.
* Share of total assets of the national banking system held by cooperative banks plus savings banks.
Source: Ayadi et al. (2018), own calculations.

with the macroeconomic crises experienced by their countries more than did transactional lenders. According to this interpretation, one could argue that, by damaging banking diversity, the new policy and regulatory/supervisory approach has dented the ability of those economies to have internal stabilizers in terms of reducing the cyclicality of credit (Ferri et al. 2014) and/or mechanisms of financial inclusion (Ayadi et al. 2010, Prieg and Greenham 2012) and/or institutions that may support local economic development and growth (Coccorese and Shaffer 2018).

Table 2 shows the percentage changes of banking diversity, population per local branch as a measure of financial inclusion (a higher population per local branch indicating lower outreach) and the Herfindahl index of banking market concentration as a measure of competition (a higher Herfindahl index indicating lower competition). The GIPSI countries with the largest declines in banking diversity—Spain (44 percent) and Greece (33 percent)—experienced the largest reduction in branch outreach (Spain: 38 percent, Greece: 53 percent) and the largest increases in the Herfindahl index (Spain: 70 percent, Greece: 86 percent). In the Netherlands (and the other Euro countries), the large reduction of outreach due to branch closures does not seem to be related to the small change in banking diversity. Only countries where banking diversity did not decline (DE, FI, FR, IE) experienced a decline in the Herfindahl index. The opposing developments of banking diversity and market concentration in the weaker GIPSI countries and the other Euro countries is striking: in the GIPSI countries, banking diversity declined by 20 percent and the Herfindahl index increased by 5 percent, while in the other Euro countries, banking diversity increased by 2 percent, and the Herfindahl index declined by 12 percent.

Table 2

Percentage changes of banking diversity, outreach and market concentration

2010–2015, 10 Eurozone member states

Country	Index of banking diversity	Population per local branch	Herfindahl index for credit institutions
AT	-0.38	5.14	3.66
DE	6.29	14.16	-9.30
ES	-44.44	38.37	69.70
FI	1.78	43.43	-23.10
FR	0.60	5.85	-3.44
GR	-33.33	53.01	85.67
IE	0	14.96	-3.14
IT	-4.26	12.03	6.10
NL	-3.38	65.50	2.68
PT	-11.72	18.38	0.66
GIPSI	-19.58	26.71	5.03
Other Euro	2.09	38.61	-11.61

AT = Austria, DE = Germany, ES = Spain, FI = Finland, FR = France, GR = Greece, IE = Ireland, IT = Italy,
NL = Netherlands, PT = Portugal.
Source: Ayadi et al. (2018), ECB (2018), own calculations.

5   Summary and conclusions

Compared to most of the institutional changes that the European Union (EU) saw in its beyond fifty years of existence, the Banking Union (BU) and the Capital Markets Union (CMU) were decided and implemented with unusual speed. The context in which the two directives emerged was indeed special. Europe had been hit by two major shocks hurting banking and finance. Though the first shock was exogenous—the Global Financial Crisis (GFC: 2008–2009) came from the US subprime mortgage crisis and the bankruptcy of Lehman Brothers—its effects ended up troubling EU banks even more than US banks. In turn, the second shock—the Euro Sovereign Crisis (ESC: 2010–2012)—was entirely homegrown triggering also a perilous doom loop between the risks of a national banking system and the risks of its government.[5] Hence, emergency called for swift repair action.

On one hand, we might commend the EU for its swift adoption of BU and CMU, helping better achieve the EU's economic goals. On the other hand, however, the emergency status led their introduction to sidestep the scrutiny of whether BU and CMU were impairing the achievement of

---

5   Brunnermeier et al. (2016) outline the following model. If the domestic banking sector holds a large amount of government securities that raises the credit risk of both the sovereign and the banking sector, a diabolic loop increases the probability of twin crises. For example, speculation on the solvency of the banking sector weakens the sovereign's soundness which, in turn, further reduces the solvency of the banking sector. This mechanism can also work in the opposite direction: speculations on the solvency of the sovereign weaken the soundness of the banking sector which, in turn, further reduces the sovereign's solvency.

other EU's goals. This paper addressed that very issue from the perspective of Banking and Banking Diversity. We accomplished this by discussing selected literature as well as reporting some original elaborations.

Table 3 summarizes our main results. The table reports by row the EU treaties, CMU, BU and Banking Diversity while by column the three overarching sets of goals of the EU—Economic goals (allocative efficiency); Social goals; Cultural goals—are reported. Indeed, the EU treaties and the Lisbon Agenda enshrine a set of economic goals—relating to allocative efficiency—on the same par as two additional sets of objectives for social goals and cultural goals. In essence, our contention is that, in various ways, the CMU has damaged the diversity of financial systems—having a bias towards capital markets—and banking diversity—with its bias towards transaction banking. The latter bias is also shared by the BU, which has impaired banking diversity too.

The policy implications of our claims are straightforward. CMU and BU should be revised to limit the damage to social and cultural goals or, else, other EU policies should be devised to restore the balance.

Table 3

Contributions of EU treaties, CMU, BU and banking diversity to economic, social and cultural goals

	Overarching goals		
	Economic goals (allocative efficiency)	Social goals	Cultural goals
EU treaties, Lisbon Agenda, Lisbon Treaty	- Internal market - Highly competitive (social) market economy - Sustainable economic growth - Information society, R&D and innovation	- Social inclusion - Social justice - Social protection - Social cohesion	- Safeguarding and enhancing cultural heritage - Respecting and preserving diversity - (Unity and) diversity in shaping economic and social policies
Capital Markets Union	- Access to capital market finance - Supply of funding - Market effectiveness	- Access to capital market finance for start-ups and social business - ESG (environmental, social and corporate governance) investments	- Less financial system diversity: bias towards capital markets - Less banking diversity: bias towards transaction banking
Banking Union	- Single market: more transparent, unified and safer market for banks		- Less banking diversity: bias towards transaction banking
Banking Diversity	- Access to finance - Competition - Stability	- Financial inclusion - Social responsibility: community and stakeholder orientation	- Safeguarding and enhancing cultural heritage of bank-based financial systems - Preserving diversity

References

— Agarwal, S., and R. Hauswald (2010): Distance and private information in lending. Review of Financial Studies, 23, 2757–2788.
— Alessandrini, P., M. Fratianni and A. Zazzaro (eds.) (2009): The changing geography of banking and finance. New York.
— Allen, F., and D. Gale (2000): Comparing Financial Systems. Cambridge, MA, MIT Press.
— Amable, B. (2003): The Diversity of Modern Capitalism. Oxford, Oxford University Press.
— Amidžić, G., A. Massara and A. Mialou (2014): Assessing Countries' Financial Inclusion Standing—A New Composite Index. IMF Working Papers 14/36. Washington, D. C., International Monetary Fund.
— Ayadi, R., G. Ferri and V. Pesic (2018): Does Business Model Instability Imperil Banks' Soundness? Evidence from Europe. Bancaria, 7-8, 22–47.
— Ayadi, R., D. T. Llewellyn, R. H. Schmidt, E. Arbak, and W. P. De Groen (2010): Investigating Diversity in the Banking Sector in Europe. Key Developments, Performance and Role of Cooperative Banks. Centre for European Policy Studies, Brussels.
— Bartoli, F., G. Ferri, P. Murro and Z. Rotondi (2013): SME financing and the choice of lending technology in Italy: Complementarity or substitutability? Journal of Banking and Finance, 37, 5476–5485.
— Bharath, S. T., S. Dahiya, A. Saunders and A. Srinivasan (2011): Lending Relationships and Loan Contract Terms. The Review of Financial Studies, 24 (4), 1141–1203. https://doi.org/10.1093/rfs/hhp064
— Bikker, J. A. and K. Haaf (2002): Measures of Competition and Concentration in the Banking Industry: A Review of the Literature. Economic & Financial Modelling, Summer 2002, Central Bank of the Netherlands.
— BMZ/IFC/CGAP (2011): Advancing Responsible Finance for Greater Development Impact 2011. Consultation Draft. 27 January, German Federal Ministry for Economic Cooperation and Development (BMZ), Consultative Group to Assist the Poor (CGAP), International Finance Corporation (IFC), Washington, D. C.
— Brunnermeier, M. K., L. Garicano, P. R. Lane, M. Pagano, R. Reis, T. Santos, D. Thesmar, S. Van Nieuwerburgh and D. Vayanos (2016): The sovereign-bank diabolic loop and ESBies. American Economic Review, 106 (5), 508–512.
— Coccorese, P., and S. Shaffer (2018): Cooperative banks and local economic growth. CAMA Working Paper 11/2018. Centre for Applied Macroeconomic Analysis, Australian National University.
— Conrad, A., A. Hoffmann and D. Neuberger (2018): Physische und digitale Erreichbarkeit von Finanzdienstleistungen der Sparkassen und Genossenschaftsbanken. Review of Regional Research, 38 (2), 255–284. https://doi.org/10.1007/s10037-018-0121-7
— ECB (2017): Report on financial structures. October 2017. European Central Bank.
— ECB (2018): Banking Union. www.bankingsupervision.europa.eu/about/bankingunion/html/index.en.html (retrieved 15.10.2019).
— EU Commission (2005a): Communication from the Commission to the Council and the European Parliament. Common Actions for Growth and Employment: The Community Lisbon Programme. Brussels, 20.7.2005 COM(2005) 330 final.
— EU Commission (2005b): Communication from the Commission to the European Parliament, the Council, the European Economic and Social Committee and the Committee of the Regions—European values in the globalised world—Contribution of the Com-

mission to the October Meeting of Heads of State and Government. Brussels, 3.11.2005, COM(2005) 525 final/2.

— EU Commission (2007): Treaty of Lisbon amending the Treaty on European Union and the Treaty establishing the European Community, signed at Lisbon, 13 December 2007. Official Journal of the European Union, 2007/C 306/01.

— EU Commission (2012): A Roadmap towards a Banking Union. Communication from the Commission to the European Parliament and the Council. Brussels.

— EU Commission (2015): Building a Capital Markets Union. Green Paper.

— EU Commission (2018): Communication from the Commission to the European Parliament, the European Council, the Council, the European Central Bank, the European Economic and Social Committee and the Committee of the Regions—Action Plan: Financing Sustainable Growth. Brussels, 8.3.2018, COM/2018/097 final.

— EU Parliament (2008): European Parliament resolution of 5 June 2008 on Competition: Sector inquiry on retail banking (2007/2201(INI)). www.europarl.europa.eu/sides/getDoc. do?pubRef=-//EP//TEXT+TA+P6-TA-2008-0260+0+DOC+XML+V0//EN&language=EN

— Ferri, G. (2017): The Evolution of Banking Regulation in the Post-Crisis Period: Cooperative and Savings Banks' Perspective. In: E. Miklaszewska (ed.): Institutional Diversity in Banking. Palgrave Macmillan Studies in Banking and Financial Institutions. Palgrave Macmillan, Cham, 1–31.

— Ferri, G., and P. Kalmi (2014): Only up: Regulatory burden and its effects on credit unions. Filene Research Institute report.

— Ferri, G., P. Kalmi and E. Kerola (2014): Does bank ownership affect lending behavior? Evidence from the Euro area. Journal of Banking & Finance, 48, 194–209.

— Ferri, G., and D. Neuberger (2014): The Banking Regulatory Bubble and How to Get out of It. Rivista di Politica Economica, Issue 2, 39–69.

— Ferri, G., and G. Pesce (2012): The Perverse Effects of Compliance Costs for the Local Cooperative Banks. In: J. Heiskanen, H. Henrÿ, P. Hytinkoski and T. KöPpä (eds.): New Opportunities for Co-operatives: New Opportunities for People. Proceedings of the 2011 ICA Global Research Conference, 24–27 August 2011, Mikkeli, Finland, University of Helsinki Ruralia Institute, November 2012.

— Flögel, F., and S. Gärtner (2018): The Banking Systems of Germany, the UK and Spain from a Spatial Perspective: Lessons Learned and What Is to Be Done? IAT Discussion Paper 18/1A.

— Hakenes, H., I. Hasan, P. Molyneux and R. Xie (2015): Small Banks and Local Economic Development. Review of Finance, 19, 653–683.

— Hall, P. A., and D. Soskice (eds.) (2001): Varieties of Capitalism: The Institutional Foundations of Comparative Advantage. Oxford, Oxford University Press.

— Kotz, H.-H., and D. Schäfer (2017a): Can the Capital Markets Union Deliver? Vierteljahrshefte zur Wirtschaftsforschung, 86 (2), 89–98.

— Kotz, H.-H., and D. Schäfer (2017b): EU Capital Markets Union: An Alluring Opportunity or a Blind Alley? The Macro-Perspective: CMU and Risk-Sharing. Vierteljahrshefte zur Wirtschaftsforschung, 86 (1), 5–7.

— Lisbon European Council (2000): Presidency Conclusions. 23 and 24 March 2000. www. europarl.europa.eu/summits/lis1_en.htm

— Michie, J. and C. Oughton (2013): Measuring Diversity in Financial Services Markets: A Diversity Index. SOAS. Discussion Paper No. 113. University of London, Centre for Financial and Management Studies.

— Nogler, L., and U. Reifner (eds.) (2014): Life Time Contracts. Social Long-term Contracts in Labour, Tenancy and Consumer Credit Law. The Hague, Eleven International Publishing.
— Pew Research Center (2014): Inequality Report. downloaded 8/1/2016 at: www.pewglobal. org/files/2014/10/Pew-Research-Center-Inequality-Report-FINAL-October-17-2014.pdf.
— Prieg, L., and T. Greenham (2012): Stakeholder Banks - Benefits of banking diversity, nef)the new economics foundation). London. https://b.3cdn.net/nefoundation/e0b3bd-2b9423abfec8_pem6i6six.pdf
— Reifner, U. (2018): Responsible Credit in European Law. The Italian Law Journal, 4 (2), 421–448.
— Rodrigues, M.J. (2009): The European Lisbon Agenda and National Diversity: Key Issues for Policy-Making. Chapter 8 in Europe, Globalization and the Lisbon Agenda, 2009 from Edward Elgar Publishing.
— Schwartz, M., T.F. Dapp, G.W. Beck and A. Khussainova (2017): Deutschlands Banken schalten bei Filialschließungen einen Gang höher – Herkulesaufgabe Digitalisierung. KfW Research, Fokus Volkswirtschaft Nr. 181. 8. Oktober 2017.

Banking sector diversity and socioeconomic structure— criteria for matching pairs

HORST GISCHER AND CHRISTIAN ILCHMANN

Horst Gischer (corresponding author), Otto-von-Guericke University Magdeburg and Forschungszentrum für Sparkassenentwicklung e. V., e-mail: horst.gischer@ovgu.de
Christian Ilchmann, Otto-von-Guericke University Magdeburg, e-mail: christian.ilchmann@ovgu.de

Summary: It has been an age-old debate whether the financial structure matters for the real economy's efficiency and therefore for real outcomes. We suppose that varying socioeconomic conditions require appropriately designed corresponding financial sectors. For providing evidence, we firstly determine the specific (quantitative) size and corporate alignments of banking sectors across Europe, based on a sophisticated cluster analysis. Secondly, we develop a coherent system of geographic, social and economic parameters to identify structural patterns within the real economy's sector. In a conclusive synthesis, we link both analytical parts and draw tentative conclusions for possible future policy implications in Europe.

Zusammenfassung: Ob die Ausgestaltung des Finanzsektors eines Landes Auswirkungen auf die Effizienz der jeweiligen Realwirtschaft und damit Einfluss auf den realen Output nimmt, ist eine in der Literatur breit diskutierte Fragestellung. Das vorliegende Papier nähert sich der beschriebenen Thematik aus zwei Richtungen: Auf der einen Seite wird eine empirische Klassifikation unterschiedlicher Bankensysteme mittels Clusteranalyse vorgenommen. Auf der anderen Seite erfolgt eine Kategorisierung verschiedener sozioökonomischer Systeme. Eine sich daran anschließende Synthese stellt beides zueinander in Beziehung. Anhand ausgewählter Kriterien werden Aussagen über Interdependenzen und Kongruenz von Bankensystemen und Realwirtschaft getroffen, woraus sich mögliche Implikationen für ordnungspolitische Entscheidungen in der EU ergeben.

→ JEL classification: E00, E02, E60
→ Keywords: European integration, economic integration, banking system structure, socioeconomic structure, Banking Union, banking business models

1   Introduction

It has been an age-old debate in the respective economic literature whether financial structure matters for the real economy's efficiency and therefore for real outcomes. The financial structure of an economy is the setting of institutions that channel funds from savers to investors by performing the following five main tasks: Lot size transformation, Risk transformation, Maturity transformation, Spatial transformation and Liquidity transformation. A first approach distinguishes between either capital-market- or bank-based-systems. According to i. a. Levine (2002) there is no clear causality between bank- or capital market-based financial systems and economic growth.

Most frequently, e. g. Germany is asserted to be overbanked. In comparison to its neighbors, Germany is supposed to have too many banks that are too small on average and—regarding their businesses—too fragmented. Hence, with the introduction of a Banking Union and Capital Markets Union, consolidation is strongly advised by a broad variety of (European) institutions as well as the introduction of a broad access to institutional capital markets for enterprises (Gischer and Ilchmann 2017).

According to Behr et al. (2013: 3473) the structure of a country's financial system develops and adapts efficiently to meet real economy's requirements. Therefore, an *overbanked* banking sector could be appropriately designed to contribute efficiently to particular financial services demanded by trade and industry. It is likely that the corporate structure determines both size and characteristics of the corresponding financial sector.

To establish matching pairs, our approach is twofold:

In section 2 we derive criteria to categorize relevant features of the financial institution's sector by applying the business model approach established by Ayadi et al. (2016). Based on a sophisticated cluster analysis, we especially determine the specific (quantitative) size and corporate alignments (in terms of retail- or capital market-orientation) of banking sectors for several chosen European countries.

In section 3 we furthermore develop a coherent system of geographic, social and economic parameters that helps to identify structural patterns within the real economy's sector.

In a subsequent synthesis of the previous analyses, we evaluate specific features of matchings in both sectors. By referring to Germany, France and Italy we examine the design of the associated matching and draw tentative conclusions for possible future policy implications.

2   Structural diversity in banking sectors—an approach to identify specific features

For a first impression of varying financial structures across Europe we consider a bank-market ratio—in line with recent literature—defined as total bank assets divided by stock market capitalization and (domestic) private bond market capitalization (Levine 2002, Langfield and Pagano

Figure 1

Bank-market ratio (2016)

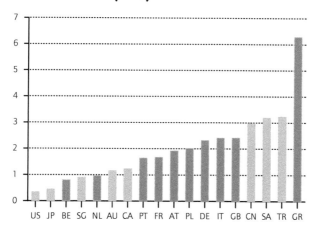

US = United States, JP = Japan, BE = Belgium, SG =Singapore, NL = Netherlands, AU = Australia, CA = Canada, PT = Portugal, FR = France, AT = Austria, PL = Poland, DE = Germany, IT = Italy, GB = United Kingdom, CN = China, SA = Saudi Arabia, TR = Turkey, GR = Greece.

Source: BIS (2018a), BIS (2018b), World Bank (2018a), own calculations.

2016). Figure 1 shows bank-market ratios for selected Countries in 2016. Smaller values indicate a more capital market-based financial system and vice versa.

At a first glance it becomes obvious that European countries (solid bars) have predominantly bank-based financial systems. While the size of the banking sector in Austria and Poland is twice the size of the capital markets (bank market-ratio of 2), the bank-market ratio in Germany comes to 2.5 and in Greece even 6.3. In comparison, other major developed (non-European) countries like the USA, Canada or Australia are way more capital market-orientated with bank market-ratios of 0.14, 1.16 and 1.22, respectively. However, that assignment does not enable for any statements regarding the (real) economic success of the respective countries as e. g. the European Union (EU) has an economic growth of 2.4 percent in 2017 on average, the US 2.3 percent, Canada 3.0 percent (World Bank 2018b).

Existing articles follow a variety of ex-post approaches to analyze patterns within the banking sector. Most commonly in Germany it is referred to an ownership-approach to identify the so called three-pillar-structure—private credit institutions, savings banks and cooperatives (Brämer et al. 2010, Gischer and Herz 2016, Gischer and Ilchmann 2017, Schmidt 2018). Furthermore, the USA are supposed to have—historically grown—a rather separated banking system as the Glass-Steagall Act remained in effect between 1933 and 1999 (Lucas 2013). In general existing structures are taken for granted.

To our knowledge there is no existing work from a banking's business perspective. We regard a banking sector as the collective of each of its individual banks. Moreover, we suppose that banks choose their *business model* (i. e. business activities) consciously and align them with the needs

Figure 2

Descriptive statistics for the focused retail banking business model

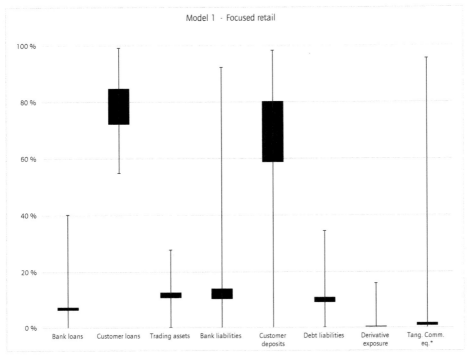

Source: Ayadi et al. (2016); own calculations.

of the real sector. To identify varying business models, we firstly utilize the state of art clustering approach established by Ayadi et al. (2016) as described below. Secondly, we examine chosen countries regarding their banking sector's composition.

Ayadi et al. (2016: 9) account for 13,040 bank-year observations between 2005 and 2014 for 2,542 banks in the European Union and Switzerland, covering more than 95 percent of relevant total assets for the cluster analysis. As business models are consciously chosen, only instruments are used, that a bank is able to control directly. The primary distinction is made "[...] *between key banking activities (i.e retail vs. market or mixed) and the funding strategies (i.e retail vs. market or mixed)*" (Ayadi et al. 2016:16). Especially bank loans, customer loans, trading assets, debt liabilities and derivative exposure are taken into account.

Based on Ward's (1973) clustering analysis and Calinski and Harabasz's (1974) pseudo-F index used as stopping rule, five different (and comprehensible) business models are derived—three retail-orientated business models (focused retail, diversified retail I, and diversified retail II) and two rather capital market-orientated business models, namely wholesale and investment. Descriptive statistics of selected models are presented below (Ayadi et al. 2016: 22 f.)

Figure 3

Descriptive statistics for the wholesale-orientated banking business model

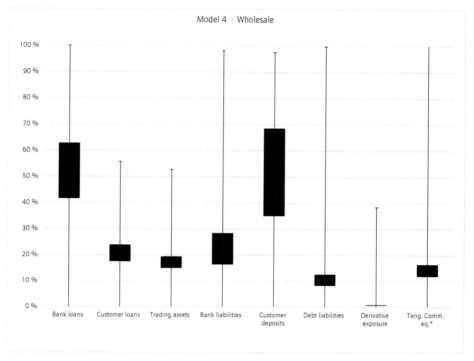

Source: Ayadi et al. (2016); own calculations.

Figure 2 shows a generic example of retail orientated business models. Retail banks are primarily involved in classical financial intermediation businesses. Focused retail banks are most active in lending to customers—customer loans represent 78.5 percent of their total assets—while customer deposits account for 69.5 percent of the total liabilities. Bank loans and trading assets are relatively limited with 7.0 percent and 11.8 percent, respectively. Meanwhile derivative exposure is nearly negligible with 0.3 percent on average. Both rather diversified retail models (type I and II)[1] have, in comparison, relatively higher trading assets with 30.9 percent and 22.6 percent as share of total assets. While the funding of type I is comparable to focused retail with a strong reliance on customer deposits (70.8 percent) type II relies most on debt liabilities with 43.3 percent of total assets.

Wholesale banks, as shown in Figure 3, are strongly involved in interbank market transactions, as bank loans account for 52.2 percent of their total assets on average and bank liabilities for 22.4 percent, respectively. Other funds are primarily used for customer loans (20.7 percent of total assets) and trading (17.1 percent).

---

1   Without illustration.

Figure 4

Descriptive statistics for the investment-orientated banking business model

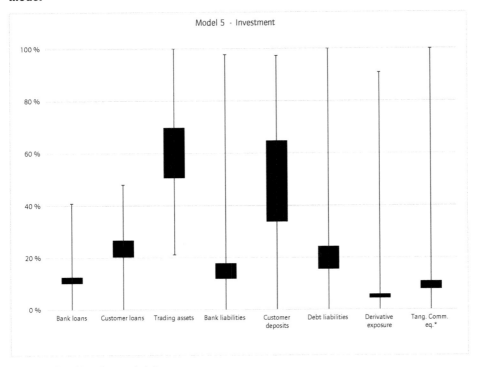

Source: Ayadi et al. (2016); own calculations.

Figure 4 shows rather investment-oriented banks that have substantial trading activities. The derivative exposures and trading assets account for 5.2 percent and 60.2 percent of total assets, respectively. Funding focus is on less stable and less traditional sources, such as debt liabilities with 19.9 percent. Meanwhile costumer deposits still play an important role (49.3 percent).

As additional contribution to the relevant area of research, we compile a current dataset[2] covering necessary data for all banks within the European Union. Furthermore, we develop a comprehensive filtering system based on the descriptive statistics of each individual business model. By doing so, we are obtaining an unambiguous assignment of the respective business model for each individual bank. To unveil the structure of the specific banking systems, we finally group the business models country wise and weight them with the corresponding total assets.

For the sake of simplicity, Figure 5 depicts the results for the six largest economies of the EU. At a first glance, a strong heterogeneity of the composition of banking sectors across Europe becomes obvious. Spain, Italy and the Netherlands have a strong reliance on (some type of) retail-oriented

---

2   The latest data available is obtained from Orbis Bank Focus for the year 2016.

Figure 5

Banking business models in 2016 (percent of assets)

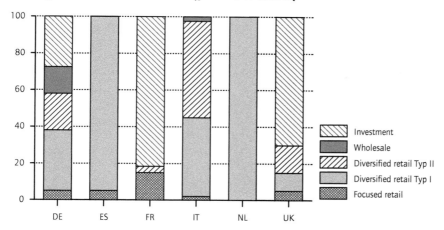

DE = Germany, ES = Spain, FR = France, IT = Italy, NL = Netherlands, UK = United Kingdom.

Source: Bureau van Dijk (2018), own calculations.

Table 1

Quantity and size of banks (2016)

	Germany	Spain	France	Italy	Netherlands	United Kingdom	Europe
Number	1,632	206	422	546	92	370	6,648
Total Assets (in billion euros)	7,083.6	3,591.2	7,216.0	2,700.4	2,533.0	10,935.8	33,398.8
Average Size (in billion euros)	4.340	17.433	17.099	4.945	27.532	29.556	5.023

Source: ECB (2017), own calculations.

banks, as they account for 95 percent, 97.5 percent and 100 percent of the country's total banking assets. In contrast, the UK and France have a strong focus on investment banks, as they account for 70 percent and 81.5 percent of total asset, respectively. Wholesale banking, i.e. interbank lending markets, seems negligible across Europe. In terms of business models, Germany has the most balanced banking system of the considered countries, as retail-orientated bank's and capital market-orientated bank's assets are nearly equal, with a slight focus on the former (58 percent versus 42 percent). These results are in line with the literature, especially Ayadi et al. (2016).

Table 1 gives an overview over various size indicators for the banking systems of the considered countries. In terms of the total number, Germany has by far the highest number of banks with 1632 institutes (24.5 percent) within the EU. In terms of (consolidated) total assets, the UK has the biggest banking sector with approx. 11 trillion euros, followed by France and Germany both having total assets of approximately 7 trillion euros. Those three countries account for almost 75 percent of total assets in the EU. While banks in Germany and Italy are rather smallish on average with 4.3 billion euros and 4.9 billion euros of total assets respectively, the Netherlands and UK have large institutes with total assets of approx. 30 billion euros on average.

3 Real economies' requirement specifications

One of the most prominent functions of the banking industry is to provide access to financial services for enterprises as well as private households. Consequently, the supply side structure should sufficiently fit to the particular demands of their potential customers. Hence, the links between both sides of the market are characterized by, at least, geographic, social and economic conditions of a country. A major challenge of the European Banking Union (EBU) is to achieve the goals of an unrestricted single market and competitive national subsystems simultaneously. In this section, we try to present a very brief impression of the variety of determining factors throughout the member states of the European Union.

3.1 Geographical considerations

Even at a first glance, the enormous differences in population and geographical size of EU-countries are more than obvious. The banking industry in Malta has to serve 476 thousand people only whereas in Germany 82.8 million inhabitants request financial products. Again, in Malta just 316 km^2 need to be covered while France spreads over 643.5 thousand km^2. Therefore, it makes sense to distinguish, somewhat analogously to banking regulations, between "significant" and "less significant" countries in the EU. Before we concentrate on the six largest EU-economies, a few additional facts may stress the position that a single or uniform industry structure is not worth striving for even in banking markets.

Although impressive on their own, the total numbers of population and sizes still veil the additional structural characteristics of the entire group. For example, when it comes to compare the member states' constitutional governance not only traditional (or historical) deviations can be observed. Germany, for instance, is organized (by name) as a "federal" republic, while France or Italy are more or less "centrally" governed. The respective repercussions are shown in Figure 6.

The picture reflects the regional organization of each EU-country on the lowest statistical level.[3] In 2016 Eurostat filed almost 1350 entities, solely 30 percent belonged to Germany. For a small number of states the dispersion in size of NUTS 3 regions is exceptionally huge (e. g. France or Finland), but even in the majority of the remaining countries the range of regional demarcation on the lowest level is significantly larger than in Germany.

---

3 NUTS stands for „Nomenclature of territorial units for statistics", level 3 comprises the smallest administrative regions in the particular countries, especially in Germany to districts ("Kreise"). See Eurostat (2018:9ff) for more detailed information.

Figure 6

Size of NUTS 3 regions (in km², 2016)

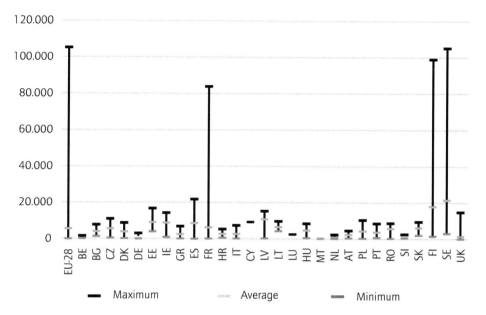

Source: Eurostat (2018).

Figure 7

Population in NUTS 3 regions (in thousands, 2016)

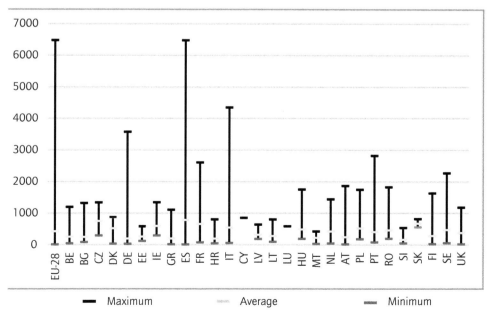

Source: Eurostat (2018).

Figure 8

Regional distribution of population (2017)

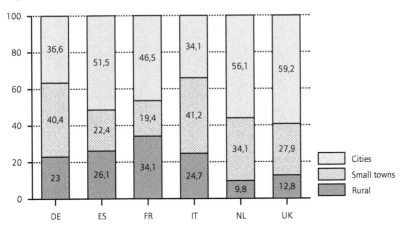

DE = Germany, ES = Spain, FR = France, IT = Italy, NL = Netherlands, UK = United Kingdom.

Source: Eurostat (2018).

Due to three rather crowded metropolitan areas (Berlin, Hamburg, and Munich) Germany also features outliers as regards population in NUTS 3 regions (Figure 7). Nevertheless, on average only Belgium and Malta have less inhabitants on this level than Germany.

An additional measure for regional disparities is the degree of urbanization (DEGRURB) (Eurostat 2018). Based on data of local administrative units the concept investigates the spatial living conditions across the EU. Figure 8 depicts the results for its six largest economies[4] for which it seems reasonable to assume that they are quite equally developed. Once again, the outcome emphasizes the renunciation from identical regional economic features. In Germany and Italy, the largest share of inhabitants lives in small towns and suburbs while in all other countries the most preferred locations are cities. Only about 10 percent of citizens decide for living in rural areas in the Netherlands and the United Kingdom whereas in Spain and France small towns and suburbs seem to be far less attractive than rural areas.

Even our cursory description reveals considerable regional discrepancies within the group of EU member states. These should be taken into account when decisions about appropriate structures of banking systems are discussed. It seems to be very unlikely that a "one size fits all-rule" could be a sensible approach.

---

4   This subsample makes up for almost two thirds of the total EU-GDP.

Figure 9

Share of gross value added by sectors (in percent, 2017)

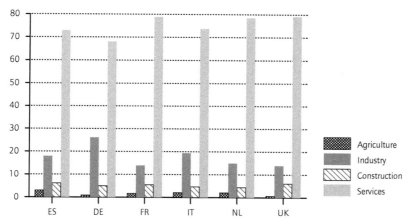

ES = Spain, DE = Germany, FR = France, IT = Italy, NL = Netherlands, UK = United Kingdom.

Source: Eurostat (2018).

3.2 Aspects of Economic Infrastructure

The respective structure of an economy's banking system not only has to match its regional features, but also should effectively support the particular country's economic infrastructure. Again, the initial situations are quite different among the EU-28 members. Even between the six largest exponents of the EU significant disparities can be observed.

Unsurprisingly, services dominate the national economies under inspection (Figure 9). Nonetheless, the respective shares differ by rather 10 percentage points between Germany and the United Kingdom. In each country, agriculture is of far least importance, while construction makes up for about 5 percent of total gross value added in the entire sample. Germany's unique characteristic is represented by its manufacturing industry. Since production facilities most frequently require specific plants and machinery, enterprises from this sector are prominent potential customers of financial intermediaries.

Of course, financial opportunities and restrictions not least depend on firm size. Large, globally operating stock companies are supposed to have direct access to institutional financial markets. They are able to acquire additional equity as well as debt capital with different time to maturity. Supplementary bank loans especially serve as short-term funds for current expenditures. Hence, the size structure of enterprises may have a significant impact on banking firms' positioning.

Frequently, the number of employees determines an enterprise's size class. Small and medium sized enterprises (MSE) range up to 249 employees, divided into four sub-classes. Firms with as many as 250 employees are referred to as large enterprises. Figure 10 visualizes the conditions for our country sample.

Figure 10

Share of gross value added by size class (2016)

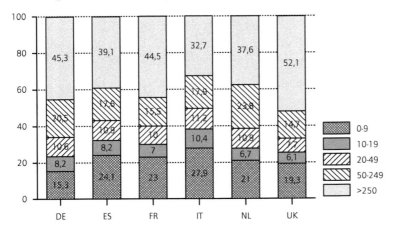

DE = Germany, ES = Spain, FR = France, IT = Italy, NL = Netherlands, UK = United Kingdom.

Source: Eurostat (2018).

Table 2

Average features of enterprises by size classes (2016)

Size	GVA	Empl.	GVA	Empl.	GVA	Empl.	GVA	Empl.	GVA	Empl.	GVA	Empl.
Total	0.7	12	0.2	4	0.3	5	0.2	4	0.3	5	0.6	9
0-9	0.1	3	0.0	2	0.1	2	0.1	2	0.1	1	0.1	2
10-19	0.5	13	0.5	13	0.8	16	0.6	13	0.9	18	0.7	14
20-49	1.4	30	1.2	30	2.0	35	1.6	30	2.5	39	1.7	35
50-249	5.6	97	5.5	102	7.4	117	6.4	96	9.8	120	6.9	114
250+	63.9	904	58.2	1,020	99.8	1,364	70.5	957	80.9	1,199	109.7	1,483

GVA = Gross value added in million euro, Empl. = Employees
Source: Eurostat (2018), own calculations.

Although the patterns seem to be similar, differences in detail exist. In Germany, the impact of very small enterprises on total Gross value added is the lowest, while in Italy the very large companies add less than one third to total Gross value added. The United Kingdom depends largely on enterprises with more than 250 employees, France and Germany, too, show very productive firms in the highest size class.

Table 2 reveals further insights. The most significant disparities between the six countries arise for the top category of enterprises. In this size class, Germany's firms are rather small although their number (11,762) is almost twice as large as in the UK (6,196). These enterprises are widely spread all over the German landscape; they are very often owner managed and comprise "hidden

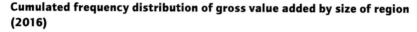

Figure 11

Cumulated frequency distribution of gross value added by size of region (2016)

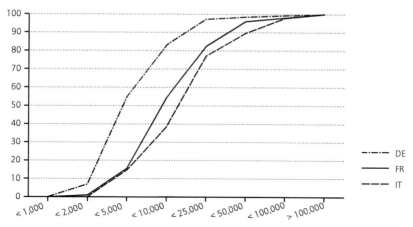

Source: Eurostat (2018), own calculations.

champions" as well as entities closely associated with multinational corporations. The majority of them has no access to institutional financial markets and, therefore, is reliant on effective credit institutions.

Figure 11 combines NUTS 3 regions with local Gross value added, respectively. For sake of simplicity, only three EU-member states are depicted. The principal result fits quite well with our findings so far. We pointed out that especially in Germany significant fractions of Gross value added are produced in rather small and remote regions. In 2016, only less than 20 percent of the total Gross value added are supplied in regions larger than 10,000 km², while in France more than 60 percent and in Italy, nearly 45 percent of total Gross value added originate from regions with a size of at least 10,000 km².

The consequences for a matching banking system are somewhat straightforward: The less centralized a country with respect to population as well as to economic activity, the more dispersed should be the respective banking sector. Hence, the frequently stated "overbanked"-accusation towards Germany does not take into consideration the facts of specific spatial distributions of population and industry.

Figure 12

Banking system characteristics

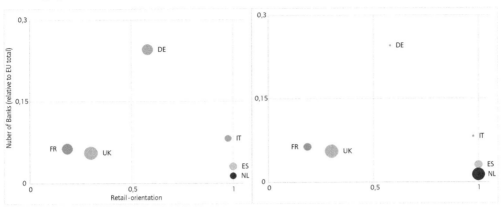

Source: Own calculations.

4   Synthesis

Figure 12 shows the combined results from the business model analysis and size indicators. While the ordinate depicts the (relative) quantity of banks for each banking system (as percent of number of EU total), the abscissa projects the influence of usiness models, where "0" implies a fully capital market-orientated banking system and "1" indicates a complete retail-orientation. The size of the dots on the left-hand side reflects the total size of the banking sectors in terms of assets, on the right-hand side the size represents the average size of individual institutes.

In summary, it can be stated that the UK and France both have large banking systems in terms of total assets with a strong capital market-orientation and rather few and also large institutes. Italy, Spain and the Netherlands have rather small banking systems and a strong focus on retail banking provided by rather few banks. Surprisingly in the Netherlands, institutes are rather small on average. The German banking sector is very different: a large banking sector in terms of total assets combined with a huge absolute number of institutes leads to rather small banks on average. Business models are balanced between retail-orientation and capital market-orientation.

We compare the particular structure of the socioeconomic parameters for the sample of Germany, France, and Italy in a similar way. Figure 13 presents the results. Again, the highest score in each of the characteristics under examination serves as a benchmark ("1.00") for the manifestation of the compared countries: Since the level of urbanization is the largest in France, Germany and Italy list significantly lower scores. Additionally, France is on top regarding average size as well as average population of the NUTS 3 regions, and Gross value added in the Service industry. Germany exhibits the most productive regions with size of less than 10,000 km², and Italy's SMEs own a comparatively large share of total Gross value added.

With a deeper look on Figure 13, distinct differences in the shapes of the respective "cobwebs" are obvious. Most prominent dispersions occur when appealing to spatial attributes. Germany

Figure 13

Socioeconomic characteristics for chosen countries

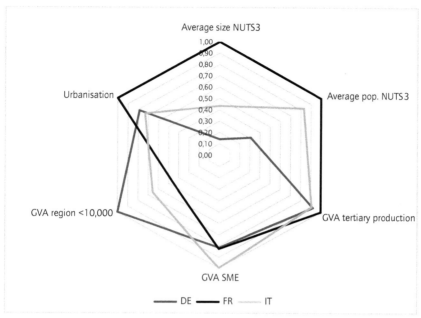

Source: Own calculations.

is by far more dependent on rather small, sparsely populated but very productive regions than France or Italy. Hence, it is not very surprising instead almost necessary to have a fitting banking system available. Consequently, German banks are quite numerous but comparatively small and predominantly regionally operating.

France, on the contrary, is much more urbanized and less regionally diversified. Even the NUTS 3 regions are relatively large and densely populated. Nevertheless, major shares of total production are provided by metropolitan centers. Consecutively, French credit institutions are larger on average with a significant focus on investment banking.

Our very brief look on a small sample of national financial markets structures highlights the relevance of socioeconomic conditions for an economy's effective institutional organization. Furthermore, it provides evidence for the hypothesis, that different socioeconomic conditions require appropriately designed corresponding financial sectors.

Irrespectively of significant progress in establishing a European Banking Union so far, the track of ongoing consolidation and (so-called) harmonization of national financial industries should be seriously reconsidered, as there are valid reasons for existing structures. "United in diversity" is not only the EU's slogan, but a desireable goal for European policy to achieve with particular emphasis on diversity.

References

— Ayadi, Rim, Willem De Groen, Ibtihel Sassi, Walid Mathlouthi, Harol Rey and Olivier Aubry (2016): Banking Business Models Monitor 2015 Europe. Centre for European Policy Studies, Brussels.

— BIS (2018a): Summary of debt securities outstanding. http://stats.bis.org/statx/srs/table/c1 (accessed December 2018).

— BIS (2018b): Consolidated banking statistics (CBS_PUB). http://stats.bis.org:8089/sta-tx/srs/table/b1?m=S&f=csv (accessed December 2018).

— Behr, Patrick, Lars Norden and Felix Noth (2013): Financial constraints of private firms and bank lending behavior. Journal of Banking & Finance, 37, 3472–3485.

— Brämer, Patrick, Horst Gischer and Toni Richter (2010): Das deutsche Bankensystem im Umfeld der internationalen Finanzkrise, List Forum für Wirtschafts- und Finanzpolitik, 36 (4), 318–334.

— Bureau van Dijk (2018): Orbis BankFocus database. https://banks.bvdinfo.com/version-20181219/home.serv?product=OrbisBanks (accessed December 2018).

— Calinski, Tadeusz, and Jerzy Harabasz (1974): A dendrite method for cluster analysis. Communications in Statistics, 3, No. 1, 1–27.

— ECB (2017): CBD2—Consolidated Banking data. http://sdw.ecb.europa.eu/browse.do?node=9689685 (accessed December 2018).

— Eurostat (2018): Eurostat regional yearbook. 2018 edition. European Commission, Brussels.

— Gischer, Horst, and Bernhard Herz (2016): Das Geschäftsmodell „Regionalbank" auf dem amerikanischen Prüfstand. Credit and Capital Markets: Kredit und Kapital, 49 (2), 175–191.

— Gischer, Horst, and Christian Ilchmann (2017): CMU—a threat to the German banking sector? Quarterly Journal of Economic Research, 86 (1/2017), 81–94.

— Langfield, Sam, and Marco Pagano (2016): Bank bias in Europe: Effects on systemic risk and growth. Economic Policy, 31 (85), 51–106.

— Levine, Ross (2002): Bank-Based or Market-Based Financial Systems: Which Is Better? Journal of Financial Intermediation, 11, 398–428.

— Lucas, Robert (2013): Glass-Steagall: A Requiem. American Economic Review, 103 (3), 43–47.

— Schmidt, Reinhard (2018): Passt das deutsche Dreisäulensystem in eine zunehmend harmonisierte Bankenstruktur für Europa? Zeitschrift für das gesamte Kreditwesen, 71, 34–37.

— Ward, Joe (1963): Hierarchical grouping to optimize objective function. Journal of the American Statistical Association, 58 (301), 236–244.

— World Bank (2018a): Market capitalization of listed domestic companies. https://data.worldbank.org/indicator/CM.MKT.LCAP.CD (accessed December 2018).

— World Bank (2018b): GDP (current US$). https://data.worldbank.org/indicator/NY.GDP.MKTP.CD (accessed December 2018).

Limited diversity— business models of German cooperative banks

ANDREAS BLEY

Andreas Bley, Bundesverband der Deutschen Volksbanken und Raiffeisenbanken e. V. (BVR) / National Association of German Cooperative Banks (BVR), e-mail: a.bley@bvr.de

Summary: The structural diversity of the German banking market and the associated variety of business models is thought to have been an important factor in the stability of the German banking market in recent decades. This diversity is manifested both in the three-pillar structure of the German banking industry and within the pillars themselves. However, empirical analysis reveals that there is limited variety within the business models used by the German cooperative banks. Almost all cooperative banks concentrate on the lending and deposit-taking business with customers. Within the traditional business model, two different types of business can be identified, one of which is more focused on lending and the other on deposit-taking.

Zusammenfassung: Die strukturelle Vielfalt auf dem deutschen Bankenmarkt und die damit verbundene Vielfalt von Geschäftsmodellen dürfte in den vergangenen Jahrzehnten ein wichtiger Stabilitätsfaktor am deutschen Bankenmarkt gewesen sein. Diese Vielfalt zeigt sich zum einen in der 3-Säulen-Struktur der deutschen Kreditwirtschaft, zum anderen aber auch innerhalb der Säulen selbst. Für die deutschen Genossenschaftsbanken dokumentiert eine empirische Analyse eine begrenzte Vielfalt der Geschäftsmodelle. Fast alle Genossenschaftsbanken konzentrieren sich auf das Kredit- und Einlagengeschäft mit Kunden. Innerhalb des traditionellen Geschäftsmodells lassen sich zwei unterschiedliche Geschäftstypen identifizieren, von denen der eine stärker aktiv- und der andere stärker passivlastig ausfällt.

→ JEL classification: G21, G32, P13
→ Keywords: German banking market, diversity, cooperative banks, business models, corporate governance

1   Introduction

The idea that the structural diversity of banking institutions is a major strength is widespread in the German banking industry. As Hans-Walter Peters, President of the Association of German Banks (BdB), puts it: "The diversity of institutions and business models has served Germany and the German financial market well" (Peters 2016). Diversity in this context is primarily understood as referring to the three-pillar model of the banking industry, represented by private banks, cooperative banks, and savings banks. But Peters also points to the variety of business models, size, and regional focus within the three individual pillars. Support for the proposition that diversity is advantageous also comes from academic literature. Making the case for diversity within banking, Schmidt (2011) says: "The three-pillar system seems [...] to be a guarantor for the stability of the banking system."

The impression that this diversity within the German banking landscape has a positive effect on the overall stability of the banking market in Germany is supported by external studies. In his book on the role of diversity in complex systems, Scott E. Page concludes: "Diversity can provide insurance, improve productivity, spur innovation, enhance robustness, produce collective knowledge, and, perhaps most important in light of these other effects, sustain further diversity" (Page 2011: 3). But, according to Page, the case for diversity comes with some caveats. Diversity is not a magic bullet and may even contribute to the instability of the system in unfavorable circumstances. It is therefore not easy to establish exactly how robust a complex system is. "The right amount and types of diversity depend on many attributes of a system—connectedness, interdependencies, and rates of adaptation—and they may change over time." (Page 2011: 255)

The question of what constitutes the optimum institutional structure of the banking industry with regard to an adequate—and, in the event of crises, robust—supply of financial services has so far received little attention in the academic literature. Schmidt et al (2016: 563) argue that savings banks and cooperative banks could play an important role in the future because diversification provides risk protection "with the same argument with wich ecologists plead for biodiversity and for safeguarding endangered species: they help us to retain a kind of social capital whose value we might overlook because we don't see it today". Policymakers should therefore not give up the diversity of the German banking structure lightly: rather, they should maintain the political and economic flexibility to ensure that this diversity is retained as part of the social capital of society.

This argument may well be justified, but it does not in itself go far enough. The case for the three-pillar system in which savings banks and cooperative banks play a major role should not be reduced to a kind of 'species protection' measure to guard against future challenges. The three-pillar structure was proven to have a stabilizing effect during the financial crisis. Ayadi et al (2009, 2010) conclude that the coexistence of purely profit-oriented commercial banks ("shareholder value banks") with the savings banks and cooperative banks, which are committed to broader objectives ("stakeholder value banks"), has contributed to the resilience of the banking industry in several European countries, including Germany. The historical persistence of the German banking industry and the absence of major banking crises in the 60 or so years from the post-war period to the global financial crisis are cited as evidence of its relative robustness (Schmidt et al. 2016).

Part of the reason why savings banks, cooperative banks, and other regional banks proved to be stable during the financial crisis was because they had relatively little exposure to toxic assets. They also had a stable deposit base and a sufficient equity base. This was primarily due to their traditional business model based on the deposit-taking and lending business with retail and corporate customers. Schmidt (2016: 116) concludes: "Despite some problems of their central financial institutions, also during the financial crisis savings banks and cooperative banks have proved to be a stabilizing factor for the German financial system and economy". Evidence of this can be found in the analysis of lending, deposit-taking, and earnings trends during the financial and sovereign debt crisis (Hofmann 2013). Both banking groups have proven to be very competitive in recent decades. Over the long term, the profits of the savings banks and local cooperative banks were above average, while the volatility of their key earnings figures was below the industry average.

Detailed studies of the banking structure provide a reliable basis for an informed assessment of the importance of institutional diversity for the stability of the banking sector. More attention has been devoted to this topic in the academic literature in recent years, especially in the form of business model analyses. In all the empirical studies, business models are analyzed on the basis of similarities between banks that are determined using a cluster analysis of key financial performance indicators (Ayadi et al. 2011, 2014, 2015, Roengpitya et al. 2014, Farné et al. 2017). Below, a simple descriptive analysis of the business models of the cooperative banks in Germany is carried out on a similar methodological basis.

2 Business models of cooperative banks in Germany

The international literature distinguishes key business models of banks based on key financial performance indicators. The study by the Bank for International Settlements (BIS 2014), for example, differentiates between (1) retail-funded commercial banks, (2) wholesale-funded commercial banks, and (3) capital-markets-oriented banks. To some extent, model (1) is further divided into a focused retail model and a diversified retail model, the latter with a lower proportion of customer loans on the assets side of the balance sheet and thus a larger proportion of trading assets and bank loans (Ayadi et al. 2015). On the equity and liabilities side, the differences are small.

In order to classify the German cooperative banks according to this typology, specific key balance sheet indicators were calculated at individual bank level for an almost complete sample. The study looked at 1,215 cooperative banks in 2007 and 912 in 2017. In its banking statistics, the Bundesbank reports a total of 1,234 and 918 cooperative banks in those two years (Deutsche Bundesbank 2008, 2018). The following analysis is based on four key figures, each in relation to the size of the balance sheet:

1. Customer lending (loans to non-banks)

2. Customer deposits (deposits and borrowing from non-banks)

3. Lending to banks

4. Deposits and borrowing from banks

The analysis does not distinguish between the different customer groups. Taking all cooperative banks together, retail and corporate customers dominate with 78 percent of loans and 86 percent

Figure 1

Scatterplot matrix of German cooperative banks balance sheet indicators

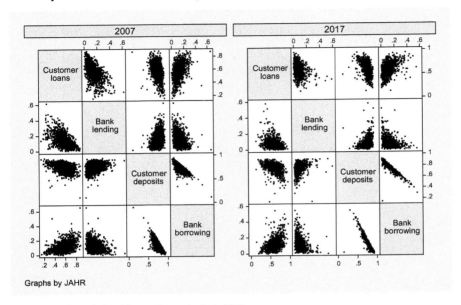

Graphs by JAHR

Source: National Association of German Cooperative Banks (BVR).

of deposits (end of 2017). Other customers include the public sector, foreign customers, and non-profit organizations, which include associations, federations, political parties, and churches.

Most German cooperative banks focus on the deposit-taking and lending business with retail and corporate customers. Consequently, the scatterplots show a very high concentration of banks with high proportions of customer loans and deposits (Figure 1). The proportion of bank loans and deposits is comparatively low. In 2017, for example, customer loans accounted for between 50 percent and 75 percent of total assets at around two-thirds of the cooperative banks; customer deposits accounted for between 70 percent and 85 percent of total equity and liabilities at over two-thirds of the cooperative banks (Figure 2a, Figure 2b).

A comparison of 2007 and 2017 shows that the balance sheet structure variables are generally highly stable over time, although there are some slight shifts. In recent years, the volume of loans as a proportion of total assets has risen moderately and the proportion of deposits within total equity and liabilities has risen slightly, but the dispersion has not noticeably increased. The shifts result from the above-average growth of the aggregated total assets of the cooperative banks by 3.5 percent per year compared with 1.7 percent across all banking groups (Deutsche Bundesbank 2008, 2018). At the same time, the share of lending to banks has declined. Despite these slight shifts, there are only a few institutions in the sample that do not fit the overall picture of a strong focus on lending and deposit-taking business with customers.

Figure 2a

Distribution of German cooperative banks customer loans as share of total assets

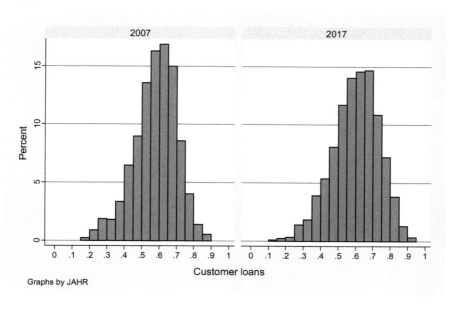

Graphs by JAHR

Figure 2b

Distribution of German cooperative banks customer deposits as share of total equity and liabilities

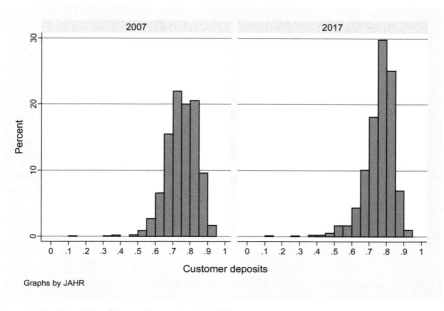

Graphs by JAHR

Source: National Association of German Cooperative Banks (BVR).

Table 1

Balance sheet indicators in relation to bank size

Total assets	Customer loans				Customer deposits				Frequency	
Million euro	Mean S. D.				Mean S. D.					
	2007		2017		2007		2017			
< 50	.57	(.13)	.55	(.10)	.80	(.07)	.82	(.06)	96	21
≥ 50 and < 100	.58	(.13)	.61	(.15)	.78	(.08)	.76	(.09)	172	70
≥ 100 and < 250	.58	(.13)	.59	(.14)	.76	(.08)	.76	(.09)	336	200
≥ 250 and < 500	.57	(.12)	.60	(.14)	.74	(.08)	.75	(.10)	299	200
≥ 500 and < 1.000	.59	(.09)	.60	(.13)	.72	(.07)	.75	(.07)	189	169
≥ 1.000 and < 2.500	.58	(.11)	.62	(.10)	.72	(.10)	.75	(.08)	92	185
≥ 2.500	.51	(.18)	.63	(.13)	.73	(.18)	.79	(.08)	31	67
Total	.58	(.12)	.60	(.13)	.75	(.08)	.76	(.08)	1215	912

Total assets	Bank lending				Bank borrowing				Frequency	
Million euro	Mean S. D.				Mean S. D.					
	2007		2017		2007		2017			
< 50	.17	(.10)	.13	(.11)	.10	(.06)	.07	(.05)	96	21
≥ 50 and < 100	.16	(.09)	.08	(.06)	.12	(.07)	.12	(.09)	172	70
≥ 100 and < 250	.15	(.08)	.09	(.08)	.13	(.06)	.12	(.08)	336	200
≥ 250 and < 500	.14	(.08)	.08	(.06)	.12	(.06)	.13	(.08)	299	200
≥ 500 and < 1.000	.13	(.07)	.07	(.05)	.13	(.05)	.13	(.07)	189	169
≥ 1.000 and < 2.500	.13	(.07)	.07	(.05)	.12	(.06)	.14	(.08)	92	185
≥ 2.500	.14	(.07)	.08	(.06)	.13	(.14)	.10	(.07)	31	67
Total	.15	(.08)	.08	(.06)	.12	(.08)	.12	(.07)	1215	912

Source: National Association of German Cooperative Banks (BVR).

Among the 'outliers' with particularly low shares of customer deposits or loans are various specialized institutions with special business models. These include, for example, BAG Hamm, which specializes in the workout of sub-performing and non-performing loans and accordingly has only a small proportion of customer deposits on its balance sheet. In contrast, there are some banks with a very high share of deposits whose customer loans represent a below-average proportion of their total assets, due either to their business model or to the regional economic structure.

Among the German cooperative banks, small and medium-sized institutions predominate. In 2017, average total assets (median) amounted to 420 million euros. The arithmetic mean was significantly higher at 948 million euros. The mean value is heavily influenced by the very large institutions and is therefore significantly higher than the median. In terms of total assets, the institutions range in size from 18 million euros (Raiffeisenbank Struvenhütten) to 44 billion euros (Deutsche Apotheker- und Ärztebank).

The obvious question is therefore whether there is a systematic difference in balance sheet structure according to the size of the institution. Table 1 lists the balance sheet indicators for seven bank size classes. This shows that the indicators are largely independent of the size of the institutions.

Table 2

Two business models of cooperative banks in 2017

	Customer loans		Customer deposits		Bank lending		Bank borrowing		Frequency
	Mean	S. D.	Mean	S. D.	Mean	S. D.	Mean	S. D.	
Cluster 1	.50	(.10)	.81	(.05)	.10	(.07)	.08	(.04)	431
Cluster 2	.70	(.08)	.72	(.09)	.06	(.04)	.17	(.08)	479
Total	.60	(.13)	.76	(.08)	.08	(.60)	.13	(.08)	910

Source: National Association of German Cooperative Banks (BVR).

Significant deviations from the average can only be observed for individual values for the highest and smallest size classes of banks, whereby the 2017 sample for the smallest banks is itself small and must therefore be interpreted with caution. The ongoing merger activities among the cooperative banks and the growth trend of banks' balance sheets meant there was a noticeable migration of banks toward the higher size classes in the ten-year period under review.

The statistics discussed above highlight the strong focus of all cooperative banks—irrespective of their size—on customer business with loans and deposits. In order to identify different business models within this general trend, the four balance sheet indicators considered can be used in a cluster analysis to search for patterns of similarity between the individual cooperative banks. The following calculations are based on a partition of the sample into a given number of clusters. Guided by the typical number of different business models in other studies, the analyses shown here were carried out for cluster sizes of two to five using a sample from 2017. The selection was based on Calinski-Harabasz statistics (Everitt et al. 2007, 2011) and showed two to be the best number of clusters.

The two clusters are based on the traditional customer-oriented business model and are of similar size, but differ in the quantitative significance of customer deposits and loans (Table 2). Banks in cluster 1 have a very high share of customer deposits (81 percent of total assets) and a below-average share of customer loans (50 percent). Overall, they are therefore more focused on deposit-taking. Due to the high proportion of deposits, borrowing from banks plays a lower than average role in their funding (8 percent). Customer loans are of above-average importance for banks in cluster 2 (70 percent of total assets), which means they are more focused on lending than those in cluster 1. Customer deposits (72 percent) play a lesser role in funding than for banks in cluster 1, with borrowing from other banks being used to a greater extent (17 percent).

Overall, the empirical analysis shows limited diversity among the business models of the cooperative banks. Almost all cooperative banks concentrate on the lending and deposit-taking business with customers. Specialized institutions with special business models are one of the main exceptions, but they have little impact on the overall picture. Within the traditional business model, two different types of business can be identified. In one of these, the banks have a stronger focus on customer deposits on their balance sheets, in the other a balance between customer loans and deposits.

3   Success factors for the cooperative banks

Institutional diversity can make a banking system more robust, provided that certain additional conditions are met. These may include a sufficiently competitive environment and the ability of banks to compete in this environment (which may involve individual institutions exiting the market). Healthy competition is important for the stability of economic systems because it leads to the elimination of inefficiencies and creates incentives for innovation (Page 2011: 214). However, the relationship between competition and stability is likely to be U-shaped, as overly intense competition can increase banks' risk appetite and make it more difficult to build up capital buffers, thereby endangering the stability of the banking system (De Jonghe et al. 2016).

Seen from the industry's perspective, competition in the German banking market has been very intense for a number of years (e. g. Oliver Wyman 2018). The economists view is less clear. The analysis by the German Council of Economic Experts (2013) of market structures in the German banking market, for example, does not include a concrete empirical assessment of the intensity of competition. But the Bundesbank also diagnoses 'intense competition', which it attributes to overcapacity in the banking market, increasing competition with non-banks, and the erosion of interest margins (Deutsche Bundesbank 2013).

3.1   Long-term viability of the business model

The German cooperative banks have thrived in this competitive environment. During the financial crisis, the growth of loans to retail and corporate customers remained stable, but in the period that followed it continuously outstripped the industry trend. The cooperative banks thus helped to ensure that there was no supply-side credit crunch for either retail or corporate customers during the crisis (Deutsche Bundesbank 2010) and prevented the recession from being any deeper. Over the ten-year period from mid-2008 to mid-2018, the cooperative banks steadily increased their market share in lending to both corporate customers (from 12 percent to 18 percent) and retail customers (from 20 percent to 24 percent) (Deutsche Bundesbank 2008, 2018).

3.2   Close market proximity and long-term profitability

The cooperative banks' business model like that of the savings banks, focuses on the traditional banking business with retail and corporate customers within a territory. In contrast to the savings banks, however, cooperative banks do not apply a strict regional principle. This is confirmed by the descriptive statistics and the cluster analysis in section 2. Both of the identified clusters correspond to this business model, one with a slightly greater focus on lending and the other with a slightly greater focus on deposit-taking. In addition, both customer groups are essentially the member base and thus also the owner base. The close proximity between the banks and their customers means the banks are intimately familiar with the market conditions in the region, an essential prerequisite for the success of the cooperative banks. The average proportion of the total assets of all cooperative banks accounted for by corporate and retail loans was 62 percent in mid-2018, while the average figure for all banks was significantly lower at 34 percent.

The earnings performance of the German cooperative banks shows that a focus on traditional banking business can be compatible with long-term profitability, or at least that this was possible in the past. The cooperative banks are now facing major challenges in the current environment of increasing regulation, persistently low interest rates, and ongoing digitalization.

The cooperative banks' solid and less volatile earnings performance compared with the rest of the banking sector is not a recent phenomenon or a product of the financial crisis. It is an expression of their sustained growth and also helps to secure their future viability. In the period between Germany's reunification and the onset of the financial crisis (1990–2007), the return on equity after taxes at the cooperative banks was 6.1 percent, with a standard deviation of 1.7. The average net income for the sector as a whole was slightly lower at 5.7 percent, with significantly higher volatility of 3.4. The above-average profitability of the cooperative banks was thus accompanied by smaller fluctuations in income. In the ten years since the peak of the financial crisis (2008–2017), the return on equity after taxes at the cooperative banks was higher still (8.3 percent) with a standard deviation of 2.6, while the industry average for net income was considerably lower (2.6 percent) with a higher volatility of 4.3. Compared to European banking groups (ECB 2018: 13), the German cooperative banks can be classed as highly profitable.

The enduring economic success of the German cooperative banks is also recognized by the rating agencies. Standard & Poor's and Fitch give the Cooperative Financial Network a very solid AA- rating. In addition to the cooperative banks, the Cooperative Financial Network also includes DZ BANK as the central institution and Bausparkasse Schwäbisch Hall, Union Asset Management Holding, R+V-Versicherung, DZ Hyp, and Münchener Hypothekenbank as specialized service providers. The rating combines all relevant assessments in the areas of business model, income, equity, liquidity, and governance structures. The banks are recognized as having a high degree of risk diversification due to the small-ticket nature of the loan receivables.

3.3 Cooperative values and collaboration in network structures

The cooperative banks' purpose is to support their members and is based on the fundamental values of self-reliance, self-management, and self-responsibility. The members of a cooperative bank join together on a voluntary basis, generally within a regional framework. One aspect of the collaboration—and part of the cooperative banks' DNA—is that it does not depend on the support of third parties such as the state. In line with the cooperative values, the banks position themselves as providers of high-quality financial services. For example, the Cooperative Financial Network is striving to provide high-quality investment advice and is plowing large sums into expanding its online presence.

However, collaboration between cooperative banks is not without its challenges. The individual institutions decide on their business policy independently but are closely linked to one another both in terms of their business relationship and through the deposit protection scheme. Economies of scale are more difficult to achieve within the network structure than in a hierarchical organization. However, the autonomy of the individual cooperative banks with their close proximity to the market remains a competitive advantage and success factor.

3.4 Risk management

Risk management plays a crucial role in ensuring the stability of the individual cooperative banks and the Cooperative Financial Network as a whole. The primary function of risk management is to correctly identify and manage risks at the level of the individual institutions. The quality of risk management is monitored by the auditing associations as part of the annual audit of the member institutions.

Beyond the banks' own individual risk management policies, the stability of the entire Cooperative Financial Network is underpinned by the protection scheme operated by the BVR (BVR 2018). The protection scheme is a central plank of the solidarity-based system of the cooperative institutions and has always guaranteed the solvency and liquidity of the affiliated banks since it was set up more than 80 years ago. The work of this scheme is strongly focused on prevention, i.e. on identifying difficulties faced by individual member institutions at an early stage and taking action to overcome them.

The strong capitalization of the cooperative banks is also an important element of risk management. On a consolidated basis, the Cooperative Financial Network's regulatory total capital ratio stood at 16.0 percent at the end of 2017 (BVR 2018). The above-average capital adequacy is reflected in a leverage ratio of 7.7 percent (including reserves under section 340f of the German Commercial Code (HGB)) and absolute equity of 104.4 billion euros.

4   Conclusion

The institutional diversity in the German banking industry is not limited to the three-pillar structure of private banks, savings banks, and cooperative banks, but also extends to the diversity within the pillars themselves. The cluster analysis based on balance sheet indicators described above illustrates the differences between the business models of Germany's cooperative banks, but at the same time also shows the clear focus on the traditional deposit-taking and lending business with retail and corporate customers.

Structural diversity enhances stability and, for this reason, economic policy and banking regulation in particular should seek to preserve and strengthen it. What can policymakers do to maintain robust structural diversity in the banking sector? The theory of complex systems suggests a cautious approach is called for: "We would be naive to believe that we can anticipate the systems level effects of artificially changing [levels of variation, amounts of diversity, and the heterogeneity of group composition] by pulling levers. But we would be equally naive to take a laissez faire approach to complex systems" (Page 2011: 254).

This means, first and foremost, that a structural policy that consciously promotes structural diversity is not the way to ensure a stable banking sector. Market competition should essentially determine which business models prevail. This must also include the possibility of individual banks exiting the market, even if they are large or systemically important in some other way.

But the lawmakers should not be completely passive either. The principle of proportionality plays a decisive role, particularly in the area of banking regulation. This states that both the requirements made of a bank's management instruments and the intensity of supervision by the banking supervisory authority should be proportionate to the risks assumed by the bank. There is clear evidence that the current system of banking regulation seriously violates this principle (e. g. Hackethal et al. 2015), thus distorting competition to the detriment of smaller credit institutions. Legislative measures are needed to eliminate such disadvantages and create a level playing field. At the same time, lawmakers should be guided by the first principle of medical ethics—'Do no harm!'—both to avoid further disadvantages for smaller institutions and with a view to preserving the structural diversity of the banking sector.

References

— Ayadi, Ram, E. Arbak and Willem de Groen (2011): Business Models in European Banking: A pre- and post-crisis screening. Centre for European Policy Studies (CEPS), Brussels.

— Ayadi, Rym, and Willem de Groen (2014): Banking Business Models Monitor 2014: Europe. Centre for European Policy Studies (CEPS), Brussels.

— Ayadi, Rym, Willem de Groen, Ibtihel Sassi, Walid Mathlouthi, Harol Rey and Olivier Aubry (2015): Banking Business Models Monitor 2015: Europe. HEC Montreal.

— Ayadi, Rym, David T. Llewellyn and Reinhard H. Schmidt (2010): Investigating Diversity in the Banking Sector in Europe. Key Developments, Performance and Role of Cooperative Banks. CEPS.

— Ayadi, Rym, Reinhard H. Schmidt and Santiago Carbó Valverde (2009): Investigating Diversity in the Banking Sector in Europe. The Performance and Role of Savings Banks. CEPS.

— Bundesverband der Deutschen Volksbanken und Raiffeisenbanken e. V. (BVR)/National Association of German Cooperative Banks (BVR) (2018): Consolidated Financial Statements 2017 of the Volksbanken Raiffeisenbanken. Cooperative Financial Network.

— De Jonghe, Olivier, Maaike Diepstraten and Glenn Schepens (2016): Competition in EU-Banking. In: Thorsten Beck and Barbara Casu (eds.): The Palgrave Handbook of European Banking. London, Palgrave, 187–211.

— Deutsche Bundesbank (2008, 2018): Banking Statistics, February.

— Deutsche Bundesbank (2010): Germany in the financial and economic crisis—Monthly Report, October.

— Deutsche Bundesbank (2013): Financial Stability Review 2013, November.

— European Central Bank (2018): SSM thematic review on profitability and business models, September.

— Everitt, Brian S., Sabine Landau, Morven Leese and Daniel Stahl (2011): Cluster Analysis. 5th Edition. John Wiley & Sons.

— Everitt, Brian, and Sophia Rabe-Hesketh (2007): A Handbook of Statistical Analysis Using Stata, 4th Edition.

— Farné, Matteo, and Angelos Vouldis (2017): Business Models of the Banks in the Euro Area. Working Paper Series No 2070, May. European Central Bank.

— German Council of Economic Experts (SVR) (2013): Annual Review 2013/14.

— Hackethal, Andreas, and Roman Inderst (2015): Auswirkungen der Regulatorik auf kleinere und mittlere Banken am Beispiel der deutschen Genossenschaftsbanken. Report commissioned by the National Association of German Cooperative Banks (BVR).

— Hofmann, Gerhard (2013): Kreditgenossenschaften – Stabilitätsanker in der Finanz- und Staatsschuldenkrise. Zeitschrift für das gesamte Genossenschaftswesen, 63 (2).

— May, Robert M, Simon A. Levin and George Sugihara (2008): Ecology for bankers. Nature, 451, February.

— National Association of German Cooperative Banks (BVR) (2018): Consolidated Financial Statements 2017 of the Volksbanken Raiffeisenbanken. Cooperative Financial Network.

— Oliver Wyman Unternehmensberatung (2018): Bankenreport 2018. Noch da? Wie man zu den 150 deutschen Banken gehört.

— Page, Scott E. (2011): Diversity and Complexity. Princeton, Princeton University Press.

— Peters, Hans-Walter (2016): Vielfalt an Instituten tut dem deutschen Finanzmarkt gut. guest contribution to the Börsen-Zeitung, November 10.

— Roengpitya, Rungporn, Nikola Tarashev and Kostas Tsataronis (2014): Bank Business Models. Quarterly Review, December 2014. Bank for International Settlements (BIS).
— Schmidt, Reinhard H. (2011): Ein Plädoyer für die Bankenvielfalt. Frankfurter Allgemeine Zeitung, May 27, 25.
— Schmidt, Reinhard H., and Patrick Behr (2016): The German Banking System In: Thorsten Beck and Barbara Casu (eds.): The Palgrave Handbook of European Banking. London, Palgrave, 541–566.

Lost diversity: Business lending in the centralised banking system of the UK

FRANZ FLÖGEL AND STEFAN GÄRTNER*

Franz Flögel, Institut Arbeit und Technik der Westfälischen Hochschule Gelsenkirchen Bocholt Recklinghausen (IAT), e-mail: floegel@iat.eu

Stefan Gärtner, Institut Arbeit und Technik der Westfälischen Hochschule Gelsenkirchen Bocholt Recklinghausen (IAT), e-mail: gaertner@iat.eu

Summary: Based on the classification of decentralised and centralised banking, this paper investigates diversity in business lending in the UK. Using expert interviews and desk research, the distance between lenders and SMEs in credit decisions for the identified types of lenders is classified. Due to the early disappearance of regional and dual bottom-line banks, today hardly any short-distance lender remains in the UK. Three different approaches have been identified to re-introduce decentralised lending to the island, though running regional banks is challenging in times of low interest rates and tightened bank regulation.

Zusammenfassung: Aufbauend auf der Klassifikation vom dezentralen und zentralen Banking untersucht dieser Beitrag die Diversität in der Unternehmenskreditvergabe des Vereinigten Königreichs. Anhand von Experteninterviews und Literaturrecherche wurde die Distanz in den Kreditvergabeentscheidungen an KMU für verschiedene Typen von Banken und anderen Finanzintermediären klassifiziert. Aufgrund des frühen Ausscheidens von regionalen und nicht rein profitorientierten Banken (Sparkassen und Genossenschaftsbanken) existieren heute kaum noch Finanzintermediäre, die Kredite dezentral, das heißt in räumlicher Nähe zum KMU-Kunden, vergeben. Drei unterschiedliche Ansätze wurden identifiziert, wie dezentrale Kreditvergabe auf der Insel wiedereingeführt werden kann. Aufgrund der Niedrigzinsphase und der verschärften Bankenregulierung ist es jedoch gegenwärtig herausfordernd, regionale Banken wirtschaftlich zu betreiben.

→ JEL classification: D43, E21, G01, G21, G38, R12
→ Keywords: Diversity in banking, SME finance in the UK, decentralised versus centralised banking, functional and operational distance

* We would like to acknowledge the financial support of the Hans Böckler Foundation and thank all the participants in the empirical study, as well as the advisory board of the project for their valuable comments on an earlier version of this article. Professor Jane Pollard kindly hosted our research stay in the UK making the empirical work for this paper possible.

I Introduction

Despite the initiatives to create a common European financial market, the banking systems of the European States vary, especially with respect to the spatial concentration of banks and other financial institutions (Klagge and Martin 2005, Gärtner and Flögel 2014, Wójcik and MacDonald-Korth 2015). Map 1 shows substantial differences in the spatial allocation of bank headquarters for the

---

Map 1

Bank headquarters locations in the euro countries in 2014 and the UK in 2017

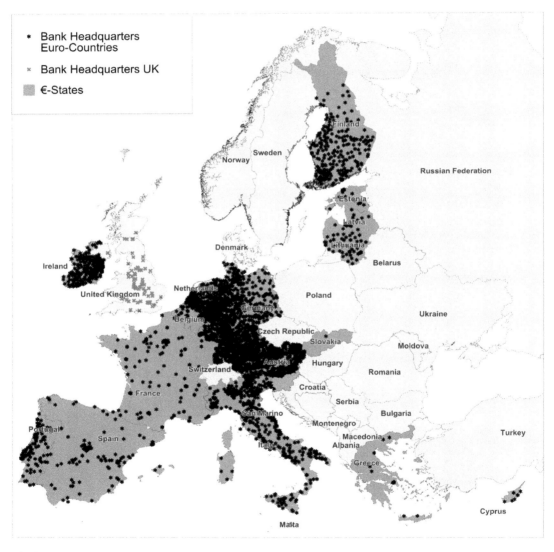

Authors' map. Sources: ECB (2014), Bank of England (2017).

---

euro countries in 2014 and the UK in 2017. Austria, Germany, Ireland, Italy and the Netherlands have a rather decentralised allocation of headquarters. In contrast, France, Spain, Belgium and the UK are seen to be rather centralised in terms of bank headquarters. The existence or non-existence of regional banks tends to account for the visual difference between the European states that is apparent in Map 1. This paper contributes to our understanding of diversity in banking in Europe by analysing business lending in the UK. As one of the most centralised countries in terms of bank headquarters (with London as the leading financial centre), the UK presents a revealing contrast to the decentralised German banking system with its more than 1300 regional savings and cooperative banks (Gärtner 2009, Gärtner and Flögel 2013). Combining interview results with a literature review, the state of centralisation in the UK's business lending, i.e. the distance of lending for different types of banks and other lenders, is explored. Section 2 introduces the theory on diversity in business lending from a spatial perspective and outlines our methods. Section 3 gives an overview of the structure and development of the UK's banking system and traces the early disappearance of regional banks. Section 4 presents our heuristic classification of distance in business lending for different types of banks and other financial providers. Instead of a conclusion, Section 5 describes different attempts to (re)establish regional banks on the island.

2   Diversity in banking from a spatial perspective: theory and methods

Because of the self-reinforcing tendencies of homogeneous and highly connected financial systems, several scholars call for diverse financial systems in the light of the global financial crisis of 2008 (Ayadi et al. 2009 2010, Schmidt 2009, Haldane and May 2011). Diversity tends to reduce the contagiousness of financial crises and thus increase the stability of the overall financial system. Ayadi et al. (2009, 2010) argue that different models of banks have advantages and disadvantages, whereas there "is a systemic advantage in having a mixed system of models" (Ayadi et al. 2009: ii). Traditionally, structural difference in financial systems is approached by distinguishing between bank- and market-based systems (Allen and Gale 2001, Demirgüc-Kunt and Levine 2001). However, misgivings about the suitability of this classification have emerged since the financial crisis (Beyer 2009, Hardie et al. 2013). There is a whole range of alternative taxonomies and concepts—like ownership structure (private vs. government/cooperative-owned) and governance (traditional versus market-based banking)—for distinguishing between financial systems (for an overview, see Gärtner 2013, Flögel, 2019). Whilst appreciating these approaches, we see one additional distinctive feature of financial and banking systems: their spatial arrangements, relating to the importance of decentralised banking compared to centralised banking.

As early as 1995, Klagge argued in favour of a classification of banking systems into decentralised and centralised systems (Klagge 1995), so our approach picks up an ongoing debate (Verdier 2002, Klagge and Martin 2005, Gärtner 2011, Gärtner and Flögel 2013 and 2017, Klagge et al. 2017). In our opinion, there are two important and related characteristics that define decentralised versus centralised banking and banking systems (Gärtner and Flögel 2014):

The first is the geographical market orientation of banks' business activities. Do banks operate on a regional level, e. g. by collecting money from regional savers and handing it to regional borrowers, or do they rely on business at the supraregional scale, whether by borrowing and investing in national or global capital markets or by operating supraregional branch systems (regional versus supraregional banks)? The theoretical foundations here lie in polarisation and post-Keynesian theories on regional banking markets and interregional flows of capital (Chick and Dow 1988, Dow and Rodríguez-Fuentes 1997, Klagge and Martin 2005, Gärtner 2009). In particular, the ability of regional banks to slow capital drains from the periphery to core regions, which is heatedly debated, suggests that regional banking may make a difference when it comes to access to finance in peripheral regions and, hence, stimulate more balanced regional development (Gärtner 2009).

The second characteristic is the place of decision-making. Do banks decide in proximity to their clients (whether to grant a loan) or are decisions made from a long distance, for example in remote headquarters (short vs. long distance)? Decentralised banking capitalises on proximity between creditors and borrowers in order to conduct investment or lending decisions. As will be explained in detail in Section 4, lending at proximity to borrowers is associated with enhanced information and therefore better access to finance, especially for small and medium-sized enterprises (SMEs). In contrast, centralised systems capitalise on proximity between the financial institutions themselves in order to facilitate financial innovation and organise and control investment decisions indirectly. Consequently, financial institutions need geographical proximity to other banks, rating agencies, lawyers, regulatory bodies and other actors, which explains the rise of financial centres (Taylor et al. 2003, Grote 2004, König et al. 2007, Schamp 2009, Gärtner 2013).

Our motivation for the research in the UK was to apply the concept of decentralised and centralised banking—developed from a German perspective (Gärtner 2009, Gärtner and Flögel 2013)—in a putatively much centralised country. To this end, we conducted a research visit to the Centre for Urban and Regional Development Studies at Newcastle University from August to September 2016, where 12 expert interviews with banking practitioners and researchers in England and Scotland and desk research were conducted.

3   Business lending in the UK

In line with recent publications (Appleyard 2013, Cable 2014, Lee and Brown 2017, Klagge et al. 2017), the history of banking in the UK is the history of the concentration and centralisation of banks and complaints about poor access to credit, especially for SMEs and enterprises in peripheral regions. In the late 1990s, the UK Treasury commissioned a report (the highly regarded Cruickshank report) that identified a lack of access to finance, above all for SMEs (Cruickshank 2000). There were also entire districts and regions lacking access to financial services (Martin

Table 1

Number of banks and branches in Germany and the UK

	Number of banks	Banks per 100,000 inhabitants	Number of branches	Branches per 100,000 inhabitants
Germany (2013)	1,827	2.25	36,287	44.79
UK (2017)	364	0.56	8,500 (the 12 largest banks)	13.28

Authors' table.
Sources: Bank of England 2017, Deutsche Bundesbank 2014, Statista 2017, ECB 2016.

1999: 20 et seqq.). Compared to Germany, one key specific feature of the UK is the almost non-existence of any types of banks other than (large) private commercial banks. Regional dual bottom-line institutions with non-private ownership (Schmidt 2009), i. e. savings and cooperative banks, have almost disappeared and the four largest banks (conducting retail business in the UK) held a market share of 90 percent of business loan volume in 2013. Table 1 displays a comparison of the number of banks and branches between Germany and the UK. Germany has 2.25 banks per 100,000 inhabitants. The high number is explained by the existence of cica 1,300 regional cooperative and savings banks. The UK has 0.56 banks per 100,000 inhabitants. The fact that London is the leading financial centre in the world with many international banks indicates that even fewer domestically focused banks per 100,000 inhabitants actually operate in the UK. Accordingly, a simple comparison of the number of banks tends to support the assertion that the banking market in the UK is highly concentrated (Cruickshank 2000, Cable 2014). Nevertheless, new banks and bank-like organisations have developed below the surface of the dominant mainstream banks. In the following different types of SME lenders are discussed.

3.1 Large banks (the big five)

Cable (2014) and several interview partners (RSA, 16 August, interview; RFP, 12 September, interview)[1] see the long period of declining credit since the financial crisis of 2008 as evidence of the insufficiency of the UK banking system. Figure 1 reports the credit volume of monetary financial institutions to the non-financial industry in the UK between 1997 and 2017. A continuous decline in credit volume between 2008 (the lending peak) and 2015 becomes visible, meaning that banks reduced credit volume by 227,558 million pounds (–35 percent). Since 2015, credit volumes have risen again. Despite the fact that the lending figures support criticism of the UK

Figure 1

Credit to the non-financial industries in millions of pounds

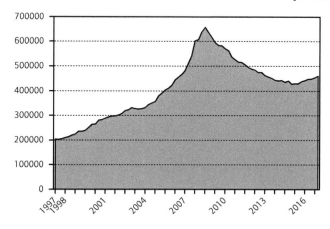

Authors' figure.
Source: Bank of England 2017.

---

1   See list of interview partners on page 16.

Figure 2

Volume shares of business loans in England and Wales[1]

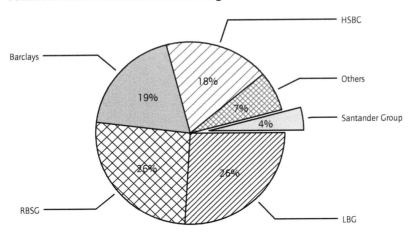

1   In Scotland and partly in Northern Ireland, other banks have a dominant position in SME lending, so the concentration is comparable to England and Wales (Löher and Schröder 2018).
Source: British Business Bank 2016.

banking system, one must also recognise the strong increase in lending, especially on the eve of the financial crisis. Against this background, Hardie and Maxfield (2013) argue that the market-based financial system has changed in the UK, as lending has become more and more important for corporate finance. However, lending banks do not act like traditional (patient) banks, but conduct market-based banking, meaning that they depend heavily on the financial market in their ability and willingness to lend. Accordingly, Hardie et al. (2013) expected substantial cyclicality of market-based lending, with excessive lending in good times and strong credit cuts in bad times (see also post-Keynesian theories on cyclicality, Chick and Dow 1988, Minsky 1992), as seen in the UK in the financial crisis.

Gärtner and Flögel (2015) outline how regional savings and cooperative banks slowed down credit cuts in Germany after the financial crisis as they increased lending, whereas the four big banks cut lending, as did the *Landesbanken*. As the Bank of England does not provide information on lending by types of banks, one cannot say for sure that the UK's large commercial banks account for the decline in lending during the financial crisis. However, their dominant position in business lending suggests this conclusion. In 2013, four large international banks dominated business lending in the UK (Figure 2). The Royal Bank of Scotland Group (RBSG) and the Lloyds Banking Group (LBG) each had a market share of 26 percent in terms of loan volume, followed by Barclays (19 percent) and HSBC (18 percent). The LBG includes the former Trustee Savings Banks (TSBs), which merged with Lloyds Bank in 1995. The RBSG has been majority-owned by the state since their bailout in the financial crisis (Greenham and Prieg, 2015). Santander UK, the UK subsidiary of the Spanish Santander Group, is in fifth place. Santander has a considerable branch network in the UK following the acquisition of several UK banks in 2010.

3.2 Challenger banks

In order to improve business lending, the government and related organisations put their confidence in new competitors, the so-called challenger banks (Cable 2014, British Business Bank 2016). "Challenger banks include new entrants to the market, spin-offs or disinvestments from large banks and existing smaller banks seeking to grow" (British Business Bank 2016: 77). Whereas challenger banks operate in several business areas, a number of banks like Aldermore and Handelsbanken focus on SMEs in particular. These new challenger banks, particularly the Swedish Handelsbanken, have a reputation for being more supportive of SMEs and are keener to maintain *Hausbank* relationships with clients compared to the big five commercial banks (RSA, 16 August, interview). Their market share in business lending is still small and accounted for approximately 20 percent of all SME lending in 2016 (British Business Bank 2017: 81). The British Business Bank tempered expectations for the forecasted rapid growth of challenger banks (British Business Bank 2017: 81). Following the EU referendum, one challenger bank has revised its plan to grow because of the resulting economic uncertainties.

3.3 Regional (savings) banks

To trace the disappearance of regional banks, i. e. the dual bottom-line banking pillars, one has to go back in time. Like in Germany and Spain, the banking system of the UK used to have a savings banks pillar. In the UK and Germany alike, aiding the poor by encouraging savings for bad times was the mission of the first savings banks established in the 19th century (Brämer et al. 2010, WSBI 2017). Savings banks in the UK were TSBs (Trustee Savings Banks), meaning that voluntary trustees, usually upstanding members of the local community, such as aristocrats and clerics, oversaw the running of the banks (WSBI 2017). Encouraged by supportive government regulations, savings banks quickly spread in the UK and their number rose to 645 by 1861. At the same time, the Savings Banks Acts restricted business activities to the safe and central investment of the clients' deposits, especially in government bonds (Batiz-Lazo and Maixe-Altes 2006). The 1976 Trustee Savings Banks Act then allowed savings banks to offer the same services as commercial banks, including lending, whereupon personal lending was introduced in 1977. At the same time, the Act demanded a reduction in the number of banks in order to enhance their competitiveness. The 16 remaining savings banks merged into one unit in 1983 in preparation for flotation on the London Stock Exchange, which took place in 1986. Only the Airdrie Savings Bank refused unification and remained an independent and local TSB until it had to shut down business in 2017 because it could not survive tightened bank regulation in the low interest rate environment as a small bank without a supportive banking association. Similarly, the natural building and loan societies in the UK petered out due to the liberalisation of their business activities, which led to M&A and demutualisation. Not a single demutualised building society survived until 2014 and most remaining mutual building societies were amalgamated (Coble 2014). Nonetheless, the mutual lenders held over 20 percent of market shares in outstanding mortgages in 2017 (BSA 2017), though they were much less significant in business lending (BBA, 17 August, interview).

As in other European countries, e. g. Spain (Gärtner and Fernandez 2018), the UK's TSBs were only granted permission to lend to clients with liberalisation in the 1970s. In contrast, savings banks in Germany were founded with the mandate to support small local firms with loans from the beginning. Hence, lending to small firms and private individuals has always been a business segment of Germany's savings banks. Here, the large commercial banks were latecomers as they targeted small private and business clients only after the Second World War (Gall et al. 1995, Historische Gesellschaft der Deutschen Bank e. V. 2009). Lending at a short distance to clients is one advantage of regional banks. Regional savings banks in the UK were only able to make use of this advantage when the permission to lend was granted in 1976.

3.4 Credit unions and responsible finance providers

Credit unions are community-based mutual societies "run as financial co-operatives" (Muqtadir 2013: 1). Today's credit unions spread to Great Britain in the mid-1960s, when credit unions from Ireland were copied in Scotland (academic expert, 7 September, interview). Like 18th-century mutual societies, credit unions were established to help their members by tackling financial exclusion. Traditionally, they are founded by members with some common bond, such as an ethnic group in a community, and volunteers conduct the business (academic expert, 7 September, interview). In 2013, there were 390 credit unions in the UK, with 1.04 million members and total assets of 957 million pounds (Muqtadir 2013). Although most credit unions are rather small and often still managed by volunteers, a trend of upscaling has become visible, especially as unions merge into larger entities. This is in line with the interests of the UK government, which is trying to support and professionalise credit unions in order to reduce financial exclusion (BBC News 2008). New regulations have relaxed the common bond requirements, enabling credit unions to target a broader customer or member base and allow lending to business and social enterprises (in 2012).

Another group of small-scale lenders are *responsible finance providers* (RFPs), who directly address micro-businesses and small businesses with their services. Previously community development finance institutions (referring to the US role model), RFPs were renamed in 2015 in order to respect their extended focus (RFA, 1 September, telephone interview). Unlike credit unions, RFPs do not take deposits from clients, but rely on government schemes (from local authorities to the EU level) and private money (including commercial bank loans) to refinance their loan books. In 2016, around 60 RFPs were members of the responsible finance association (RFA). In addition to the business lenders, a mix of personal and social lenders also belong to the association. According to survey data of the RFA, in 2016 the responsible finance sector provided credits of 242 million pounds, of which 103 million pounds went to 9,600 small businesses (RFA 2017). This represents a 5 million pounds increase in business lending compared to 2015 (RFA 2016), though the RFA market share in business lending only accounts for 0.023 percent in terms of total bank and non-bank lending (see Figure 1).

4 Distance in lending decision-making

Distance matters for lending decisions as banks face difficulties in transmitting so-called soft information across distances (Pollard 2003, Klagge and Martin 2005, Agarwal and Hauswald 2007, DeYoung et al. 2008, Alessandrini et al. 2009, 2010). For Stein (2002, 1982), "soft information cannot be directly verified by anyone other than the agent who produces it", so its transmission within hierarchical structures or across distances (such as via ICTs) causes difficulties. In contrast, the transmission of so-called hard information is not subject to any restrictions. Actors unambiguously verify hard information such as financial statements, payment history and account information. According to Alessandrini et al. (2009), the distance between two actor-pairs matters for bank-based SME lending: firstly, between SME customers and their customer advisors (called operational distance) and, secondly, between customer advisors and supervisors, e.g. head offices (called functional distance). As Flögel (2018) argues, the incorporation of distance in the Stein (2002) model implies the following relations. Whereas short operational distance eases customer advisors' ability to access soft information, short functional distance is associated with enhanced bank-internal use of soft information, which encourages local staff to collect soft information in the first place.

Several studies indicate worse access to finance for SMEs in peripheral areas of the UK (Lee and Brown 2017). Applying Alessandrini et al.'s (2009) approach, Zhao and Jones-Evans (2017) analyse the influence of distance on financial constraints. The authors identify functional distance (measured as distance between branch and headquarters) as one of the reasons for the higher financial constraints found in the periphery, whereas operational distance (number of branches) tends to be unrelated to SMEs' access to credit. Interestingly, the study also identifies the "abnormality of London", as firms in London face 7.6 percent higher loan constraints than in the East of England. With a similar study design, Degryse et al. (2015) show that it is only since the financial crisis that functional distance has led to an increase in the financial constraints of SMEs, whereas this variable was insignificant for the period from 2004 to 2007. Overall, the studies suggest uneven spatial access to finance, i.e. a firm's geographical location has an impact on its ability to gain access to bank credit. Remarkably, however, there is not only less access to finance in peripheral areas, but also in London (where most banks have their headquarters), which suggests that other effects apart from the metric distance to branches and headquarters influence SMEs' access to bank debt. A purely metric understanding of distance explains information transmission insufficiently, as short geographical distance is neither a necessary nor a sufficient condition for facilitating knowledge exchange between actors (Boschma 2005, Torre and Rallet 2005, Bathelt and Henn 2014). Instead, other dimensions of closeness such as social and organisational embeddedness and cognitive affinity must be considered to fully understand the effect of distance in banking (Uzzi and Lancaster 2003, Klagge and Martin 2005, Alessandrini et al. 2009, 2010). Nonetheless, short geographical distance eases the transmission of soft information because it facilitates face-to-face interaction and supports other forms of closeness like social embeddedness. This is one reason why several authors argue that regional banks operating at short geographical distances should conduct superior screening and monitoring of informationally opaque SMEs (Klagge 1995, Gärtner 2009, Alessandrini et al. 2010). We now turn to the geographical and non-geographical aspects of distance in the credit decision-making of different types of banks and other financial providers in the UK.

Figure 3 displays the functional and operational distance of the lenders studied. The position of these organisations on the x- and y-axis are estimated heuristically. The font size of their names indicates the lending volume to business to give an impression of the comparative importance of the lenders (see Section 3 for the discussion of market shares in business lending). The positions in the axis are not calculated but are classified in short, medium and long distance, based on our qualitative empirical work.

Figure 3

A heuristic classification of distance in SME finance of banks and other financial providers of the UK
(font size illustrates the volume of business loans)

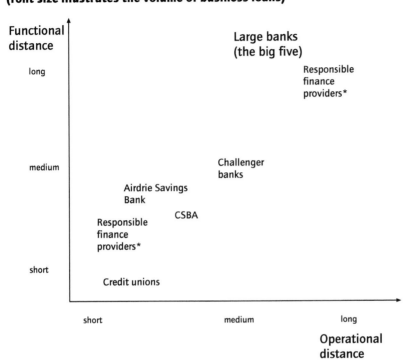

*Depending on the scheme, responsible finance providers approve loans at rather short or rather long functional and operational distance.
Source: Authors' figure.

4.1   Large banks (the big five)

The interview partners outlined a major change in business lending by the large commercial banks approximately in the mid-1990s. The old system was characterised by close relationships between clients and local managers (customer advisors) in the branches. The local customer advisors enjoyed considerable lending autonomy and approved credit on the basis of trust and local knowledge. In contrast, today local customer advisors sell loans and other services on the basis of predefined criteria, such as credit scores, and have very limited discretion (RSA, 16 August, interview; CSBA, 12 September, interview; academic expert, 18 August, interview; BBA, 17 August, interview; RFA, 1 September, telephone interview; academic expert, 13 September, interview). This lack of local lending authority among the large commercial banks is criticised because central lending limits fail to take specific local circumstances into consideration, for example (RSA, 16 August, interview), and make it harder to take local and soft information into account. On the other hand, the British Bankers' Association (BBA) also points out that the old system was rather conservative and prone to error, arbitrariness and discrimination (BBA, 17 August, interview). The general curtailing of lending authority from local branches and their managers is well document-ed (Leyshon and Thrift, 1999, Leyshon and Pollard 2000, Mason 2010, Vik 2016). The following details concerning operational and functional distance have been observed[2]:

Starting with *operational distance*, the long term and continuing trend of branch closures among the large banks is well documented in the UK (French et al. 2008, Prestridge 2017). Altogether, the big five banks still had approximately 6,600 branches in 2017 (The Daily Telegraph 2017), although precise figures are not available. Turning to non-geographical aspects of operational distance, according to the interviewed experts, larger SME-clients (with a turnover of over 1 or 2 million pounds) tend to have a designated local customer advisor, whilst smaller SMEs have no fixed personal advisor and rely instead on alternative service channels like online applications and call centres (BBA, 17 August, interview; Löher and Schröder (2018) report similar statements from interviews). In reaction to the new challenger banks, especially Handelsbanken, the large banks have put more effort into personal customer advisors. As such, "what is often said is that the big four banks have now decided that they want to copy Handelsbanken" (RSA, 16 August, interview). Accordingly, operational distance in terms of embeddedness depends on the size of the SME, as only larger firms have designated customer advisors.

Concerning *functional distance,* one expert from an NGO (the Royal Society of the Arts [RSA]), voiced his frustration with centralisation trends in the UK:

> *"All regional anything in this country is being merged to bigger and bigger institutions. And I think there is still this general bias that it is dangerous to give too much power to have local stan-dalone institutions"* (RSA, 16 August, interview).

The interview partners consistently described the authority of the large banks' local customer advi-sors, meaning local decision-making, as limited (RSA, 16 August, interview; CSBA, 12 September, interview; academic expert, 18 August, interview; BBA, 17 August, interview; RFP, 12 September, interview). Banks set lending criteria centrally, which can hinder appropriate lending from the perspective of local circumstances:

> *"The credit criteria have been set globally. It doesn't take into account the circumstances [...] so, that's one of the dangers that this setting of a probably quite sensible analysis of this global or national level has: it doesn't take into account any of those [local] circumstances. [...] The amount of the loan which local managers can take a decision over is now small, [...]"* (RSA, 16 August, interview).

Due to the limited authority of local advisors, their job is a "no-brainer", since they may come to a lending decision based on the hard and soft information they gather about a client but cannot use the information because the headquarters, or central lending criteria or credit scores, determine lending. This is why the old generation of customer advisors have left the large banks and the new generation is trained to sell products. Therefore, the interview partner from the RSA is sceptical

---

2   Interviews with employees from a large bank were not possible. Thus, the following report relies on statements of other interviewed experts (e. g. regional bankers, banking associations and academic experts).

about possible attempts to delegate more authority to local customer advisors, as he fears the new generation of customer advisors lacks the ability of screening on the basis of soft information.

Studies on discretion in lending decisions depict a more nuanced picture of the large banks in the UK (Wilson et al. 2007, Deakins et al. 2010, Wilson, 2015). According to these studies, "gut feeling" and personal judgment by the customer advisors still matter, also because the advisors have the right to decline credit directly at the client's first request. Deakins et al. (2010) report that Scottish customer advisors possess the most discretion in granting medium-sized loans because banks decide on small credits (ca. 50,000 pounds) using standardised credit scores, and large loans in the headquarters, so the customer advisors have most autonomy in decisions about medium-sized loans. Nevertheless, Löher and Schröder (2018) report that banks have increased centralisation and standardisation in SME lending in response to new banking regulations enacted by the UK government (aimed at increasing competition in SME lending) since the financial crisis. The studies of Wilson (2015) and Deakins et al. (2010) do not consider these new changes.

Overall, the studies and interview results indicate that large commercial banks in the UK tend to operate from a medium operational distance and long functional distance (Figure 3). However, functional distance differs between firms depending on the characteristics of the firms applying and the credit amount, a result we have also found for large banks and to a lesser extent for savings banks in Germany (Flögel 2018, Flögel and Gärtner 2018). Whereas the functional distance of the UK's large commercial banks might be comparable with that of large banks in Germany, operational distance tends to be shorter in non-geographical terms in Germany, as rather small SMEs also have personal customer relationship managers there (Flögel and Gärtner 2018, Flögel 2018).

4.2   Challenger banks and Airdrie Savings Bank

The interviewees mentioned challenger banks as an alternative to large banks for financing SMEs (RSA, 16 August, interview; BBA, 17 August, interview; Airdrie Savings Bank, 7 September, interview; CSBA, 12 September, interview) because they tend to operate with a more decentralised (short-distance) business model. Short distances in lending are partly explained by the smaller size of the newer challenger banks. Furthermore, they tend to strive for *Hausbank* relationships with SMEs. In particular, the UK subsidiary of the Swedish Handelsbanken was mentioned as a good example of a decentralised bank (RSA, 16 August, interview; BBA, 17 August, interview), even though it is "only" a branch of a foreign bank.

Handelsbanken ran 207 branches in the UK and lent 11.4 billion pounds to firms in 2017 (Martin 2017). According to Kroner's (2009) portrayal of Handelsbanken, the success of the business model lies in its decentralised organisation, together with its prudence or risk aversion and slow-growth strategy. "'The branch is the bank' is the summary of Handelsbanken's strategy" (Kroner 2009). The branch managers wield substantial decision-making authority, not only with respect to lending, but also concerning pricing, marketing, customer segmentation and back-office work. Interestingly, Handelsbanken conducts regional market segmentation (every branch has its designated market area and lending outside the area is not permitted) and even supports regional savings-investment cycles (branches are rewarded for equalising their (virtual) balance sheet).

Turning to functional distance, Handelsbanken grants local branch managers considerable authority (local staff members always have the initial right to reject regardless of the size of the loan application), but closely monitors performance. According to Kroner (2009), this is motivated by the consideration that local branches possess the most information on clients and local markets, which enhances lending decisions. Non-performing loans are dealt with in the branches (and not processed in a separate department like in most large banks), so customer advisors remain responsible for their lending decisions. Of course, local branches do not wield unlimited authority. Different hierarchical levels become involved in the lending decision depending on the size of the loan and on the experience of the branch manager. The hierarchical level following the branch is the so-called regional bank. All branches belong to one of the two regional banks in the UK. The regional bank level monitors and coaches its branches and their managers. About 3–4 percent of Handelsbanken's loan applications need approval at the CEO level in Stockholm. This is a low percentage in the industry according to Kroner (2009). Overall, Handelsbanken can be considered a rather decentralised bank. Nonetheless, we classified Handelsbanken and all challenger banks to show a medium operational and functional distance (Figure 3) as they tend to have longer operational and functional distances than the "real" regional savings and cooperative banks in Germany. Moreover, it should be noted that the ability of Handelsbanken and the other challenger banks to improve SME finance in the UK is somewhat limited, because they tend to target rather larger and wealthier SMEs that are not as risky. These clients are more profitable than the mass market of medium-sized enterprises and especially small and micro businesses (CSBA, 12 September, interview; RFA, 1 September, telephone interview). As argued by Flögel (2018), smaller SMEs and firms in financial distress tend to gain the most from lending at short distances, as in these cases soft information can really make a difference in lending decisions.

Other than Handelsbanken, *Airdrie Savings Bank* targeted smaller business clients before it closed business in 2017. The savings bank had three branches (four branches had already been closed) and around 70 employees in 2016. It operated approximately 30,000 accounts and 1,800 business loans. The TSB did not restrict its market area, but had business clients in central Scotland, though most clients were located near the town of Airdrie. A team of 12 credit officers were in charge of business lending and clients had no fixed credit officer. However, the bank was so small that all clients usually knew all credit officers and vice versa. Likewise, there was no division between the front and back offices: the credit officer team served the clients and conducted the back-office work. The credit officers had limited lending authority. Instead, a credit sanctioning committee (in which the CEOs and others participated) decided on larger credit applications. To ensure timely lending decisions, the sanctioning committee met ad-hoc on demand and credit officers discussed lending decisions in advance with the CEO, because it was a small bank with close relationships between staff and CEO. A rating system was not applied. Rather, the bank conducted risk analysis by hand (for example, risk classification was conducted by the degree of collateralisation of loans). Due to the small size of Airdrie Savings Bank, lending was restricted to smaller credit volumes (less than 2 or 3 million pounds). Surprisingly, the bank also applied rather pronounced sector restrictions. Overall, Airdrie Savings Bank is classified as a short-distance bank in terms of functional and operational distance, especially because of its small size and the resulting short (functional) distance between credit officers and decision makers.

4.3 Non-bank lenders

"*Credit unions* were traditionally just savings and loans. So you joined and became a member and then, if you wanted a loan you would have to save traditionally for six weeks or so, and then you could get a loan double to what was in your savings" (academic expert, 7 September, interview). Membership in a credit union was a long-term relationship and becoming a member was a restricted and long-lasting process. Credit unions replace pawnbrokers, payday lenders and commercial banks by serving their lower income members and are generally more client-oriented lenders. In this respect, the interest rates of credit unions are rather high, ranging up to 3 percent per month, as they only gain money from short-term lending. Today, some credit unions tend to develop the lending approach of a more "ordinary bank". Overall, the traditional lending model of credit unions tends to be local and community-based, with very short operational and functional distances. Nevertheless, no information about the new segment of business loans was gained in the interviews. Here credit unions still tend to be very new lenders.

For the *RFP* interviewed, the geographical reach in lending depends on the scheme; some schemes have a local focus (e.g. the business growth loan scheme,) whereas under other schemes the RFP lend across the whole of England (e.g. the start-up loan scheme) (RFP, 12 September, interview). The business growth loan scheme targets existing businesses that need capital to invest in growth. Lending of up to 150,000 pounds is permitted. Four business advisors from the RFP conduct the screening and monitoring. They receive the initial contact, usually by e-mail or telephone, and help the business owners to put together the application. The business advisors check the applications and if they seem promising, they invite the applicants to a personal meeting. If positively impressed, advisors forward the application for approval. The CEO of the RFP approves loans of up to 10,000 pounds. All other requests go to an external committee, meaning a local panel of stakeholders including local bankers and business organisations where the applicants submit their proposals in person. According to the interviewed CEO, the committee meetings work somewhat like *Dragons' Den* (the British reality TV-show where start-ups bid for VC investment), since the business owners have to convince the committee to grant them the loan (RFP, 12 September, interview). Each business advisor is responsible for his or her credit applications and often also advises the clients after they have received the loan. The RFP gives loans for growing the business only to less risky proposals because it has to carry a significant share of the default risk. Considering the fact that the RFP interviewed approves a large share of loans under the start-up loan scheme (RFP, 12 September, interview) we split the classification of RFPs in Figure 3. Lending under schemes like the business growth loan tends to be short in terms of operational and functional distance, whereas the start-up loan scheme suggests long distance in the lending process organisation because at the end of the day a scoring system decides.

5   Regional banks for the UK?

Overall, the heuristic classification developed in Section 4 illustrates the lack of important short-distance lenders in the UK. Credit unions and RFPs (depending on the scheme) can be considered short-distance lenders. However, in terms of credit volume, they lend much less than 500 million pounds to business in total. Challenger banks seem to lend at shorter distances than the big five commercial banks and have increased lending significantly, especially to SMEs. Still, they tend to target larger and more affluent SMEs. Given these observations, it is not surprising that several organisations are attempting to re-establish regional banks (The Economist 2012, Greenham and Prieg 2015, Community Savings Banks Association 2016). The decentralised German banking system tends to be a role model in this context. Thus, following the example of the German savings and cooperative banking groups, such calls demand dual bottom-line regional banks for the UK that should form a banking group supported by a strong banking association (Greenham and Prieg 2015). Three different ways to (re)create regional banks have been identified.

The New Economic Foundation, Civitas and ResPublica, published a seemingly smart approach that would create a regional and public banking group with a substantial market share in one stroke (Greenham and Prieg 2015). In essence, the proposal calls for the restructuring of the RBSG into a network of local banks with a public service mandate. This proposal is feasible due to the government's majority ownership of the RBSG since its bailout in the financial crisis. The RBSG could be split into 130 local banks in England, which would cooperate in one financial group. Furthermore, the business of the new regional banks should be focused on retail banking and local stakeholders should control each of the local banks (Greenham and Prieg 2015). We interviewed one of the authors of the proposal, who explained that as far as he knows it would not currently work because the RBSG has an outdated ICT system that would hinder segregation of the customer database (RSA, 16 August, interview). Hence, at the time of the interviews in 2016, it seemed unlikely that the proposal would take shape. Moreover, the government had started gradually selling off small pieces of the RBSG.

The second suggestion is to re-create regional banks entirely from scratch with the help of a new association that would provide economies of scale and knowledge in order to enable local people to create their local banks. Two organisations, Local First (http://local-first.org.uk) and the Community Savings Bank Association (CSBA, www.csba.co.uk), are trying to push this idea independently of each another. We interviewed a key person from the CSBA (CSBA, 12 September, interview) and outline the CSBA's idea below.

At the time of the interviews, the CSBA was in the process of creating a "bank in a box", which means a regional bank concept ready for local application. The "bank in a box" includes a bank licence, ICTs, lending process organisation, legal form, market intelligence, etc. (CSBA, 12 September, interview). For the creation of the "bank in a box", the CSBA literally copied Airdrie Savings Bank by using the documents of Airdrie's existing bank licence (around 1,000 pages long) in community savings banks' (CSBs) licensing processes with UK bank supervision. Unlike Airdrie Savings Bank, however, the CSBs should be founded as cooperative banks that are only allowed to conduct business with their members. The cooperative ownership helps to gain the necessary equity capital and entails tax advantages. Following the example of the Handelsbanken lending process organisation, CSBs should grant substantial authority to the local branches. Here, two individuals should be involved in the lending decisions to SMEs: the customer advisor (who is usually the head of the branch because SME clients are under his or her responsibility) and the credit officer, who is also located in the local branch. Credit officers' performance should be compensated in line with the default rates of their credit portfolios. Only very large credit engagements should need approval from high-level supervisors outside the branch. To gain sufficient information about the customers, CSBs should try to build *Hausbank* relationships with clients, which includes keeping their current accounts. Compared to Handelsbanken, CSBs should be more retail-oriented, targeting smaller clients with modern ICTs and simple products. Here, the interview partner also saw an economic advantage over Airdrie Savings Bank, as substantial earnings should come from payment transactions and other retail services in order to reduce dependency on interest surplus (CSBA, 12 September, interview).

A third way to establish local banking in the UK involves the upscaling of credit unions and RFPs. Interestingly, each of these finance providers already has a specific trade association, lobbying in the interest of its members. Here, credit unions may be closer to regional banks as accepting customers' savings makes them less reliant on government money. Learning from the historical experience of the TSBs as well as Spanish savings banks (Gärtner and Fernandez 2018), we would advise the introduction (maintenance) of a regional principle, meaning regional market segregation. A regional principle reduces the decline in the number of institutions, limits competition within the financial groups (thereby allowing a strong association to be formed) and enables lending decisions at shorter distances to clients, which is associated with better access to soft and local information and, therefore, less risky lending.

Overall, all three attempts to (re)establish regional banks in the UK are promising, although despite being attractive, the RBSG proposal seemed less realistic at the time of our interviews. Nevertheless, the current low interest rate environment and increased complexity in banking regulations (both resulting from actions that were taken to tackle the financial and economic crisis) make running regional banks challenging (for Germany, see Gärtner and Flögel 2017), as underlined by the closure of the last savings bank in the UK. If it is in the public interest to re-establish a decentralised banking system, it may be appropriate to find means to support regional banks.

List of interview partners

(all interviews have been conducted in 2016)

Academic expert, 13 September, interview: Newcastle University
Academic expert, 3 August, interview: University of Glasgow
RSA, 16 August, interview: Royal Society of Arts
Academic expert, 17 August, interview: London School of Economics and Political Science
BBA, 17 August, interview: British Bankers Association
Academic expert, 18 August, interview: Lancaster University
RFA, 1 September, telephone interview: Responsible Finance Association
Airdrie savings bank, 7 September, interview: Airdrie Savings Bank
Academic expert, 7 September, interview: University of Glasgow
Academic expert, 8 September, interview: University of Glasgow
CSBA, 12 September, interview: Community Savings Bank Association
RFP, 12 September, interview: Responsible Finance Provider

References

— Agarwal, S., and R. Hauswald, R. (2007): Distance and Information Asymmetries in Lending. (Working Paper).
— Alessandrini, P., A. F. Presbitero and A. Zazzaro (2009): Global banking and local markets: a national perspective. Cambridge Journal of Regions, Economy and Society, 2 (2), 173–192.
— Alessandrini, P., A. F. Presbitero and A. Zazzaro (2010): Bank size or distance: what hampers innovation adoption by SMEs? Journal of Economic Geography, 10 (6), 845–881.
— Allen, F., and D. Gale (2001): Comparative financial systems: a survey. Wharton School, University of Pennsylvania, Philadelphia, PA.
— Appleyard, L. (2013): The geographies of access to enterprise finance. The case of the West Midlands. UK. Regional Studies, 47 (6), 868–879.
— Ayadi, R., D. T. Llewellyn, R. H. Schmidt, E. Arbak and W. P. Groen (2010): Investigating Diversity in the Banking Sector in Europe: Key Developments, Performance and Role of Cooperative Banks. Centre for European Policy Studies, Brussels.

— Ayadi, R., R. H. Schmidt, S. C. Valverde, E. Arbak and F. R. Fernandez (2009): Investigating Diversity in the Banking Sector in Europe. The Performance and Role of Savings Banks. Centre for European Policy Studies, Brussels.

— Bank of England (2017): List of reporting MFI. www.bankofengland.co.uk/statistics/Pages/reporters/institutions/default.aspx

— Bathelt, H., and S. Henn (2014): The geographies of knowledge transfers over distance: toward a typology. Environment and Planning, A 46 (6), 1403–1424.

— BBC News (2008): Credit union rules 'to be eased'. http://news.bbc.co.uk/2/hi/business/7480418.stm.

— Beyer, J. (2009): Varietät verspielt? Zur Nivellierung der nationalen Differenzen des Kapitalismus durch globale Finanzmärkte. In: J. Becker and C. Deutschmann (ed.): Wirtschaftssoziologie. Wiesbaden, VS Verlag (Kölner Zeitschrift für Soziologie und Sozialpsychologie Sonderheft, 49 2009).

— Boschma, R. (2005): Proximity and Innovation: A Critical Assessment. Regional Studies, 39 (1), 61–74.

— Brämer, P., H. Gischer, A. Pfingsten and T. Richter (2010). Der öffentliche Auftrag der deutschen Sparkassen aus der Perspektive des Stakeholder-Managements. Zeitschrift für öffentliche und gemeinwirtschaftliche Unternehmen: ZögU/Journal for Public and Non-profit Services, 311–332.

— British Business Bank (2016): Small Business finance markets report 2015-16. Online available at: http://british-business-bank.co.uk/research/small-business-finance-markets-report-201516/

— British Business Bank (2017): The British Business Bank's Enterprise Finance Guarantee at: http://british-business-bank.co.uk/ourpartners/supporting-business-loans-enterprise-finance-guarantee/

— BSA (Building Societies Association) (2017): Mortgage Lending at: https://www.bsa.org.uk/statistics/mortgages-housing

— Cable, V. (2014): Observations on the UK Banking Industry in: International Review of Financial Analysis 36(2014), pp. 84–86.

— Chick, V. and S. C. Dow (1988): A post-Keynesian perspective on the relation between Banking and Regional Development in: P. Arestis (ed.): Post-Keynesian monetary economics. Alderhots, Hants, pp. 219–250.

— Community Savings Banks Association (2016): website. Available online at: www.csba.co.uk.

— Degryse, H., K. Matthews and T. Zhao (2015): SMEs and Access to Bank Credit: Evidence on the Regional Propagation of the Financial Crisis in the UK. (Working Paper).

— Demirgüc-Kunt, A. and R. Levine (2001): Bank-Based and Market-Based Financial Systems: Cross- Country Coparisons. In: A. Demirgüç-Kunt, and R. Levine (eds.): Financial Structure and Economic Growth. A Cross-Country Comparison of Banks, Markets and Development. Cambridge, 81–140.

— DeYoung R., D. Glennon and P. Nigro (2008): Borrower–lender distance, credit scoring, and loan performance: Evidence from informational-opaque small business borrowers. Journal of Financial Intermediation, 17 (1), 113–143.

— Dow, S. C., and C. F. Rodríguez-Fuentes (1997): Regional Finance: A Survey. Regional Studies, 31 (9), 903–920.

— Flögel, F. (2018): Distance and modern banks' lending to SMEs: ethnographic insights from a comparison of regional and large banks in Germany. Journal of Economic Geography, 18 (1), 35–57.

— Flögel, F. (2019): Distance, Rating Systems and Enterprise Finance. Ethographic insights frim a comparison of regional and large banks in Germany. London.
— Flögel, F., and S. Gärtner (2018): The Banking Systems of Germany, the UK and Spain from a Spatial Perspective: The German Case. IAT Discussion Paper 18 (04).
— French, S., A. Leyshon, and P. Signoretta (2008): All Gone Now: The Material, Discursive and Political Erasure of Bank and Building Society Branches in Britain. Antipode, 40 (1), 79–101.
— Gall, L., G.D. Feldman, H. James, C.-L. Holtfrerich and H.E. Büschgen (1995): Die Deutsche Bank 1970–1995. München.
— Gärtner, S. (2009): Balanced Structural Policy: German Savings Banks from a Regional Economic Perspective. Perspectives, (58), June 2008.
— Gärtner, S. (2011): Regionen und Banken: Gedanken im Lichte der Krise. Informationen zur Raumentwicklung, 2, 153–167.
— Gärtner, S. (2013): World capitals of capital, cities and varieties of finance systems: internationality versus regionally oriented banking. K. Fujita (ed.): Cities and crisis: new critical urban theory. London, Sage, 147–187.
— Gärtner, S., and J. Fernandez (2017): The Banking Systems of Germany, UK and Spain from a Spatial Perspective: The Spanish Case.
— Gärtner, S. and F. Flögel (2013): Dezentrale versus zentrale Bankensysteme. Geographische Marktorientierung und Ort der Entscheidungsfindung als Dimensionen zur Klassifikation von Bankensystemen. Zeitschrift für Wirtschaftsgeographie, 57 (3), 105–121.
— Gärtner, S. and F. Flögel (2014): Call for a spatial classification of banking systems through the lens of SME finance—decentralized versus centralized banking in Germany as an example. Institut Arbeit und Technik (IAT Discussion Paper, 14/01).
— Gärtner, S. and F. Flögel (2015): Dezentrale Banken – ein Vorteil für die Unternehmensfinanzierung in Deutschland? Geographische Rundschau, 67 (2), 32–37.
— Gärtner, S. and F. Flögel (2017): Raum und Banken. Zur Funktionsweise regionaler Banken. Baden-Baden.
— Greenham, T. and l. Prieg (2015): Reforming RBS, Local Banking for the public good. New Economic Foundation, London.
— Grote, M.H. (2004): Die Entwicklung des Finanzplatzes Frankfurt. Eine evolutionsökonomische Untersuchung. Berlin, Duncker & Humblot.
— Haldane, A.G., and R.M. May (2011): Systemic risk in banking ecosystems. Nature 469 (7330), 351–355.
— Hardie, I., D. Howarth, S. Maxfield and A. Verdun (2013): Introduction: Towards a Political Economy of Banking. In: I. Hardie and D. Howarth (eds.): Market-Based Banking and the International Financial Crisis. Oxford, 1–21.
— Hardie, I. and S. Maxfield (2013): Market-Based Banking as the Worst of All Worlds: Illustrations from the United States and United Kingdom. In: I. Hardie and D. Howarth (eds.): Market-Based Banking and the International Financial Crisis. Oxford, 56–78.
— Historische Gesellschaft der Deutschen Bank e.V. (2009): Wünsche warden Wirklichkeit: Die Deutsche Bank und ihr Privatkundengeschäft. München.
— Klagge, B. (1995): Strukturwandel im Bankenwesen und regionalwirtschaftliche Implikationen. Konzeptionelle Ansätze und empirische Befunde. Erdkunde, 49 (3), 285–304.
— Klagge, B., and R. Martin (2005): Decentralized versus centralized financial systems: Is there a case for local capital markets? Journal of Economics Geography, 14 (3), 387–421.
— Klagge, B., R. Martin and P. Sunley (2017): The spatial structure of the financial system and the funding of regional business: a comparison of Britain and Germany. In: R. Martin

and J. Pollard (eds.): Handbook on the Geographies of Money and Finance. Cheltenham, Edward Elgar, 125–156.

— König, W., E. W. Schamp, R. Beck, M. Handke, J. Prifling and S. H. Späthe (2007): Finanzcluster Frankfurt. Eine Clusteranalyse am Finanzzentrum Frankfurt/Rhein-Main. Frankfurt a.M., Books on Demand.

— Kroner, N. (2009): A Blueprint For Better Banking: Svenska Handelsbanken and a Proven Model for More Stable and Profitable Banking. Petersfield, Harriman House.

— Lee, N., and R. Brown (2017) Innovation, SMEs and the liability of distance: the demand and supply of bank funding in UK peripheral regions. Journal of Economic Geography, 17, 233–260.

— Leyshon, A., and J. Pollard. (2000): Geographies of Industrial Convergence: The Case of Retail Banking. Trans Inst Br Geog, 25 (2), 203–220.

— Leyshon, A., and N. Thrift (1999): Lists come alive: electronic systems of knowledge and the rise of credit-scoring in retail banking. Economy and Society, 28 (3), 434–466.

— Löher, J., and C. Schröder (2018): Einfluss des Regionalbankensystems auf die Mittelstandsfinanzierung. IfM Materialien 267.

— Martin, B. (2017): Rival branch closures boost Handelsbanken UK. The Telegraph, 8 February 2017. www.telegraph.co.uk/business/2017/02/08/rival-branch-closures-boost-handelsbanken-uk/

— Martin, R. (1999): The new economic geography of money. In: R. Martin (ed.): Money and the Space Economy. Chichester, Wiley, 3–27.

— Martin, R. (ed.): (1999): Money and the Space Economy. London.

— Mason, C. (2010): Entrepreneurial finance in a regional economy in: Venture Capital 12 (3): pp. 167-172.

— Minsky, H. P. (1992): The Financial Instability Hypothesis. Levy Economics Institute of Bard College (Working Paper 74).

— Muqtadir, M (2013): Introduction to Credit Unions Statistics. Bank of England.

— Pollard, J. (2003): Small firm finance and economic geography. Journal of Economic Geography, 3 (4), 429–452.

— Prestridge, J. (2017): Bank and building society branches are vanishing all over Britain: Is your local branch about to shut? We reveal the full list of closures for 2017. The Mail, Sunday, 13 Feburary 2017. www.thisismoney.co.uk/money/saving/article-4166954/Bank-building-society-branches-closing-UK.html#ixzz4qgbo18IU

— RFA (2016): Responsible Finance. The industry in 2015.

— RFA (2017): Responsible Finance. The industry in 2016.

— Schamp, E. W. (2009): Das Finanzzentrum – ein Cluster. Ein multiskalarer Ansatz und seine Evidenz am Beispiel von Frankfurt/RheinMain. Zeitschrift für Wirtschaftsgeographie, 53 (1-2), 89–105.

— Schmidt, R. H. (2009): The Political Debate About Savings Banks. Business Review, 61, 366–392.

— Stein, J. (2002): Information Production and Capital Allocation: Decentralized versus Hierarchical Firms. The Journal of Finance, (57) 5, 1891–1921.

— Taylor, P., J. Beaverstock, G. Cook, N. Pandit, K. Pain and H. Greenwood (2003): Financial Services Clustering and its significance for London. Extended Report. Loughborough University, Manchester Business School.

— The Economist (2012): What Germany offers the world. Germany's economic model. The Economist, 14 April.

— Torre, A., and A. Rallet (2005): Proximity and localization. Regional Studies, 39 (1), 47–59.

— Uzzi, B., and R. Lancaster (2003): Relational embeddedness and learning: The case of bank loan managers and their clients. Management Science, 49 (4), 373–399.
— Verdier, D. (2002): Moving money. Banking and finance in the industrialized world. Cambridge, Cambridge University Press.
— Vik, P. (2016): 'The computer says no': the demise of the traditional bank manager and the depersonalisation of British banking, 1960–2010. Business History, 59 (2), 231–249.
— Wilson, F. (2016): Making Loan Decisions in Banks. Straight from the Gut? Journal of Business Ethics, 137 (1), 53–63.
— Wilson, F., S. Carter, S. Tagg, E. Shaw and W. Lam (2007): Bank Loan Officers' Perceptions of Business Owners. The Role of Gender. Br J Management, 18 (2), 154–171.
— Wójcik, D., and D. MacDonald-Korth (2015): The British and the German financial sectors in the wake of the crisis: size, structure and spatial concentration. Journal of Economic Geography, 15 (5), 1033–1054.
— WSBI (2017): Trustee savings banks in the UK 1810-1995. www.wsbi-esbg.org/About-us/History/Pages/HistoryUK.aspx
— Zhao, T., and D. Jones-Evans (2016): SMEs, banks and the spatial differentiation of access to finance. Journal of economic geography, 17 (2017), 791–824.

Post-financial crisis times: Only a short phase of re-intermediation and re-direction to boring banking business models? Regulatory burden, fintech competition and concentration processes

KARL-PETER SCHACKMANN-FALLIS AND MIRKO WEISS

Karl-Peter Schackmann-Fallis, Deutscher Sparkassen- & Giroverband (German Savings Banks Association, DSGV), e-mail: karl-peter.schackmann-fallis@dsgv.de
Mirko Weiß, Deutscher Sparkassen- & Giroverband (German Savings Banks Association, DSGV)

Summary: The analysis highlights the aspects of diversified market structures and of local, low-distance banking as advantageous for financial stability. Heterogeneity protects from uniform market behaviour. Local banking can better overcome the problem of asymmetric information, particular in SME lending. Moreover, connections to other socio-political aspects must be factored into the assessment: financial inclusion, presence in rural areas, and depletion of regional disparities. The vast regulation and Europeanisation of supervision, however, —so far neglecting differences in risk profiles and bank sizes—have imposed a higher minimum business size, which led to an extensive merger trend, especially negatively affecting smaller and regionally focussed credit institutions. So it seems that the process of re-intermediation and re-directing banking business back to deposit-based lending, taken place in the aftermath of the financial crisis, was of short length only. Regarding recent developments, we argue that FinTech applications are expected to complement, not to replace, existing banking and financial services. However, we warn against existing regulatory loopholes and regulatory arbitrage for FinTech applications and BigTech approaches.

Zusammenfassung: Die Analyse beleuchtet die Aspekte diversifizierter Marktstrukturen sowie regional ausgerichteter Geschäftsmodelle als vorteilhaft für Finanzstabilität. Heterogenität schützt vor gleichgerichtetem Marktverhalten. Regionale Kreditinstitute können das Problem asymmetrischer Informationen besser überwinden, insbesondere bei der Kreditvergabe an KMU. Darüber hinaus sind weitere gesellschaftspolitische Aspekte

→ JEL classification: D82, E51, G14, G21, G28, L11, O16
→ Keywords: Financial intermediation, business models of banks, regional development, small- and medium-sized enterprises, financial regulation, fintechs

in die Bewertung einzubeziehen: finanzielle Einbindung, Präsenz in ländlichen Gebieten und der Abbau regionaler Disparitäten. Die umfangreiche Regulierung und Europäisierung der Aufsicht – bislang unter Vernachlässigung von Unterschieden im Risikoprofil und Institutsgrößen – erzwang jedoch eine höhere Mindestinstitutsgröße, was zu einem umfassenden Fusionstrend führte, der insbesondere kleinere und regional ausgerichtete Kreditinstitute negativ traf. Es scheint daher, dass der Prozess der Re-Intermediation und Wiederausrichtung des Bankgeschäfts auf einlagenbasierte Kreditvergabe, der nach der Finanzmarktkrise zu beobachten war, nur kurz währte. In Bezug auf jüngere Entwicklungen argumentieren wir, dass FinTech-Anwendungen vorhandene Bank- und Finanzdienstleistungen ergänzen, aber nicht ersetzen werden. Wir warnen jedoch vor bestehenden Regelungslücken und Möglichkeiten regulatorischer Arbitrage für FinTech-Anwendungen und BigTech-Ansätze

Introduction
Prospects of a comeback of intermediation and "Boring Banking" in the light of recent regulation and financial innovations

In the aftermath of the financial crisis, there seemed to be a consensus among legislators across countries that the banking system should be reduced to its traditional functions, revitalizing "boring" business models of deposit-based lending across the board.[1] The structural flaws inherent in a highly disintermediated financial system could no longer be ignored after the crisis had revealed moral hazard and capital misallocation as shortcomings.

Analysis of the crisis implicitly challenged (see Turner et al. 2010, Capelle-Blancard and Labonne 2011, Rousseau and Wachtel 2011, Law and Singh 2014 or Cecchetti and Kharroubi 2015, among others) the assumption that a growing financial industry[2] benefits the real economy (see Goldsmith 1969 and, synoptically, Levine 2005 as well as Ang 2008). A more critical view has regained traction among financial system analysts. In their opinion, a large financial sector ties up an excessive share of an economy's resources, or drains them from the real sector, and boosts credit cycles until debt ratios become unsustainable (as stated by Tobin as early as 1984, and Minsky 1992). Moreover, the general public has become aware of the risks and unfair competition posed by institutions considered systemically important or too big to fail.[3] The fiscal cost resulting from implicit government liability for such institutions has given rise to profound scepticism among taxpayers about parts of the financial industry and of business models prevalent in investment banking.

---

1   See Finance Watch 2014: 68, as an example representative of Europe's civil society: *"the crisis did not show that all banks were too risky and that we consequently need more capital markets. It showed instead that some universal and investment banks were too risky and that we need more traditional banks. It is essential to distinguish between business models and promote those that have proven both more robust and more useful for the financing of the real economy."*

2   The value of global financial assets grew from USD 14 trillion in 1980 to 206 trillion in 2007. Relative to the gross world product (GWP), it trebled from 120 percent to 365. Source: United Nations Conference on Trade and Development 2013: 17.

3   On excessive risk-taking by too big to fail (TBTF) institutions (respectively too systemic to fail institutions), see Barrell et al. 2010, Brewer and Jagtiani 2013, Marques et al. 2013, among others. On lower funding cost and the extent of supposed government liability for TBTF institutions, see, for instance, Boyd and Gertler 1993, Soussa 2000, Fecht et al. 2008, Völz and Wedow 2009, Gandhi and Lustig 2010, Ueda and Di Mauro 2012, Siegert and Willison 2015.

The impact of the wave of post-crisis bank regulation is going to be manifold. It cannot be assessed conclusively yet.[4] What we see, however, is a strong trend among financial institutions to deleverage, that is, reduce their borrowed capital level. Many lines of the banking business are considerably less profitable now than they were before the crisis. Reasons range from writing down non-performing loans, through cost increases due to tighter regulation, to incomes declining because of low global interest rates.[5] In addition, earnings are coming under pressure across the industry due to the digitalization of customer relations, new competitors especially in the payments business[6] and the proliferation of shadow banks such as crowdfunding platforms or private debt funds (for details, see German Council of Economic Experts 2015 as well as Rehm 2016, for instance).

As regards organizational structures, reregulation has prompted financial institutions to reinforce their risk management and compliance departments. By effectively stepping up the minimum size required of a bank's business, regulators have set off a wave of mergers among small institutions, in particular.[7] Alessandrini et al. 2016: 17, cast a critical look at the situation in Europe: *"Given that a large part of meeting regulation is a fixed cost, its burden falls proportionally more on small, local banks than large banks. While this asymmetric burden is recognized and in part corrected in the United States, it is instead almost ignored in the European Union, where the 'one-size fits all' rule prevails. [...] There is an apparent contradiction between the policy of banking consolidation and retrenchment and the objectives of financial stability and economic development."*

Policymakers have succeeded in rehabilitating loan securitization.[8] To check the moral hazards associated with securitization, article 405 of the European Capital Requirements Regulation (CRR) obliges originators to retain a minimum of five percent of the nominal value of the securitized exposure or the first-loss tranche.[9] It remains doubtful, though, whether risk retention to that tune will suffice to overcome the information asymmetry that notoriously tempts originators to securitize bad risks, above all.

---

4   See Kotz 2009, 2011 and 2014, among others, for insights into the political debates and economic necessities of a Europeanization of regulation and banking supervision.

5   For empirical research on interest rate levels, yield curves and the profitability of banks, see Demirgüç-Kunt and Huizinga 1999, Alessandrini and Nelson 2015, Borio et al. 2015, among others.

6   On current trends in the German and European payments industry, see Schiereck 2018, among others.

7   In the European Union (EU-28, fixed composition), the number of credit institutions declined by 2,050 or 25 percent from January 2008 to January 2018. In the Euro area (19 members, fixed composition), it fell by 1,695 or 26 percent. In Germany, the number of credit institutions dropped by 396 during that time (source: ECB Statistical Data Warehouse (SDW), Financial Corporations/Total Number of Credit Institutions). In parallel, the size of German cooperative banks increased by 92 percent from 506 million euros to 970 on average, while the average size of Sparkassen grew by 35 percent from 2.3 billion euros to 3.1 (source: Deutsche Bundesbank, Banking Statistics, table I.3).

8   See Basel Committee on Banking Supervision and International Organization of Securities Commissions 2015. The European Commission's initiative to revive securitization forms part of its capital markets union (CMU) action plan adopted in September 2015. It led to Regulation on Laying Down a General Framework for Securitisation and Creating a Specific Framework for Simple, Transparent and Standardised Securitisation (EU/2017/2402) and to lower risk weights in equity requirement for so-called STS securitisations according to Regulation EU/2017/240.

9   In the wake of the financial crisis, Germany introduced a retention rate of 10 percent (KWG banking act, § 18a, repealed version). When the CRR came into force, that rate was reduced to 5 percent.

Against that backdrop, the question is whether and to what extent legislators have met their primary post-crisis objective of making banks more "boring" again (see Krugman 2009 and 2010). Must we admit that many in our industry have relapsed into pre-crisis thinking habits already? The issue is becoming even more urgent given the rise of crowd equity and crowdlending as new business models compromised by information asymmetry quite like securitization.

This article looks at such issues (see in detail as well Schackmann-Fallis et al. 2017). Drawing on the lessons learnt from the financial crisis, chapter 2 discusses the key functions banks[10] perform in an economy and reflects on whether it is possible to get a highly disintermediated financial system to work without friction. Against this background, chapter 3 works out the market structures required for banks to mediate a steady flow of borrowed capital to small and medium-sized enterprises (SMEs). More specifically, the chapter highlights the structural advantages local banks have when lending to SMEs, such as access to first-hand and nonstandard information, and to regional resources. Furthermore, local banking serves a number of sociopolitical purposes, among them the mitigation of regional disparity, the provision of a financial infrastructure in rural areas, and financial inclusion.

Chapter 4 focuses on the institutional structure of the regional constituents of Germany's banking market and underlines that the business models of local banking and deposit-based lending are sufficiently profitable to ensure financial stability. Finally, chapter 5 looks at emerging business models powered by financial technology (fintech), their potential impact on incumbent competitors and intermediated relations, and discusses the need for regulatory actions. The article concludes by suggesting measures of economic policy that seem necessary to promote or, at least, preserve "boring banking" business models.

1 Disintermediation: Consequences of doing without traditional banking services

1.1 How disintermediation was to overcome banking risks—and failed

In the 1980s, growing concern about the risks of traditional banking, comprising interest rate risk, funding risk and default risk, sparked a global disintermediation trend that continued to the onset of the financial crisis in 2007/8. Disintermediation, in that context, refers to a shift from bank borrowing to raising funds on the securities market directly, which results in a transition toward a financial system that relies on capital markets.

In the global race for deregulation, disintermediation and banking market concentration were high on the agenda of economic policy makers.[11] Market failure such as asymmetric or incomplete information appeared to be of minor importance. Instead, markets seemed capable of regulating

---

10   In this article, we use the terms *bank* and *credit institution* synonymously. On their distinction in German prudential terminology, see KWG §§ 39 ff.

11   For details, see Alessandrini et al. 2016: 3, for instance: *"we have had two peaks of financial regulation, the first in the wake of the GD [Great Depression] of the 1930s and the second after the GFC [Great Financial Crisis] of 2008–2009. Between these two peaks we have experienced a long wave of deregulation that started in the 1980s and progressed in the 1990s."*

themselves. Policymakers favoured size and globality. Bringing forth national champions was considered the way to get there.[12] A traditional banking sector focused on deposit-based lending appeared to be obsolete, even harmful to financial stability.

Technically, disintermediation was enabled by the rapid advancement of information technology, global connectivity of markets and real-time data availability. From an academic viewpoint, the new disciplines of financial engineering and the art of securitization provided a mathematical and statistical foundation on which to redesign financial transactions.

In the course of disintermediation, more and more banks confined themselves to acting as brokers between clients and capital markets. While, in the customer's eye, banks continued to be lenders, in fact they were applying a business model known as "originate to distribute", hastening to sell their credit assets rather than keep them on their books as they used to. Consequently, investment banking became more important to financial institutions, as reflected on their income statements by a shift from net interest earnings to commissions.

Apart from the overarching benefits attributed to deregulation in general, disintermediation was regarded as an opportunity for lenders to increase their risk-bearing capacity by spreading risks broadly across capital markets. Those markets seemed to be preferable as sources of corporate finance, too, for being more liquid, more risk-tolerant and almost limitless in terms of quantity.[13]

1.2   Disintermediation and the crisis

As hammered home by the crisis, the core problem of disintermediation consists in adequately dealing with the associated increase in information asymmetry, and the resultant moral hazard and adverse selection. Neither balance sheets nor credit ratings turned out as readily available and reliable as would be necessary for a market-driven financial system to work in a sustainable manner.[14]

Specifically, since it was legal for issuers to securitize loans at large scale without retaining either the first-loss tranche or an adequate percentage of the exposure's value, lending solvency assessments were lax. This practice proved particularly problematic in the case of subprime or NINJA (no income, no job, no assets) lending in the United States. The failure of rating agencies to assess risks reliably, which proved them unequal to taking over the monitoring function so far performed by banks, is rooted in the rating market's fundamental structural flaws, especially its legal exemption from liability (see in detail Stuwe et al. 2012 as well as Kotz and Schäfer 2013, among others).

---

12   On consolidation and concentration in the banking industry, see, for instance, White 1998, Berger et al. 1999 or Berger et al. 2000. Verdier 2002, among others, looks back on the evolution of banking systems including the influence of legislators in shaping them, and relates it to either unitary or federal forms of government.

13   On the classification of bank- versus market-based financial systems, see, for instance, Allen and Gale 2000, Demirgüç-Kunt and Levine 2001 or, critically, Hardie and Howarth 2013.

14   In the wake of the financial crisis, interest has grown in Ireland, among others, in facilitating access to financial services outside major cities for SMEs, in particular. Establishment of municipal savings banks similar to those in Germany has been discussed in a report on local public banking issued in July 2018 by the treasury and the department of rural development (see Government of Ireland 2018). Further examination has been announced.

Structures established in the course of disintermediation thus turned out ineffective in reducing information asymmetry.[15] Inadequate or omitted rating of the borrower's creditworthiness or the solidity of the investment resulted in misallocation of capital and a solvency crisis among institutional market participants. The same structures proved just as unsuited to handling the funding risk ensuing from macroeconomic maturity mismatches.

Looking at the fiscal cost of the financial crisis and the drop in aggregate production, and for fear of a protracted crunch in SME lending, legislators began to question what, if any, economic sense disintermediation was making. The traditional macroeconomic role of an intermediary banking sector, reflected in the buzzword of "boring banking", regained the favour of economic policy theorists and makers.

1.3 Credit intermediation: Reduction of information asymmetry and moral hazard

Just as transforming sizes, maturities and risks, and keeping the macroeconomic circular flow of income running, the reduction of information asymmetry is one of the banking sector's vital economic functions (For details, see Mishkin 2016, among others). Banks are in a better position to deal with information asymmetry than securities market participants or individual economic agents whenever the following conditions are met:[16]

- Local knowledge: credit institutions with a regional focus are better informed about local borrowers (see Mookherjee 2006, among others), which reduces information asymmetry ex ante and makes moral hazards ex post easier to deal with.

- Relationship banking, that is, long-standing business ties with a credit institution of first resort (referred to as "house bank" in German speaking countries). By providing first-hand knowledge of the borrower's financial situation and behaviour, such a relationship neutralizes almost any information asymmetry (see, for instance, Hodgman 1960, Boot 2000, Puri et al. 2011, Van Hoose 2010), and enables the bank to spot any sign of mismanagement or credit misuse immediately.

Another advantage of relationship banking is that the institution of choice is more likely to keep credit available in hard times.[17] A "house bank" has a large stake in helping borrowers stay solvent, capitalizing on its detailed customer insight and tapping cross-selling potential. Capital markets, by contrast, tend to respond abruptly and indiscriminately to rumours or hints of crisis as information is more asymmetric or incomplete, thus making the formation of a boom and bust cycle more likely.[18]

---

15   The European property bubble which materialized, besides in Ireland, to an even greater extent in Spain, was also the outcome of flawed, politically imposed structural changes. Abolition of the regional focus of Spanish savings banks (cajas or caixas) triggered boundless expansionism and ruinous competition, which combined with insufficient knowledge of other regions led to high-risk credit assets. For details, see Gärtner and Fernandez 2018, among others.

16   For details, see Allen and Gale 2000, a fundamental work that various later studies on information asymmetry draw on.

17   On relationship banking, see Fried and Howitt 1980, Petersen and Rajan 1995, Boot 2000, Handke 2011, among others.

18   This pattern is macroeconomically significant because lending standards vary procyclically with the conjunctival cycle (see, for example, Anastasious et al. 2018). Thus, the house bank relationship counteracts the endogenous boosting boom-bust cycles.

Lastly, relationship banking ideally ties a bond of trust between an institution and its clients, which counters moral hazard on the borrowers' side. By applying their distinctive capability of reducing information asymmetry, credit institutions contribute to mitigating market failure.

2 Banking market structure: SME lending, regional disparity and social infrastructure

Lessons learnt from the financial crisis, notably from the stability of Germany's economy in spite of it, combined with political recognition of the systemic relevance of large enterprises even in the real economy sector, have improved the SME community's standing with economic policy makers on the European level, too. Legislators have become aware of the fact that small and medium-sized enterprises contribute the lion's share both to the gross value added and to employment not only in Germany but across the continent.[19] Moreover, SMEs have been instrumental in mitigating regional disparity, paving the way for economically underdeveloped regions to catch up. That is why dependable SME funding is a sociopolitical concern as well.

Raising a loan from a bank causes an SME substantially lower transaction cost than issuing a bond. Corporate borrowers are subject to less onerous disclosure requirements than bond issuers. This is particularly relevant to family businesses, most of which prefer to keep internal data to themselves. Borrowers need neither an external credit rating nor any expensive issuance support services. Loans are also the instrument of choice for raising smaller amounts.[20] Conversely, it is almost exclusively large enterprises that tap capital markets directly since they are more likely to recover the high fixed cost it involves.[21]

2.1 Local banking: First-hand, nonstandard information and regional resources

For SMEs to reap the potential benefits of credit finance, their demand must be reflected on the supply side of the market structure. The loan portfolio of a small or medium-sized bank with a regional focus differs from that of a major credit institution. The percentage of SME loans, for instance, is significantly higher on the books of smaller banks. Besides, large banks' portfolios tend to be biased against peripheral or economically underdeveloped regions. Recent literature abounds with econometric analyses that confirm and explain such observations (see Alessandrini et al. 2016 for a synopsis, as well as Bellucci et al. 2017, Zhao and Jones-Evans 2017, Lee and Brown 2017).

---

19   In 2017, SMEs in the EU-28 contributed 57 percent to the aggregate real-economic value added and 66 percent to employment, see European Commission 2018: 14. For figures on Germany, see German Federal Ministry of Economic Affairs 2013, for instance.

20   From 2010 to 2015, the amounts of bonds issued by German SMEs averaged 48 million euros. By comparison, the median principal lent to corporate customers of German Sparkassen was half a million. Those figures exemplify the range of funding needs, see Hauschild and Kral 2013.

21   For an overview including minimum requirements on corporate bond issuance, see "Best Practice Guide: Entry-Standard für Unternehmensanleihen" (corporate bonds), published by Deutsche Börse in 2014 not least in response to defaults and other disruptions in the SME bond segment. On page 5, the guide recommends that prospective issuers should be generating an annual revenue of 100 million euros at least. By that standard, the majority of issuers of supposed SME bonds exceed current SME definitions.

The differences in the composition of the loan books of small versus large banks are mainly due to their organizational characteristics, which are indicative not only of the level of complexity of an institution's business but also of the geographic and social distance between loan applicants and credit decision makers (see, for instance, Radner 1993, Clark and O'Connor 1997, Stein 2002, Dessein 2002, Pollard 2003, Crémer et al. 2007, Alonso et al. 2008, Alessandrini et al. 2009, Flögel and Gärtner 2018). Those factors determine the operational, functional, sociocultural and cognitive distance between a bank and its customers.[22]

Especially when lending to tradespeople, craftspeople or farmers, soft facts are of the essence.[23] Yet such information and opinions tend to be lost on the way from the branch office to the central credit decision maker, or cannot by conveyed at all. What is more, since staff turnover is generally high in complex organizations such as large banks, local soft facts cease to be available in the long run, or employees do not feel any motivation to capture such data.[24] Staff turnover thus leads to a preference of short-term projects at the expense of local start-ups and regional economic development (see Stein 2002 or Palley 1997). Besides, gathering soft facts requires a minimum of sociocultural and cognitive affinity with the region (see Uzzi and Lancaster 2003, for instance).

Alternatively, large banks could standardize SME lending decisions based on financial ratios. But as SMEs are exempt from extended accounting requirements, and do not, as a rule, have a vast quantitative controlling system in place, that approach turns out inviable. Central credit decision makers hence have to deal with a high level of information asymmetry.[25] Last but not least, it is less costly and easier for a decentralized organization to spot and curb ex-post moral hazards in credit misuse.

Owing to the limited availability and evaluation of soft or local information, and the higher cost of punishing credit misuse, large banks hold a smaller percentage of SME loans relative to the total loan portfolio (for empirical analyses, see Cole et al. 2004, Scott 2004, Berger et al. 2005, Uchida et al. 2012, Ogura and Uchida 2014, for instance). This, in turn, goes at the expense of SME operations and regional economic development (see Bonaccorsi and Dell'Ariccia 2001, Black and Strahan 2002, Alessandrini et al. 2003: 33 ff, among others).

Similarly, in cases two medium-sized credit institutions merge or a large bank acquires a small one, the ensuing loss of local information channels will mostly result in a drop in the percentage of SME loans (see, for instance, Strahan and Weston 1998, Bonaccorsi and Gobbi 2001, Focarelli et al. 2002). The decline in the capture and usage of soft facts is chiefly due to the geographic and

---

22   For a quantitative analysis of geographic concentration in the banking industry, and of operational as well as functional distance, see Flögel and Gärtner 2018: 15 ff.

23   Kay 2015: 155 ff: *"Obtaining finance for a small business has never been easy. [...] But as financialisation gathered pace, and the traditional bank manager retired, or was made redundant, business lending operations were removed from bank branches [...]. More professional analysis of business plans replaced information gained at the nineteenth hole. [...] But the financing of small business is not only, or primarily, a matter of judging the numbers."*

24   See Ferri 1997, among others. Flögel and Gärtner 2018: 27, emphasize the importance of time for collecting soft information facts: *"The long time that it took to legally allow the savings banks of Spain and the UK to offer loans made them latecomers to universal banking [...]. Therefore, savings banks in the UK and Spain could not capitalise on soft and local informational advantages in short distance lending, which had implications for both their profitability and corporate finances."*

25   For empirical research on decentralized decision-making in credit processing, see Liberti and Mian 2009, Benvenuti et al. 2013, Cotugno et al. 2013, Skrastins and Vig 2014, among others.

cultural distance that mergers or acquisitions put between credit decision makers and those who interact with clients (see Mian 2006, DeYoung et al. 2008, Liberti and Mian 2009, Filomeni et al. 2016, among others). Empirical data also shows that withdrawal from SME lending does not necessarily lift the profitability of merged institutions as it affects borrowers regardless of their credit standing (see Sapienza 2002, Degryse et al. 2011, Presbitero et al. 2014, among others). Since mergers increase the information asymmetry in credit relationships, the market becomes less functional, which materializes as a mismatch between supply and demand, and resultant deadweight loss (see Alessandrini et al. 2008).

Differences in the loan books of small versus large banks can also be explained as follows. In large institutions, allocation of available own funds and refinance to branch offices is driven not only by local credit demand, but also by subjective sociocultural judgements of decision makers in the headquarters. Their decisions tend to be biased against economically underdeveloped regions.[26]

Large banks whose organizational structures are marked by geographic and functional distance typically give preference to their country or region of domicile. Empirical literature has documented this home bias for the period of the financial crisis as well. Corporate clients from regions other than the bank's domicile are subject to higher interest rates, lending restrictions or even credit crunches (see, among others, Giannetti and Laeven 2011, Popov and Udell 2012, De Haas and Van Horen 2013, Gambacorta and Mistrulli 2014, Gobbi and Sette 2015). This is partly due to global or multinational banks' tendency to respond to liquidity shocks by overdraining liquid assets from peripheral markets into the region of domicile (see Cetorelli and Goldberg 2012, Berrospide et al. 2013, Dekle and Lee 2015, International Monetary Fund 2015, for instance).

2.2 Lending policy of foreign banks during the crisis

In Germany, too, both foreign branches and centralized large domestic banks displayed a home bias and resultant volatile lending during the financial crisis (Figure 1). Regional Sparkassen and cooperative banks, by contrast, kept their lending steady, which had a levelling effect.[27] Commanding a market share of 47 percent, those regional institutions are the principal lenders to businesses and self-employed persons.[28, 29]

---

26   See Scharfstein and Stein 2000, Landier et al. 2009, for instance. Regional savings and investment cycles, and the risk of a capital drain from peripheral markets have been discussed by Myrdal 1957 already.

27   For details, see Gischer and Reichling 2010, among others. For an analysis of lending stability over multiple economic cycles, see Behr et al. 2017: *"We find that banks with a public mandate are 25% less cyclical than other local banks"* (ibidem: 64). Flögel and Gärtner 2018: 12: *"Germany's savings and cooperative banks account for this smoothing in lending as they increased credit volumes in the crisis. This actually leads to the uncommon observation that large companies (typically clients of larger banks) faced heavier financial constraints than smaller SMEs (typically clients of decentralised savings and cooperative banks) at the apogee of the financial crisis in Germany."*

28   In Q3 2018, lending to businesses and self-employed persons totalled 1.477 trillion euros, including 416 billion from Sparkassen and 278 billion from cooperative banks (source: Deutsche Bundesbank [banking statistics, tables I.7.a and b]).

29   A survey conducted by the Center for Financial Studies (CFS) at Goethe University Frankfurt among some 400 executives confirms the relevance of regional Sparkassen and cooperative banks to corporate finance, see CFS 2017. 62 percent of the respondents agreed that the three-pillar system of Germany's credit industry, comprising Sparkassen, cooperative and private commercial banks, had proven its worth. 43 percent saw Sparkassen as crucial for funding domestic SMEs, another 47 percent considered them important. Agreement was similar regarding cooperative banks. By contrast, only 20 percent of the respondents said that private commercial banks were crucial for SME funding.

Figure 1

**Lending to domestic enterprises and self-employed persons in Germany
(year-on-year rate of change of selected types of banks)**

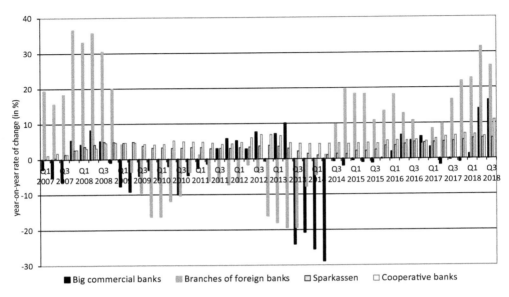

Source: Deutsche Bundesbank (banking statistics, table I.7.b), own illustration.

2.3 Local banking: reduction of regional disparity, provision of infrastructure and structure of real economy

Empirical research shows that the special lending focus of small and medium-sized banks spurs regional economic growth (see Lucchetti et al. 2001, Berger et al. 2004, Usai and Vannini 2005). Looking at economically underdeveloped regions in Germany, Hakenes et al. (2015) have found that funding from local credit institutions increases the number of new business registrations. A decentralized banking system thus helps reduce regional disparity (see Gärtner 2009, for instance), whereas a geographically centralized system endogenously stimulates the formation of highly concentrated financial clusters.[30]

Moreover, the political assessment has to take into account that, small and medium-sized regional banks perform important socioeconomic functions such as local availability, or the financial inclusion of low-income households. Their branches often become nuclei of rural or urban development, contribute to the preservation of urban infrastructure and stimulate the social interaction that such projects involve. When economic policy decisions compromise the business model of

---

30   Since centralized banking systems lack the means of capturing information from regional lending, they need to rely on third-party information providers and contract specialists such as credit rating agencies or law firms. This dependence promotes the formation of business clusters of credit institutions and other financial service providers, see Thrift 1994, Grote 2004, Schamp 2009, among others.

small and medium-sized regional banks, the latter's fulfilling of socioeconomic functions, too, will be at risk.

Their unique ability to accumulate information on local credit markets makes regionally focused small or medium-sized banks vital for funding SMEs and mitigating socioeconomic disparity (see Gehrig 2011). In that sense, the structure of a country's banking market contributes greatly to achieving sociopolitical goals.[31] In particular, dynamic interdependences has to be considered: if strengthening real-sector SMEs is on the economic policy agenda, the financial system must furnish suitable, that is, bank-based, structures (for details, see Schackmann-Fallis and Weiß 2014).

3 Regional elements in Germany's banking market

Globally, Germany's banking market stands out for its variety of business models, legal forms, and the complementarity of institutions large and small. Business models with a regional focus and decentralized responsibility have been the domain of Sparkassen and cooperative banks, and, to a lesser extent, of private commercial banks.[32] Among the latter, however, large institutions operating internationally command the lion's share, accounting for 59 percent of aggregate total assets at the end of 2018.

3.1 Public-law credit institutions and the idea of a financial services network

A key constituent of Germany's banking market are public-law credit institutions such as Sparkassen with their regional focus and extensive branch networks, and DekaBank, a provider of investment funds and other capital market products for Sparkassen' customer business.[33] An additional part of the market segment under public law are the Landesbanken, which mainly engage in wholesale banking. Landesbanken also provide services that complement Sparkassen' product range for corporate clients, such as underwriting, derivatives and price hedging, large-scale or syndicated lending, or international banking.

In Germany, there are 385 Sparkassen (end of 2018), established under public law and operating under municipal trusteeship (*Trägerschaft*)[34] in their vast majority, but also including a small

---

31 On the underlying politico-economic debate about historical differences among equally suited, economically successful institutional arrangements, see Hall and Soskice 2001.

32 For a detailed description of the structures of the German banking market, see Schmidt and Tyrell 2004, Behr and Schmidt 2016, among others.

33 For details, see Civitas 2013, Ayadi et al. 2009: 113 to 138, Schmidt 2009, Schmidt et al. 2016, among others. For a comparison of Sparkassen with US community banks, see Gischer and Herz 2016, for instance. For a description of the structures of regional credit institutions in Europe, see Bülbül et al. 2013, among others.

34 The legal form of public-law institution (Anstalt des öffentlichen Rechts), and the concept of municipal trusteeship, as opposed to ownership, were established in the wake of the German economic crisis from 1931. Sparkassen then ceased to be dependent public utilities under direct municipal influence, which, in turn, has made it impossible for municipalities to misuse their Sparkasse for propping up their budgets.

number of so-called "freie Sparkassen".[35] Trusteeship, in that context, differs from ownership in that municipalities may not sell local Sparkasse ad libitum, nor interfere in the latter's day-to-day business. The trustee is neither liable for an institution's debts (as was the case until 2001) nor obliged to provide financial support.[36] Still, by nominating some of the members of the supervisory board (Verwaltungsrat), the municipality participates in setting the principles of the institution's business policy and oversees the work of the executive board,[37] yet without making any operational decisions.

While most Sparkassen were founded by municipalities, they basically own themselves. The name of a Sparkasse refers to the municipality where it is located, that is, a city, town or rural district. German Sparkassen focus their business on their municipality's jurisdiction, especially as regards branch location, corporate banking and, to a lesser extent, retail banking.

Legally, this so-called *regional principle* (Regionalprinzip) follows from the municipalities' legal competences under article 28(2) of Basic Law for the Federal Republic of Germany (Grundgesetz), but the regional and administrative limitation of each municipal jurisdiction. As to SME lending, the regional principle effects a close operational and functional proximity of information sources in terms both of gathering intelligence (operational) and of forwarding it to credit decision makers (functional). Besides, it is in the interest of an institution operating regionally that the local economy should thrive, because it cannot evade regionally.

Sparkassen are credit institutions under section 1(1) of German Banking Act (Kreditwesengesetz, KWG) and article 4, paragraph 1(1), of the EU Capital Requirements Regulation. As such, they are subject to German and EU prudential regulation as well as to supervision by Deutsche Bundesbank, the Federal Financial Supervisory Authority (Bundesanstalt für Finanzdienstleistungsaufsicht [BaFin]) and the European Central Bank (ECB). At the end of 2017, German Sparkassen held total assets of 3.1 billion euros on average, with individual figures ranging from 44 billion at Hamburger Sparkasse (Haspa) to a mere 132 million at Stadtsparkasse Bad Sachsa in Lower Saxony. Sparkassen' mainstay is retail banking, in other words, deposit-based lending to non-affluent consumers and SMEs. Capital market products and international banking can be provided via the central institutions, the DekaBank and the Landesbanken.

---

35   There are five Sparkassen in Germany that are not public-law institutions. They were founded at the end of the 18th and at the beginning of the 19th century by civically engaged individuals. Though their governance structures differ from those of their public-law counterparts, those *freie Sparkassen*, too, are committed to their regions and to the common welfare.

36   As a fall-back construction the trustees (municipalities or federal states) guaranteed the debts of the Sparkassen or Landesbanken in the event of insolvency (so-called *Gewährträgerhaftung*). The rationale behind it was to pretend depositors from "bank running". Historically, the trustee's guarantee was an institutional provision to secure (savings) deposits when lending restrictions were lifted. German Sparkassen were thus able to lend to businesses and become diversified universal banks much earlier than those in other countries such as Britain (1976) or Spain (1977). To promote competition between public-law and private commercial banks, the guarantee was abolished in July 2001. The transitional period ended in July 2005, insuring liabilities by no later than the end of 2015.

37   For details, see Gischer and Spengler 2013, for instance. For an analysis of corporate governance structures in Germany's banking market, see Kotz and Schmidt 2017. In reply to the occasional criticism of the allegedly insufficient expertise of supervisory board members appointed by municipalities, Schäfer 2018 asks on page 952: *"But then, were the many supposed experts on the supervisory boards of faltering large banks able to prevent multi-billion euro bailouts? The standards of supervision do not hinge on supervisors and supervisees being birds of a feather. In fact, it can be detrimental when they are. What is crucial, though, is that supervisors be willing to ask tough questions and insist on plausible answers. Besides, local politicians, too, have access to experts whom they can consult."*

Constitutive of German Sparkassen is their public mandate, also referred to as double bottom line or dual purpose (see Schmidt 2009 or Brämer et al. 2010), which implies a basic commitment to the common good. Sparkassen are expected to make a profit, but not to maximize it. More specifically, they are mandated to grant low-income households access to financial services, to promote private savings and financial literacy, to maintain an extensive branch network that covers rural regions as well and, above all, to keep lending to regional businesses[38], credit ratings permitting.[39] Furthermore, Sparkassen have been sponsoring social projects, the arts and sports in their regions of domicile.

Sparkassen are thus an integral part of Germany's public services infrastructure. By choosing to have them operate under public law and municipal linkage,[40] legislators refrained both from immediate public ownership or public-sector production and from delegating production to private businesses, which would involve drafting complex contracts to align the latter's strategies with political objectives.[41]

German Sparkassen are allied with Landesbanken and DekaBank in the Sparkassen-Finanzgruppe (Finance Group).[42] Unlike its official name suggests, it is not a unified corporate group (Konzern) but a network of autonomous credit institutions and insurance companies. Such a financial services network is a specific form of interbank cooperation. It differs from a corporate group in being a bottom-up organization, with members remaining legally and financially self-reliant. They cooperate, however, in several aspects and have set up a joint institutional protection scheme (IPS) under article 113(7) CRR.[43] Regional Sparkassen associations and the DSGV as their national umbrella organization coordinate cooperation within the network, but do not have any formal authority.

Cooperation within the network includes sharing a common logo and brand as well as conjointly IT systems and back office services to comply with prudential requirements, for instance. Products not sold by Sparkassen themselves are provided by the head institutions. Financial products

---

38   Brei and Schclarek 2013 confirm in an international setting that credit institutions with a public mandate, especially in times of crisis, have stable lending, while the lending behavior of private credit institutions is highly cyclical.

39   As banks under public law, Sparkassen can be seen as a specific institutional arrangement of strategic coordination in a coordinated market economy as described in Hall and Soskice 2001. Due to its close market proximity and stable market presence, such an arrangement helps economic agents to share information and commit to each other credibly even when contracts are incomplete. More recently, the concept of regional credit institutions, which is rooted in institutional economics, and the historical sociopolitical idea of Sparkassen and cooperative banks have reappeared in the economics of development finance as microfinance and inclusive banking (for details, see Schmidt et al. 2016 as well as Schmidt 2018).

40   Legislators were thus abiding by the views of Georg Friedrich Hegel, Max Weber and the historical school of economics, who saw a democratically controlled bureaucracy acting in an organized, rational manner as a suitable institutional arrangement for creating mechanisms that would ensure an adequate supply of goods and services of public interest. For more on this subject, see Sekera 2016.

41   Given its lower capital, contract and coordination costs, public production makes sense in providing goods and services of general public interest, especially as there is no a priori reason to assume that government involvement in the production of such goods or services should per se be inefficient, see Hall and Nguyen 2018. On the fundamental debate about government intervention when markets fail, in the production of goods and in meeting demand, see De Grauwe 2017, Raworth 2017, Sekera 2018 and Wedel 2018, among others.

42   In Germany, systems of voluntary cooperation among autonomous businesses exist outside the banking industry as well, for instance in retail trade.

43   The option of entering into an IPS under article 113(7) CRR is available to credit institutions of any legal form including private sector banks. In Germany, cooperative banks have formed another financial services network and protection scheme, the Genossenschaftliche FinanzGruppe Volksbanken Raiffeisenbanken.

and services which are not produced by Sparkassen themselves are complementary provided by the central institutions. Sparkassen associations and central institutions also ensure the regional banks' operational and informational connection to financial centres and capital markets.

The idea behind a financial services network is to benefit from centralization without giving up the advantages of a decentralized organization. Networking enables credit institutions to tap synergies in areas such as IT, brand building and maintenance, development of bank management tools or financial products, while preserving their decentralized decision-making powers. This is particularly important in lending to SMEs and self-employed persons, where customer focus combines with local presence, knowledge and decision-making powers to produce stable credit supply and sustainable credit decisions.

3.2 Preference of long-term borrowing

Credit institutions have always been the mainstay of Germany's financial system, even though their GDP share is below international average. The ratio of lending to real-sector businesses divided by corporate bonds in circulation was 4.7 (3rd quarter 2018), considerably higher than in Britain or the United States (see Schackmann-Fallis and Weiß 2014, for instance). In other words, German businesses heavily rely on banks for funding by international comparison as well.

Figure 2

Lending to domestic enterprises and private households in Germany by maturity

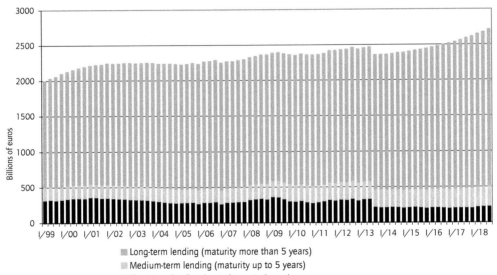

Source: Deutsche Bundesbank (banking statistics database: lending by MFIs in Germany to domestic enterprises and households), own illustration.

Figure 3

Long-term lending (maturity more than five years) to domestic enterprises and private households in Germany; shares of selected types of banks

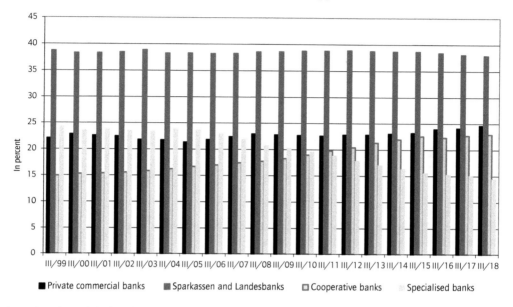

■ Private commercial banks   ■ Sparkassen and Landesbanks   ☐ Cooperative banks   Specialised banks

Source: Deutsche Bundesbank (banking statistics database: lending by MFIs in Germany to domestic enterprises and households); own illustration.

The minor importance of capital market funding in Germany has two reasons. First, the vast prevalence of SMEs and the fact that regarding for those enterprises bank borrowing incurs lower transaction cost than using capital market instruments. Second, the ubiquity of credit institutions with a regional focus, which is conducive to stable banking relationships (see Behr et al. 2013 as well). As a result, there is little need to resort to other sources of debt capital.

Typical of Germany's credit market is borrowers' strong preference for long-term loans. At 78 percent on average from 1999 to 2018, loans running for over five years have been prevailing, with rising tendency. At the end of 2018, 81 percent of outstanding loans to domestic enterprises and private households, totalling 2.708 trillion euros, had a maturity of more than five years (Figure 2).

At 38 percent, Sparkassen and Landesbanken account for the largest share of long-term loans (Figure 3). Also visible is the growing exposure of cooperative banks to long-term lending. Their share in that market segment rose from 15 percent in the first quarter of 1999 to 23 in the first quarter of 2018.[44]

---

44   The very long maturities of German Sparkassen' and cooperative banks' lendings are a consequence of their regional focus, deposit-based funding and specific governance models. Regional focus, in turn, is either based on the regional principle laid down in the federal states' legislation on Sparkassen or, regarding cooperative banks, mandated by their members. Those institutions' long-term lending to domestic enterprises and private households accounted for 56 percent of total assets or 55 percent respectively; at private commercial and

In particular, to SMEs, mostly having only a limited number of business areas, long credit maturities and fixed interest rates are advantageous because they make financial planning easier and more reliable. The banking sector, conversely, is heavily involved in maturity transformation. Supervisory authorities therefore need to keep tabs on funding and interest rate risks.

3.3   Profitability of "boring" business models

As regards Germany, empirical research rebuts the occasional doubts raised in the early literature (Verdier 2002, for instance) as to whether regional credit institutions operating in peripheral markets can be sufficiently profitable (for regional studies, see Christians 2010 as well as Christians and Gärtner 2014, among others) (Figure 4). If anything, the regional principle is a key factor of success because it makes for strong customer relationships and minimizes information asymmetry.

Figure 4

Profit or loss for the financial year before tax; selected banking market segments in Germany

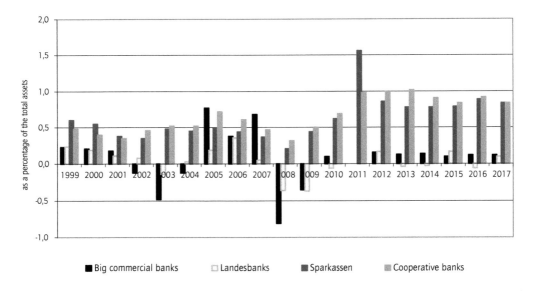

Source: Deutsche Bundesbank, "The performance of German credit institutions", Monthly Report September (multiple years), own illustration.

large banks, by contrast, that ratio is only 17 percent (September 2018, source: Deutsche Bundesbank, banking statistics database [lending by MFIs in Germany to domestic enterprises and households]). Sparkassen and cooperative banks, and their interconnection as networks rather than corporate groups, thus form a vital institutional arrangement that provides long-term finance as quasi-public good.

By adopting a policy of negative interest rates, the ECB has been accelerating the projected tendency for banks' net interest income to decline in a global low-interest-rate environment. Monetary policy itself has thus become a risk to the stability of the banking system (for details on this debate, see International Monetary Fund 2016 or Deutsche Bundesbank 2015, for instance). It has also been compromising the earnings potentials of classic business models focused on deposit-based lending, forcing banks to expand their commission and fee-earning business, or resort to negative deposit rates to maintain their interest margins.

However, economic policy makers would be ill-advised to push for a general shift toward fee and commission revenue, as the International Monetary Fund (IMF) and others have long since been advocating. While such a shift would, indeed, make earnings less contingent on maturity transformation and less susceptible to zero-interest monetary policies, we must take into account that fees and commissions, too, are subject to subsequent imponderables such as legal risks.

Moreover, given the moral hazard inherent in pure selling, pushing fees and commissions across the industry seems unwise. If it succeeds, banks will be less involved in size, maturity and risk transformation. But since that function is vital to the economy, it would inevitably be assumed by providers less experienced therein than banks. Incidentally, the IMF's country-specific advice also reflects differences in basic attitudes toward finance. The continental system has always been bank-based. Banks are intermediaries proper that take risks and generate income from interest margins. The IMF's approach, by contrast, is geared more toward capital markets.

4   Fintechs: Business strategies and the need for regulatory action

The emergence of innovative ICT-driven financial products has been almost as disruptive as the disintermediation of depositor and borrower relations through securitization and capital market orientation. Fintech products are challenging the business models of conventional intermediation. Prime examples are brokerage or crowd platforms featuring standardized query capabilities. But as the latter fail to provide soft facts, they reinforce information asymmetries rather than mitigate them. Other fintech instruments such as cryptocurrencies were expressly designed to bypass the traditional intermediation and monetary system.

4.1   Fintechs and digitalization in the financial market

The term *fintech* mostly refers to start-up companies that target technophile consumers with products based on state-of-the-art information technology or algorithms.[45] Such businesses typically act as highly specialised intermediaries catering to niche markets.

Fintechs pick individual lines of business rather than offer the gamut of services that incumbent credit institutions provide. This trend is also known as *unbundling* of banks. By interfacing with third parties, though, fintechs manage to establish a market presence notwithstanding their fragmented production chains. Their lines of business essentially comprise the following five:

---

45   See Financial Stability Board (FSB) 2017: 7: "*Fintech is defined as technology-enabled innovation in financial services that could result in new business models, applications, processes or products with an associated material effect on the provision of financial services.*"

- *Payment solutions* such as mobile or instant payment, payment initiation services, account information services or cryptocurrency exchanges.

- Fintech business models include the replacement of classic forms of funding, notably bank loans, by recruiting large numbers of capital suppliers among the "crowd" of web users. *Crowdfunding* variants—crowd-investing, crowd-lending und crowd-funding—range from crowd equity and debt capital lending through preselling a product to collecting donations. Since none of them matches classic intermediation between depositors and borrowers, crowdlenders run a high risk of losing their money.

- *Crowd platforms* do not perform the basic macroeconomic function of maturity and risk transformation. By applying credit scoring methods that consider data from multiple public sources, for instance, some platform providers help capital raisers and potential funders reduce the information asymmetry between them. But unless providers are held liable for the scores they issue or have a skin in the game via participation in lending, it remains doubtful whether such methods are incentive-compatible and thus reliable. Nor do providers monitor how the funds raised on their platforms are used.

- Use of *robo-advisers* to automate sales of investment and asset management services.

- A number of platforms engage in *loan, deposit and insurance brokerage.*

- *Cryptocurrencies* have declared their intentions to replace entire monetary systems including payments and deposits.

4.2   Impact on incumbent competitors and intermediation ties

Focusing on just one or two of the lines of business typically bundled in a credit institution enables fintechs to offer highly specialised products which have been attracting more attention than those of incumbent competitors. Unlike the latter, many fintechs aim for rapid expansion across Europe. By standardizing their business processes and generating economies of scale, they expect to make sufficient profit even from minimal margins.

Splitting off any of the lines of business so far bundled in one institution exposes the latter to the risk of their customers turning away from habitual one-stop finance to sourcing stand-alone services from a multitude of specialised providers. Unbundling also results in a loss of information synergy. Besides, standardized and automated processing does not lend itself to capturing soft facts. Consequently, information asymmetry is likely to grow alongside the fintech industry. While in personal banking that asymmetry can be offset by big data analysis, in working with SME clients it probably cannot.

In the medium term and comparable to the so-called new economy around the turn of the millennium, it is to be assumed that fintech market and fintech business ideas will shake out. In that process and regarding market structure, some fintech protagonists are likely to grow or merge into larger technology providers (bigtechs), or be swallowed by conventional banks or insurance companies. The market will be characterised by bigtechs with standardised processes on the one hand and genuine financial intermediaries using soft information factors on the other hand.

In view of all that, incumbent credit institutions, notably regional banks, should identify and nurture competitive advantages like their geographic proximity to customers. Where those advantages turn out insufficient, banks ought to cooperate with specialists. In addition, they should consider offering services that complement their core business, such as identity verification, capitalizing on the fact that consumers are more inclined to trust a credit institution than to rely on an online platform. Especially the latter's inability to provide soft facts continues to hold market potential that traditional credit institutions can tap.

Disruptive technological innovations, notably distributed ledgers as typified by blockchains, must be assessed separately from the multitude of current fintech solutions. Because such innovations are applicable to a plethora of purposes beyond the financial sector.

4.3   Prudential treatment of fintechs

The debate on what would be an adequate regulatory treatment of fintechs and their products has just begun (See, for instance, European Banking Authority (EBA) 2014, 2015 and 2017, FSB 2017, Basel Committee on Banking Supervision 2018). Priorities for action include the following:

Adherence to the principle of same risk, same rules

For the sake of fair competition, consumer protection and financial stability it is imperative that fintechs and incumbent financial institutions are regulated by the same standards without exception. Hence neither a so-called regulatory sandboxes nor dedicated soft fintech laws are the way to go. To prevent regulatory arbitrage in chartering a fintech, EU-wide harmonization of the licensing and registration requirements is of the essence.

Crowdfunding: Questionable leapfrog strategy

Crowdfunding and its varieties involve a series of critical regulatory issues. Lending platforms have assumed the intermediary role of credit institutions, matching capital in search of investment with the needs of loan applicants. But this happens outside the insured or regulated relations between depositors and lenders, or investors and issuers, respectively.

Crowdplatforms have been capitalizing on generous exemptions from prospectus requirements. Their business model thus reveals a wide gap in investor protection and clearly serves to circumvent the legal provisions applicable to deposit banking, credit lending and the issuance of capital market products. Moreover, capital raised on a crowdfunding platform is mostly junior, which translates into high losses for funders when users become insolvent. In addition, information available on such platforms is often insufficient.

Moreover, Germany's aggregate crowdfinancing volume has been negligible, at less than 150 million euros in 2016, including 77 million in lending, as well as 37 million investments in real estate projects and 16 million equity investments in start-ups (source: Für-Gründer.de 2017). Those numbers and the average principal of 17,254 euros per project (ibidem) are indicative of the impossibility to rely on the crowd for stable SME finance. At best, some forms of crowdfunding can serve start-ups, in particular, to bridge minor financial gaps.

Need for transparency in brokering processes/information privacy/addressing cyber risks

When fintechs act as brokers, they must be required to make that known to potential customers. They must avoid any impression of being credit institutions, lest they or their products illicitly capitalize on the faith that customers tend to have in the highly regulated financial services market. Supervisors ought to keep such grey areas under surveillance, send cease-and-desist letters to offenders, and bill them directly for any administrative cost thus incurred. Any regulated institution that has a stake in a brokerage platform must be identifiable at first glance.

Whatever their lines of business, most fintechs heavily rely on customer information processing and analyses. This makes data protection particularly challenging regarding fintech business models. Supervision of their compliance with information privacy laws is hence of utmost importance. Users' need for information security and privacy must be met without reserve.

Last but not least, cyber risk, too, is on the rise. To preserve the fragile bond of trust with their customers, fintechs and credit institutions must ensure a high level of protection from cybercrime, which is going to require increasing investment. But while IT security remains, first and foremost, a responsibility for the financial industry itself to meet, it also concerns public infrastructure, making it urgent for governments, too, to devote more attention and resources to it.

In-depth analysis of risks to financial stability

New lines of business entail new risks. Since analysis of threats to financial stability arising from fintech business models and products has been insufficient, it would be desirable for macroprudential supervisory authorities to study such risks in depth to complement regular microprudential surveillance.

Exemption from fees distorts competition

Prudential supervision of the fintech market, and the risks to financial stability and investor protection emanating from that industry, should be exercised both at the European and at national levels. On the EU level, EBA, ESMA and, macroprudentially, the European Systemic Risk Board (ESRB) would be in charge. In Germany, the fintech industry should be supervised by the Federal Financial Supervisory Authority (Bundesanstalt für Finanzdienstleistungsaufsicht [BaFin]) and, macroprudentially, by the Financial Stability Committee (Ausschuss für Finanzstabilität [AFS]).

Since only incumbent market players have been subject to prudential supervision and pertinent fees so far, the administrative cost of monitoring the fintech industry would be borne by them. However, exempting fintechs from contributing to the fee-based funding of regulatory and supervisory agencies distorts the competition. Hence fintechs must not only appear on the regulatory radar but also pay their fair share of their supervisors' operating budget.

Cryptocurrencies: Prone to laundering, speculative and bad for the economy

With an eye to consumer protection, digital currencies are highly speculative. They are also problematic in that they are not covered by current legislation on the prevention of using of the financial system for the purposes of money laundering or terrorist financing. On top of that, their taxability is anything but clear.

The vast use of digital currencies as medium of exchange is nowhere to be seen. Their high volatility makes them unsuitable as means of payment. Neither to be neglected are the resources required, and the pollution caused, to generate the electricity needed to mine additional cryptocurrency units.

Moreover, digital currencies are inappropriate to keep price level stable. Founders have capped the number of currency units that can be mined. Once the limit has been reached, deflation will rise as the economy grows. Additionally, absent any central governing body to control them, cryptocurrencies are unamenable to monetary policy, permitting neither any countercyclical measures to stabilize the economy nor any intervention as lender of last resort in the event of a liquidity crunch in the financial sector. In summary, it can be stated that from economic point of view, cryptocurrencies are neither able to replace traditional currencies and monetary systems nor would it be preferable.[46]

5   Conclusion and economic policy implications

Strengthening regional SMEs is a core concern of German and European economic policy. Its agenda ranges from easing the bureaucratic burden, through issues of taxation, social security contributions and the risk tolerance of society as a whole, to the stability of financing facilities and hence bank regulation.

In continental Europe, credit institutions have always been a primary source of corporate finance. To the benefit of both sides, this tradition has resulted in long-term business ties which have been providing banks with deep customer insight enabling them to understand a client's credit risk better than anyone else. Since credit agreements and bond indentures are incomplete contracts of limited enforceability, the wealth of information from relationship banking gives lending institutions an edge over capital markets not only in credit rating but also in usage monitoring and, if need be, renegotiation.

For SMEs, in particular, there are two more reasons to prefer bank loans to capital market-based funding: transaction cost and corporate governance. Market-based financing involves publication and rating costs, and forces the board, which in most SMEs comprises members of the owning family, to focus on shareholder value and cede a substantial measure of control. Given the prevalence of SMEs in Germany's economy, stable credit institutions providing competitive corporate lending and banking services are vital for the country's prosperity.

Institutions whose business models are based on deposit banking and decentralized decision-making have proven to be particularly loyal lenders, not least because they draw on stable funding themselves. The geographic proximity to their borrowers provides regional institutions with the above mentioned wealth of soft facts that enable them to rate their clients' credit better and for longer terms. The possible disadvantage of small and regional credit institutions of not achieving economies of scale and of not offering a broad range of financial services and products can

---

46   EBA has recommended specific legislative measures concerning cryptoassets and demanded the European Commission for acting (see European Banking Authority 2019 in detail).

be overcome by cooperation within a financial services network. Key features of a functional regionally focussed and decentralized banking system include: "*I. Short distance and embeddedness in (supportive) regional bank associations* [...] *II. Real decentralised universal banks* [...] *III. Regional principle, regional embeddedness and regional balance*".[47]

Yet despite its many merits, the business model of deposit-based lending is under threat, or has at least been complicated, by certain aspects of economic policy, such as undifferentiated regulation or central banks' prolonged zero-interest policy.

The current regulatory framework puts small and medium-sized banks at a competitive disadvantage. On the one hand, implicit government guarantees are still helping TBTF-institutions to refinance themselves at better terms, which they can pass on to their customers. On the other hand, since regulatory costs are mainly fixed administrative expenses, the price that small and medium-sized institutions pay for the current one-size-fits-all approach to regulation is out of proportion.[48] Banks solid enough to weather the crisis might now turn out too small to survive regulation. The asymmetric impact of the cost of post-crisis re-regulation forces smaller institutions to merge, which increases distances in customer relationships. That, in turn, goes at the expense of SMEs and peripheral or economically underdeveloped regions.

Other existing threats to the "boring banking" business model as well as to stability in SME lending arise from gathering quantitative requirements on loan origination and increasingly burdensome regulatory reporting obligations. The growing dominance of an approach to supervision that looks at financial ratios, above all, dismisses the soft facts which are so decisive in SME lending. Moreover, that quantitative approach gives supervisors a false sense of security, blinding them to new risk factors, and tempts supervised institutions to come up with workarounds that make even dubious business practices formally compliant with regulatory thresholds. What would make more sense, then, is a qualitative, subtle supervision that only intervenes when necessary, as laid down under the second pillar of Basel II.

In addition, regulation has become a central element of strategic and operational business decisions, making the business behaviour of credit institutions much more homogeneous and thus making the overall financial system more prone to macroprudential shock (see Schumacher et al. 2019).

On the whole, the European Union's regulatory framework has so far turned out ineffective in fostering heterogeneous and small-scale market structures and in fostering business models of deposit-based lending. In other words, regulators have been counteracting the legislative goal of cutting the proliferation of financial business models back to boring banking across the board.

---

47   Flögel and Gärtner 2018: 21 ff. Moreover, Flögel and Gärtner 2018: 27, argue that there is no need for protecting regional credit institutions from competition but a need for political support of the principles of regionalism and interbank networking: "[...] *governments do indeed matter, but less so in preventing centralised banks from wiping decentralised banks off the market with overwhelming competiveness. Rather, governments matter to protect decentralised banks from damaging their own factors of success by restricting them to their regional markets. In Spain, the abolishment of the regional principle tended to initiate the end of savings banks*". Likewise, see Schmidt et al. 2016.

48   See Alessandrini et al. 2016: 5, for instance: "*The uniformity of regulation penalizes local banks relative to larger banks because the implementation of complex regulation is to a large extent a fixed cost.*" Likewise, see Koch (2013), Hackethal and Inderst (2015), Schackmann-Fallis et al. 2016, Lange and Paul 2017, Schumacher et al. 2019. For an estimate of additional regulatory costs incurred by US community banks, see Feldman et al. 2013 and Ash et al. 2015, among others.

The good news is that CRR II is to differentiate regulatory requirements in favour of small and non-complex institutions somewhat more than its predecessor (For details on differentiation in US bank regulation, see Hoskins and Labonte 2015). Easing the burden of reporting and disclosure, in particular, concerns institutions with total assets under 5 billion euros and along several criteria for being non-complex (article 4(114a) CRR II). In doing so, Europe is following the US-led path of differentiating bank regulation (see Schackmann-Fallis et al. 2016 and Loeper 2017 for the concept of a so-called small and simple banking box).

The problem with absolute thresholds, however, is that they are eroded by inflation, and disregard the differences in size among national economies. A more balanced choice would have been a relative threshold, such as assets totalling up to one percent of the GDP of a bank's domicile, along with classification pursuant to supervisory criteria for identifying systemic importance. Still, the threshold under consideration is a step in the right direction and should be applied consistently in the technical standards and guidelines to be adopted by EBA.

Besides the regulatory framework, the other determinant of the future of boring banking are market trends. Europe and Germany are turning into a digital economy. This evolution is taking place in all sectors and affects all parts of society. Financial technology specialists, or fintechs for short, are disrupting the market by launching financial innovations and outsourcing the value chain. Incumbent institutions must compete with fintechs' ideas and be receptive to their solutions, enabling technical progress to reach the entire market. All things considered, products and processes developed by fintechs are more likely to complement than to replace conventional banking transactions and financial services.

Bank loans have long had to stand their ground against financial innovations and fashions. After the rise and fall of SME bonds (see Mausbach and Simmert 2016, among others), crowdfunding and its varieties have become the latest hype. Technically it resembles bond financing, although crowdassets are not fungible. Making the savings of others accessible to prospective borrowers on an online platform is subject to a high level of information asymmetry since traditional sources of information such as customer relationships or extensive disclosure requirements are unavailable. Nor is there any opportunity to renegotiate.

Although fintech products have been pushing innovation across the economy, they must be appraised as critically as conventional banking in terms both of financial stability and of investor protection. Subsuming financial innovations launched by fintechs under the current prudential regime based on a qualitative comparison of their features is the right approach in that it prevents market distortion resulting from regulatory arbitrage. Should this subsumption fail, however, the introduction of specific regimes to regulate crowd platforms, investment brokerage platforms and cryptocurrencies will be inevitable.

References

— Alessandrini, P., G. Calcagnini and A. Zazzaro (2008): Asset Restructuring Strategies in Bank Acquisitions: Does Distance Between Dealing Partners Matter? Journal of Banking and Finance, 32 (5), 699–713.

— Alessandrini, P., M. Fratianni, L. Papi and A. Zazzaro (2016): Banks Regions and Development after the Crisis and under the new Regulatory System. Credit and Capital Markets, 49 (4), 535–561.
— Alessandrini, P., M. Fratianni and A. Zazzaro (2009): The Changing Geography of Banking and Finance: The Main Issues. In: P. Alessandrini, M. Fratianni and A. Zazzaro (eds.): The Changing Geography of Banking and Finance. New York, 1–14.
— Alessandrini, P., and B. Nelson (2015): Simple Banking: Profitability and the Yield Curve. Journal of Money Credit and Banking, 47 (1), 143–75.
— Alessandrini, P., L. Papi and A. Zazzaro (2003): Banks, Regions and Development. BNL Quarterly Review, 56 (224), 23–55.
— Allen, F., and D. Gale (2000): Comparing Financial Systems, Cambridge, Mass. [et al.]
— Alonso, R., W. Dessein and N. Matouschek (2008): When Does Coordination Require Centralization? American Economic Review, 98 (1), 145–179.
— Anastasious, D., K. Drakos and S. Giannoulakis (2018): Are Bank Credit Standards Affected by the Business Cycle? Evidence from the Euro Area. Applied Economics Quarterly, 64 (1), 5–16.
— Ang, J. B. (2008): A Survey of Recent Developments in the Literature of Finance and Growth. Journal of Economic Surveys, 22 (3), 536–576.
— Ash, P., C. Koch and T. F. Siems (2015): Too Small to Succeed?—Community Banks in a New Regulatory Environment, Dallas Fed: Financial Insights, 4 (4), 1–4.
— Ayadi, R., R. H. Schmidt, S. C. Valverde, E. Arbak and F. R. Fernandez (2009): Investigating Diversity in the Banking Sector in Europe: The Performance and Role of Savings Banks. Brussels.
— Barrell, R., E. P. Davis, T. Fic and D. Karim (2010): Is there a Link from Bank Size to Risk Taking? National Institute of Economic and Social Research Discussion Papers, No. 367.
— Basel Committee on Banking Supervision/International Organization of Securities Commissions (2015): Criteria for Identifying Simple, Transparent and Comparable Securitisations. Basel.
— Basel Committee on Banking Supervision (2018): Sound Practices: Implications of Fintech Developments for Banks and Bank Supervisors. Basel.
— Behr, P., L. Norden and F. Noth (2013): Financial Constraints of Private Firms and Bank Lending Behavior. Journal of Banking and Finance, 37 (9), 3472–3485.
— Behr, P., D. Foos and L. Norden (2017): Cyclicality of SME Lending and Government Involvement in Banks. Journal of Banking and Finance, 77, 64–77.
— Behr, P., and R. H. Schmidt (2016): The German Banking System. In: T. Beck and B. Casu (eds.): The Palgrave Handbook of European Banking. London, 541–566.
— Bellucci, A., A. Borisov, and A. Zazzaro (2017): Bank Orgainzation and Loan Contracting in Small Business Financing. In: D. S. Siegel, and N. Dai (eds.): The World Scientific Reference on Entrepreneurship. Volume 2: Entrepreneurial Finance—Managerial and Policy Implications. Singapore, 171–199.
— Benvenuti, M. ,L. Casolaro, S. Del Petre and P. Mistrulli (2013): Loan Officer Authority and Small Business Lending: Evidence from a Survey. University Library of Munich MPRA Papers, No. 26475.
— Berger, A. N., R. S. Demsetz and P. E. Strahan (1999): The Consolidation of the Financial Services Industry: Causes, Consequences, and Implications for the Future. Journal of Banking and Finance, 23 (2–4), 135–194.

— Berger, A. N., R. De Young, H. Genay and G. F. Udell (2000): Globalization of Financial Institutions: Evidence from Cross-Border Banking Performance. Brookings Wharton Papers on Financial Services, 3, 23–120.

— Berger, A. N., I. Hasan and L. Klapper (2004): Further Evidence on the Link between Finance and Growth: An International Analysis of Community Banking and Economic Performance. Journal of Financial Services Research, 25 (2), 169–202.

— Berger, A. N., N. H. Miller, M. A. Pertersen, R. G. Rajan and J. C. Stein (2005): Does Function Follow Organizational Form? Evidence from the Lending Practices of Large and Small Banks. Journal of Financial Economics, 76 (1), 237–269.

— Berrospide, J. M., L. K. Black and W. R. Keeton (2013): The Cross-Market Spillover of Economic Shocks through Multi-Market Banks. Federal Reserve Board Finance and Economics Discussion Series, No. 52.

— Black, S. E., and P. E. Strahan (2002): Entrepreneurship and Bank Credit Availability. The Journal of Finance, 57 (6), 2807–2833.

— Bonaccorsi, E. and G. Dell'Ariccia (2001): Bank Competition and Firm Creation. IMF Working Paper, No. 21.

— Bonaccorsi, E. and G. Gobbi (2001): The Changing Structure of Local Credit Markets: Are Small Businesses Special? Journal of Banking and Finance, 25 (12), 2209–2237.

— Boot, A. W. A. (2000): Relationship Banking: What Do We Know? Journal of Financial Intermediation, 9 (1), 7–25.

— Borio, C., L. Gambacorta and B. Hofmann (2015): The Influence of Monetary Policy on Bank Profitability. BIS Working Papers, No. 514.

— Boyd, J., and M. Gertler (1993): U.S. Commercial Banking: Trends, Cycles and Policy. NBER Macroeconomics Annual, 8, 319–367.

— Brämer, P., H. Gischer, A. Pfingsten and T. Richter (2010): Der öffentliche Auftrag der deutschen Sparkassen aus der Perspektive des Stakeholder–Managements. Zeitschrift für öffentliche und gemeinwirtschaftliche Unternehmen, 33 (4), 313–334.

— Brei, M., and A. Schclarek (2013): Public Bank Lending in Crisis Times. Journal of Financial Stability, 9 (4), 820–830.

— Brewer, E., and J. Jagtiani (2013): How Much Did Banks Pay to Become Too–Big–To–Fail and to Become Systemically Important? Journal of Financial Services Research, 43 (1), 1–35.

— Bülbül, D., R. H. Schmidt and U. Schüwer (2013): Savings Banks and Cooperative Banks in Europe. SAFE White Paper Series, No. 5.

— Capelle-Blancard, G., and C. Labonne (2011): More Bankers, More Growth? Evidence from OECD Countries. CEPII Working Paper, No. 22.

— Cecchetti, S., and E. Kharroubi (2015): Why Does Financial Sector Growth Crowd Out Real Growth? CEPR Working Paper, No. 10642.

— Center for Financial Studies (2017): CFS–Umfrage: Das Drei-Säulen-Modell der deutschen Kreditwirtschaft hat sich bewährt – Für die Finanzierung des deutschen Mittelstands sind Sparkassen und Genossenschaftsbanken entscheidend. Frankfurt a. M.

— Cetorelli, N., and L. Goldberg (2012): Banking Globalization and Monetary Transmission. Journal of Finance, 67 (5), 1811–1843.

— Christians, U. (2010): Zur Ertragslage der Sparkassen und Genossenschaftsbanken in den strukturarmen Regionen Ostdeutschlands. In: U. Christians and K. Hempel (eds.): Unternehmensfinanzierung und Region: Finanzierungsprobleme mittelständischer Unternehmen und Bankpolitik in peripheren Wirtschaftsräumen. Hamburg, 231–253.

— Christians, U., and S. Gärtner (2014): Kreditrisiko von Sparkassen in Abhängigkeit vom regionalen Standort und geschäftspolitischen Variablen. Zeitschrift für das gesamte Kreditwesen, 67 (12), 620–626.

— Civitas: Institute for the Study of Civil Society (2013): The German Sparkassen (Savings Banks): A Commentary and Case Study. London.

— Clark, G. L., and K. O'Connor (1997): The Informational Content of Financial Products and the Spatial Structure of the Global Finance Industry. In: K. R. Cox (ed.): Spaces of Globalization: Reasserting the Power of the Local. New York, 89–114.

— Cole, R. A., L. G. Goldberg and L. J. White (2004): Cookie-Cutter versus Character: The Micro Structure of Small Business Lending by Large and Small Banks. Journal of Financial and Quantitative Analysis, 39 (2), 227–251.

— Cotugno, M., S. Monferra and G. Sampagnaro (2013): Relationship Lending, Hierarchical Distance and Credit Tightening: Evidence from the Financial Crisis. The Journal of Banking and Finance, 37 (5), 1372–1385.

— Crémer, J., L. Garicano and A. Prat (2007): Language and the Theory of the Firm. Quarterly Journal of Economics, 122, 373–407.

— De Grauwe, P. (2017): The Limits of the Market: The Pendulum between Government and Market. Oxford/New York.

— De Haas, R., and N. Van Horen (2013): Running for the Exit: International Banks and Crisis Transmission. Review of Financial Studies, 26 (1), 244–285.

— Degryse, H., N. Masschelein and J. Mitchell (2011): Staying, Dropping, or Switching: The Impacts of Bank Mergers on Small Firms. Review of Financial Studies, 24 (4), 1102–1140.

— Dekle, R., and M. Lee (2015): Do Foreign Bank Affiliates Cut their Lending more than the Domestic Banks in a Financial Crisis? Journal of International Money and Finance, 50 (1), 16–32.

— Demirgüç-Kunt, A., and H. Huizinga (1999): Determinants of Commercial Bank Interest Margins and Profitability: Some International Evidence. World Bank Economic Review, 13 (2), 379–408.

— Demirgüç-Kunt, A., and R. Levine (2001): Bank-Based and Market-Based Financial Systems: Cross-Country Comparison. In: A. Demirgüç-Kunt and R. Levine (eds.): Financial Structure and Economic Growth. A Cross-Country Comparison of Banks, Markets and Development. Cambridge, 81–140.

— Dessein, W. (2002): Authority and Communication in Organizations. The Review of Economic Studies, 69 (4), 811–838.

— Deutsche Börse (2014): Best Practice Guide: Entry Standard für Unternehmensanleihen – Empfehlungen für Anleiheemissionen. Frankfurt a. M.

— Deutsche Bundesbank (2015): Risks in the German Banking Sector. Financial Stability Review, 29–40.

— DeYoung, R., D. Glennon and P. Nigro (2008): Borrower–Lender Distance, Credit Scoring, and Loan Performance: Evidence from Informational-Opaque Small Business Borrowers. Journal of Financial Intermediation, 17 (1), 113–143.

— European Banking Authority (EBA) (2014): EBA Opinion on 'Virtual Currencies'. EBA/Op/2014/08.

— European Banking Authority (EBA) (2015): Opinion of the European Banking Authority on LendingBased Crowdfunding. EBA/Op/2015/03.

— European Banking Authority (EBA) (2017): Discussion Paper on the EBA's Approach to Financial Technology. EBA/DP/2017/02.

— European Banking Authority (EBA) (2019): Report with Advice for the European Commission on Crypto-Assets. London.
— European Commission (2018): Annual Report on European SMEs 2017/2018. Luxemburg.
— Fecht, F., K. G. Nyborg and J. Rocholl (2008): The Price of Liquidity: Bank Characteristics and Market Conditions. Deutsche Bundesbank Discussion Paper Series 1: Economic Studies, No. 30.
— Feldman, R., K. Heineckeand and J. Schmidt (2013): Quantifying the Costs of Additional Regulation on Community Banks. Federal Reserve Bank of Minneapolis Economic Policy Papers, No. 3.
— Ferri, G. (1997): Branch Manager Turnover and Lending Efficiency: Local vs. National Banks. BNL Quarterly Review, 50 (March), 229–247.
— Filomeni, S., G. F. Udell and A. Zazzaro (2016): Hardening Soft Information: How Far Has Technology Taken Us? University Ancona Money and Finance Research Group Working Paper Series, No. 121.
— Finance Watch (2014): A Missed Opportunity to Revive "Boring" Finance? Brussels.
— Financial Stability Board (FSB) (2017): Financial Stability Implications from FinTech: Supervisory and Regulatory Issues that Merit Authorities' Attention. Basel.
— Flögel, F., and S. Gärtner (2018): The Banking Systems of Germany, the UK and Spain from a spatial perspective: Lesson learned and what is to be done? IAT Discussion Paper, No. 1A.
— Focarelli, D., F. Panetta and C. Salleo (2002): Why Do Banks Merge? Journal of Money, Credit and Banking, 34 (4), 1047–1066.
— Fried, J., and P. Howitt (1980): Credit Rationing and Implicit Contract Theory. Journal of Money, Credit and Banking, 12 (3), 471–487.
— Für-Gründer.de (2017): Crowdfinanzierung in Deutschland Nr. 1/2017. Friedberg.
— Gambacorta, L., and P. E. Mistrulli (2014): Bank Heterogeneity and Interest Rate Setting: What Lessons have we Learned since Lehman Brothers? Journal of Money, Credit and Banking, 46 (4), 753–778.
— Gandhi, P., and H. Lustig (2010): Size Anomalies in US Bank Stock Returns: A Fiscal Explanation. NBER Working Papers, No. 16553.
— Gärtner, S. (2009): Balanced Structural Policy: German Savings Banks from a Regional Economic Perspective. Brussels.
— Gärtner, S., and J. Fernandez (2018): The Banking Systems of Germany, the UK and Spain from a spatial perspective: The Spanish Case. Gelsenkirchen (forthcoming).
— German Council of Economic Experts (2015): Stability Risks from Low Interest Rates. Annual Report 2015/16. Wiesbaden, 180–200.
— German Federal Ministry of Economic Affairs (2013): German Mittelstand: Engine of the German Economy. Berlin.
— Giannetti, M., and L. Laeven (2011): The Flight Home Effect: Evidence from the Syndicated Loan Market during Financial Crises. Journal of Financial Economics, 104 (1), 23–43.
— Gischer, H., and B. Herz (2016): Das Geschäftsmodell „Regionalbank" auf dem amerikanischen Prüfstand. Credit and Capital Markets, 49 (2), 175–191.
— Gischer, H., and P. Reichling (2010): The German Banking System and the Financial Crisis. In: B. Gup (ed.): The Financial and Economic Crisis: An International Perspective. Cheltenham, 69–78.
— Gischer, H., and T. Spengler (2013): Verwaltungsrat einer Sparkasse: Aufgaben, Zusammensetzung und Herausforderungen. In: R. Hölscher and T. Altenhain (eds.): Handbuch

Aufsichts- und Verwaltungsräte in Kreditinstituten: Rechtlicher Rahmen – Betriebswirtschaftliche Herausforderungen – Best Practices. Berlin, 201–214.

— Gobbi, G., and E. Sette (2015): Relationship Lending during a Financial Crisis. Journal of the European Economic Association, 13 (3), 453–481.

— Goldsmith, R. W. (1969): Financial Structure and Development. New Haven.

— Government of Ireland (2018): Local Public Banking in Ireland: An Analysis of a Model for Developing a System of Local Public Banking in Ireland. Dublin.

— Grote, M. H. (2004): Die Entwicklung des Finanzplatzes Frankfurt: Eine evolutionsökonomische Untersuchung. Berlin.

— Hackethal, A., and R. Inderst (2015): Auswirkungen der Regulatorik auf kleine und mittlere Banken am Beispiel der deutschen Genossenschaftsbanken. Frankfurt a. M.

— Hakenes, H., I. Hasan, P. Molyneux and R. Xie (2015): Small Banks and Local Economic Development. Review of Finance, 19 (2), 653–683.

— Hall, P. A., and D. Soskice (2001): An Introduction to Varieties of Capitalism. In: P. A. Hall and D. Soskice (eds.): Varieties of Capitalism: The Institutional Foundations of Comparative Advantage. Oxford [et al.], 1–70.

— Hall, D., and T. A. Nguyen (2018): Economic Benefits of Public Services. Real-World Economics Review, No. 84, 100–153.

— Handke, M. (2011): Die Hausbankbeziehung. Institutionalisierte Finanzlösungen für kleine und mittlere Unternehmen in räumlicher Perspektive. Berlin [et al.].

— Hardie, I., and D. Howarth (2013): Framing Market-Based Banking and the Financial Crisis. In: I. Hardie and D. Howarth (eds.): Market-Based Banking and the International Financial Crisis. Oxford, 22–55.

— Hauschild, S., and S. Kral (2013): Mittelstand setzt weiter auf Bankkredit. Betriebswirtschaftliche Blätter. 06.12.2013.

— Hodgman, D. R. (1960): Credit Risk and Credit Rationing. The Quarterly Journal of Economics, 74 (2), 258–278.

— Hoskins, S. M., and M. Labonte (2015): An Analysis of the Regulatory Burden on Small Banks. Congressional Research Service Reports, R43999.

— International Monetary Fund (2015): International Banking after the Crisis: Increasingly Local and Safer? Global Financial Stability Report, April, 55–91.

— International Monetary Fund (2016): Impact of Low and Negative Rates on Banks. Global Financial Stability Report, April, 44–46.

— Kay, J. (2015): Other People's Money: Masters of the Universe or Servants of the People? London.

— Koch, C. (2013): Regulatory Burden Rising. Federal Reserve Bank of Dallas: Annual Report 2012, 35–37.

— Kotz, H.-H. (2009): Finanzstabilität und Liquidität: Der Geldmarkt als Kristalisationspunkt. In: A. Belke, H.-H. Kotz, S. Paul and C. M. Schmidt (eds.): Wirtschaftspolitik im Zeichen europäischer Integration: Festschrift für Wim Kösters anlässlich seines 65. Geburtstages, 247–262.

— Kotz, H.-H. (2011): Enhancements in EU Financial Regulation: Have We Done Enough? In: Oesterreichische Nationalbank (ed.): 39th Economics Conference—The Future of European Integration: Some Economic Perspectives, 98–109.

— Kotz, H.-H. (2014): SSM and ECB: Supra-Nationalization of Banking Politics. In: Oesterreichische Nationalbank (ed.): 42nd Economics Conference—Toward a European Banking Union: Taking Stock, 136–144.

— Kotz, H.-H., and D. Schäfer (2013): Rating–Agenturen: Fehlbar und überfordert. Viertel-jahrshefte zur Wirtschaftsforschung, 82 (4), 135–162.
— Kotz, H.-H., and R. H. Schmidt (2017): Corporate Governance of Banks—A German Alter-native to the ‚Standard Model'. Goethe University Frankfurt, SAFE White Papers, No. 45.
— Krugman, P. R. (2009): Making Banking Boring. The New York Times, 10 April 2009.
— Krugman, P. R. (2010): Good and Boring. The New York Times, 1 February 2010.
— Landier, A., V. B. Nair and J. Wulf (2009): Trade-Offs in Staying Close: Corporate Decision Making and Geographic Dispersion. Review of Financial Studies, 22 (3), 1119–1148.
— Lange, M., and S. Paul (2017): Kumulative Auswirkungen der Bankenregulierung auf die Geschäftsmodelle von Genossenschaftsbanken. Zeitschrift für das gesamte Genossen-schaftswesen, 67 (4), 218–244.
— Law, S. H., and N. Singh (2014): Does too much Finance Harm Economic Growth? Journal of Banking and Finance, 41 (April), 36–44.
— Lee, N., and R. Brown (2017): Innovation, SMEs and the Liability of Distance: The Demand and Supply of Bank Funding in UK Peripheral Regions. Journal of Economic Geography, 17 (1), 233–260.
— Levine, R. (2005): Finance and Growth: Theory and Evidence. In: P. Aghion and S. Durlauf (eds.): Handbook of Economic Growth 1A. Amsterdam [et al.], 865–934.
— Loeper, E. (2017): Zwingen aufsichtliche Anforderungen zu anderen Betriebsgrößen? Praxis Sparkassen Management, No. 72, 16–23.
— Liberti, J. M., and A. R. Mian (2009): Estimating the Effect of Hierarchies on Information Use. Review of Financial Studies, 22 (10), 4057–4090.
— Lucchetti, R., L. Papi and A. Zazzaro (2001): Banks' Inefficiency and Economic Growth: A Micro-Macro Approach. Scottish Journal of Political Economy, 48 (4), 400–424.
— Marques, L. B., R. Correa and H. Sapriza (2013): International Evidence on Government Support and Risk Taking in the Banking Sector. IMF Working Paper, No. 94.
— Mausbach, C., and D. B. Simmert (2016): Wie geht es weiter mit dem Markt für Mittel-standsanleihen? – ein Blick in die Glaskugel. Zeitschrift für das gesamte Kreditwesen, 69 (12), 591–593.
— Mian A. (2006): Distance Constraints: The Limits of Foreign Lending in Poor Economies. Journal of Finance, 61 (3), 1465–1505.
— Minsky, H. P. 1992): The Financial Instability Hypothesis. Levy Economics Institute of Bard College Working Papers, No. 74.
— Mishkin, F. S. (2016): The Economics of Money, Banking, and Financial Markets. 11th edi-tion. Boston [et al.].
— Mookherjee, D. (2006): Decentralization, Hierarchies, and Incentives: A Mechanism De-sign Perspective. Journal of Economic Literature, 44 (2), 367–390.
— Myrdal, G. (1957): Economic Theory and Under-developed Regions. London.
— Ogura, Y., and H. Uchida (2014): Bank Consolidation and Soft Information Acquisition in Small Business Lending. Journal of Financial Services Research, 45 (2), 173–200.
— Palley, T. L. (1997): Managerial Turnover and the Theory of Short-Termism. Journal of Economic Behavior and Organization, 32 (4), 547–557.
— Petersen, M., and R. Rajan (1995): The Effect of Credit Market Competition on Lending Relationships. Quarterly Journal of Economics, 110, 407–443.
— Pollard, J. S. (2003): Small Firm Finance and Economic Geography. Journal of Economic Geography, 3 (4), 429–452.
— Popov, A., and G. F. Udell (2012): Cross–Border Banking, Credit Access, and the Financial Crisis. Journal of International Economics, 87 (1), 147–161.

— Presbitero, A. F., G. F. Udell and A. Zazzaro (2014): The Home Bias and the Credit Crunch: A Regional Perspective. Journal of Money, Credit and Banking, 46 (s1), 53–85.
— Puri, M., J. Rocholl and S. Steffen (2011): On the Importance of Prior Relationships in Bank Loans to Retail Customers. ECB Working Papers, No. 1395.
— Radner, R. (1993): The Organization of Decentralized Information Processing. Econometrica, 61 (5), 1109–1146.
— Raworth, K. (2017): Doughnut Economics: Seven Ways to Think like a 21st–Century Economist. London.
— Rehm, H. (2016): Perspektiven der künftigen Bankenstruktur. Zeitschrift für das gesamte Kreditwesen, 69 (12), 582–587.
— Rousseau, P. L., and P. Wachtel (2011): What is Happening to the Impact of Financial Deepening on Economic Growth? Economic Inquiry, 49 (1), 276–288.
— Sapienza, P. (2002): The Effects of Banking Mergers on Loan Contracts. Journal of Finance, 57 (1), 329–367.
— Schackmann–Fallis, K.-P., and M. Weiß (2014): Régulation des marchés financiers et financement des entreprises. Revue d'économie financière, n° 114 (juin), 209–231.
— Schackmann–Fallis, K.-P., M. Weiß and H. Gischer (2016): Differenzierte Regulierung – ein Plädoyer aus der Perspektive deutscher Sparkassen. Zeitschrift für das gesamte Kreditwesen, 69 (21), 1052–1055.
— Schackmann-Fallis, K.-P., H. Gischer and M. Weiß (2017): A Case for Boring Banking and Re-Intermediation. FEMM Working Papers (Faculty of Economics and Management, University Magdeburg), No. 18.
— Schäfer, D. (2018): Sparkassen als nächster Krisenherd? Wohl eher nicht! DIW Wochenbericht, 85 (43), 952.
— Schamp, E. W. (2009): Das Finanzzentrum – ein Cluster: Ein multiskalarer Ansatz und seine Evidenz am Beispiel von Frankfurt/RheinMain. Zeitschrift für Wirtschaftsgeographie, 53 (1–2), 89–105.
— Scharfstein, D. S., and J. C. Stein (2000): The Dark Side of Internal Capital Markets: Divisional Rent-Seeking and Inefficient Investment. Journal of Finance, 55 (6), 2537–2564 .
— Schiereck, D. (2018): Von der Bargeldzahlung zur digitalen Transaktion: Zur Zukunft des Bezahlens und der Zahlungsverkehrspartner. Bonn.
— Schmidt, R. H. (2009): The Political Debate about Savings Banks. Business Review, 61, 366–392.
— Schmidt, R. H. (2018): Microfinance—Once and Today. Credit and Capital Markets, 51 (2), 183–203.
— Schmidt, R. H., H. D. Seibel and P. Thomes (2016): From Microfinance to Inclusive Banking: Why Local Banking Works. Weinheim.
— Schmidt, R. H., and M. Tyrell (2004): What Constitutes a Financial System in General and the German Financial System in Particular? In: J. P. Krahnen and R. H. Schmidt (eds.): The German Financial System. Oxford, 19–68.
— Schumacher, S., M. Lange and S. Paul (2019): Kumulative Auswirkungen der Regulierung auf die Geschäftsmodelle deutscher Sparkassen: Eine qualitativ-empirische Analyse. Credit and Capital Markets (forthcoming).
— Scott, J. A. (2004): Small Business and the Value of Community Financial Institutions. Journal of Financial Services Research, 25 (2/3), 207–230.
— Sekera, J. A. (2016): The Public Economy in Crisis: A Call for a New Public Economics. SpringerBriefs in Economics. Springer International Publishing.

— Sekera, J. A. (2018): The Public Economy: Understanding Government as a Producer. A Reformation of Public Economics. Real-World Economics Review, No. 84, 36–99.
— Siegert, C., and M. Willison (2015): Estimating the Extent of the 'Too big to fail' Problem – Review of Existing Approaches. Bank of England Financial Stability Paper, No. 32.
— Skrastins, J., and V. Vig (2015): How Organizational Hierarchy Affects Information Production. Institute for Monetary and Financial Stability University Frankfurt Working Paper Series, No. 92.
— Soussa, F. (2000): Too Big to Fail: Moral Hazard and Unfair Competition? In: L. Halme (ed.): Selected Issues for Financial Safety Nets and Market Discipline: Financial Stability and Central Banks. London, 5–31.
— Stein, J. C. (2002): Information Production and Capital Allocation: Decentralized versus Hierarchical Firms. Journal of Finance, 57 (5), 1891–1921.
— Strahan, P. E., and J. P. Weston (1998): Small Business Lending and the Changing Structure of the Banking Industry. Journal of Banking and Finance, 22 (6–8), 821–845.
— Stuwe, A., M. Weiß and J. Philipper (2012): Rating Agencies: Are They Necessary, Superfluous, a Necessary Evil or Harmful? Bonn.
— Thrift, N. (1994): On the Social and Cultural Determinants of International Financial Centres: the Case of the City of London. In: S. Corbridge, N. Thrift and R. Martin (eds.): Money, Power and Space. Oxford/Cambridge.
— Tobin, J. (1984): On the Efficiency of the Financial System. Lloyd's Bank Review, 153, 1–15.
— Turner, A., A. Haldane, P. Wooley, S. Wadhwani, C. A. Goodhart, A. Smithers and A. Large et al. (eds.) (2010): The Future of Finance. London.
— Uchida, H., G. F. Udell and N. Yamori (2012): Loan Officers and Relationship Lending to SMEs. Journal of Financial Intermediation, 21 (1), 97–122.
— Ueda, K., and B. Weder di Mauro (2012): Quantifying Structural Subsidy Values for Systemically Important Financial Institutions. IMF Working Papers, No. 128.
— United Nations Conference on Trade and Development (UNCTAD) (2013): Trade and Development Report 2013. Geneva.
— Usai, S., and M. Vannini (2005): Banking Structure and Regional Economic Growth: Lessons from Italy. Annals of Regional Science, 39 (4), 691–714.
— Uzzi, B., and R. Lancaster (2003): Relational Embeddedness and Learning: The Case of Bank Loan Managers and their Clients. Management Science, 49 (4), 383–399.
— Van Hoose, D. (2010): The Industrial Organization of Banking: Bank Behavior. Market Structure, and Regulation. Berlin [et al.].
— Verdier, D. (2002): Moving Money: Banking and Finance in the Industrialized World. Cambridge.
— Völz, M., and M. Wedow (2009): Does Banks' Size Distort Market Prices? Evidence for Too-Big-To-Fail in the CDS Market. Deutsche Bundesbank Discussion Paper Series 2: Banking and Financial Studies, No. 6.
— Wedel, J. R. (2018): Bureaucracy Shouldn't Be a Dirty Word: The Role of People-Responsive Bureaucracy in a Robust Public Economy. Real–World Economics Review, No. 84, 154–169.
— White, W. R. (1998): The Coming Transformation of Continental European Banking? BIS Working Papers, No. 54.
— Zhao, T., and D. Jones-Evans (2017): SMEs, Banks and the Spatial Differentiation of Access to Finance. Journal of Economic Geography, 17 (4), 791–824.

Finance and growth— shortly reconsidered

MECHTHILD SCHROOTEN

Mechthild Schrooten, Hochschule Bremen, e-mail: mechthild.schrooten@hs-bremen.de

Summary: In the 1980s and 90s of the last century, one economic paradigm gained power: financial develop-ment was considered as a major determinant of economic growth and productivity (Levine, Loayza and Beck 2000). Typically, paradigms are based on assumptions. Reality made a reconsideration of the former results necessary. With the international crisis 2007 it became clear that financial development and credit booms might not only support growth but jeopardize the whole economic system. While there exists a huge literature on the finance growth nexus before the international financial crisis analyses on post-crisis developments are rare. In this empirical paper, we focus on these post-crisis developments and find that the finance-growth nexus has widely disappeared after crisis. This might go back to a deeper understanding of systemic and financial risk.

Zusammenfassung: In den 1980ern und 90ern entwickelte sich ein neues ökonomisches Paradigma: Finanz-märkte – so wurde angenommen – haben einen erheblichen Einfluss auf das Wirtschaftswachstum und die Produktivitätsentwicklung (Levine, Loayza und Beck 2000). Paradigmen kommen in der Regel auf Annah-men zurück. Solche Annahmen bieten eine gute Voraussetzung für Zirkelschlüsse. Mit der internationalen Finanzkrise 2007 wurde klar, dass der Finanzsektor nicht nur einen Einfluss auf das Wirtschaftswachstum hat, sondern im schlimmsten Fall das gesamte System gefährden kann. Während es eine umfangreiche Literatur zum Zusammenhang zwischen Finanzsystem und Wachstum vor der internationalen Finanzkrise gibt, ist dieser Untersuchungszweig nach der Krise verkümmert. In diesem Paper steht die Nachkrisenzeit im Mittelpunkt. Dabei wird klar, dass sich der vormals vorhandene Zusammenhang inzwischen kaum noch finden lässt. Dies mag auch darauf zurückgehen, dass es inzwischen ein besseres Wissen um den Zusammenhang zwischen Größe des Finanzsystems und Risiken gibt.

→ JEL classification: O16, O40
→ Keywords: Growth, financial development, credit booms

I   Introduction

The interdependence between economic growth and finance is an interesting field of research—and far from being clear. The famous female economist Joan Robinson argued that finance follows the real sector development (Robinson 1952: 56).Other economists considered the development of and in the financial sector to be crucial for the economic outcome. This point of view emerged first in the context of development economics (McKinnon 1973). However, in the 80ies and 90ies a strand of literature arose considering the finance and growth nexus as extremely relevant not only for developing countries but also for the developed world (King and Levine 1993a, 1993b). Thus, finance and money were considered as to be rare. It was assumed that financial sector decides about the allocation of financial resources and is very productive. Nevertheless, this specific "financial productivity" could not be measured directly. However, it was argued that indirect effects of the performance of the financial sector on growth result at least partly from its selection of real sector innovations.

Most of the studies in the 80ies and 90ies offered a lot of empirics. Many of these empirical studies showed the predicted results. In simple words, the differences in performance of the domestic financial sector can be made responsible for differences in growth rates even among industrialized countries (Levine, Loayza and Beck 2000). In addition, a simple rule was developed: the larger the financial system, the better the growth perspectives are—this was a widely accepted view. Rajan and Zingales explained: "A number of studies have identified a positive correlation between the level of development of a country's financial sector and the rate of growth of its per capita income. As has been noted elsewhere, the observed correlation does not necessarily imply a causal relationship. This paper examines whether financial development facilitates economic growth by scrutinizing one rationale for such a relationship; that financial development reduces the costs of external finance to firms" (Rajan and Zingales 1998). Other authors argued that lower financial transaction costs in the financial sector lead to higher growth rates (Pagano 1993). These academic findings had a far reaching impact on existing financial systems. Many countries—among them Germany—started to liberalize their financial system. Newly developed, sophisticated and complex financial products entered the international markets. The world was in a financial rush.

With the international financial crash 2007/2008 this view changed (Beck 2012). Today, the finance-growth nexus is seen much more critically. Obviously real world developments questioned the above mentioned academic findings. With the international financial crisis, the society as well as policy advisers claimed for stronger regulations—the time for financial liberalization is over. Why did the studies not focus on the potential harm of financial sector development? This is an open question for those who focus on history of academic thoughts.

Here, we are in the empirics. Reality made a reconsideration of the former results necessary. Using a panel of 50 countries over 30 years Cecchetti and Kharroubi (2012) showed in their paper that *"as is the case with many things in life, with finance you can have too much of a good thing"* Cecchetti and Kharroubi (2012: 1). According to them, in a developed country more credit and banking result in lower real sector growth rates. Later, using a smaller country set these authors showed that financial development crowd out real sector growth (Cecchetti and Kharroubi 2015). According to these authors unlimited financial sector growth is harmful especially for RandD intensive economies—in times of crisis as well as in tranquil times.

Here, we take a different approach. We focus on the linkages between finance and growth *after* the harsh international crisis 2007. The basic idea behind this is that the finance and growth linkages changed after the destabilization of the international financial system. The post-crisis changes in financial regulation lead to higher transaction costs for financial intermediaries. Does the formerly reported finance-growth nexus still exist? In other words, we want to analyze whether the formerly reported finance and growth linkages were distorted by the endogenous shock. The data are taken from The Worldbank (The Worldbank 2019). The paper is organized as follows: In the next section, we deliver some descriptive statistics and compare them to the results of former studies. In section three, we explain the general results of the simple cross-section regressions. Section four concludes.

2 Data description

The Worldbank offers data for a broad set of countries. Economic growth rates as well as many other indicators are included. For this paper we take data from 151 countries (Table 1) and consider the years 2008–2017. All data are taken as averages, thus we argue on the base of a cross-country approach.

The countries under consideration differ widely in terms of economic growth. The lowest average annual economic growth rate for the years 2008–2017 was reported for Ukraine followed by Central Africa. The highest average annual growth rate was found in Quatar followed by China. The numbers clearly show that the economic slowdown after the international financial crisis hit developed countries more than emerging economies. The average annual growth rate in the country set under consideration for the years 2008–2017 was 3 percent (Table 2). This is a remarkable result. In other words, the world recovered soon from the international financial crisis. Many countries enjoyed an average growth rate above 5 percent, most of them are so-called emerging economies. The reported standard deviation is comparably high. Thus this rich cross-country variation gives a good base for analyzing the link between finance and growth.

Turning now to the financial sector development it becomes clear that the countries under consideration differ widely. Claims on central governments in percent of GDP (GOVERN)[1] are on average very low or even negative. This result might be surprising. Nevertheless, the highest figure is reported for Japan where this ratio reaches more 120 percent. Domestic credit to the private sector in percent of GDP (PRIVATE) shows a high degree of variation too. The highest value is found for Japan, followed by Cyprus and the US. Foreign direct investment (FDI) as percent of GDP differs widely among the countries. The country with the highest rate of FDI is Lithuania with an average of about 52 percent of GDP. Another indicator for economic growth is Gross capital formation in percent of GDP (CAPITAL) which reflexes investment activities. Here we find emerging economies at the top—some of them reached more than 40 percent. Taking the effects of the overall monetary policy into account the indicator MONEY (broad money in percent of GDP) provides us some insights to the general financial conditions of a given economy. However, the number of observation here is lower due to the fact that The Worldbank does not report single figures for the

---

[1] Claims on central government take loans to central government institutions net of deposits (The Worldbank 2019).

Table 1

Country set

Afghanistan	Bolivia	Costa Rica	Georgia	Jamaica	Mongolia	Poland	Sudan
Albania	Bosnia and Herzegovina	Cote d'Ivoire	Germany	Japan	Montenegro	Portugal	Suriname
Algeria	Botswana	Croatia	Ghana	Jordan	Mozambique	Qatar	Sweden
Antigua and Barbuda	Brazil	Cyprus	Guatemala	Kazakhstan	Myanmar	Romania	Switzerland
Argentina	Brunei Darussalam	Czech Republic	Guinea	Kenya	Namibia	Russian Federation	Tajikistan
Armenia	Bulgaria	Denmark	Guinea-Bissau	Korea, Republic	Nepal	Samoa	Tanzania
Aruba	Burkina Faso	Dominica	Guyana	Kuwait	Netherlands	Saudi Arabia	Thailand
Australia	Burundi	Dominican Republic	Haiti	Kyrgyz Republic	New Zealand	Senegal	Togo
Austria	Cabo Verde	Ecuador	Honduras	Latvia	Nicaragua	Serbia	Trinidad and Tobago
Azerbaijan	Cambodia	Egypt, Arab Republic	Hong Kong SAR, China	Lebanon	Niger	Seychelles	Turkey
Bahamas, The	Cameroon	El Salvador	Hungary	Liberia	Nigeria	Sierra Leone	Uganda
Bahrain	Central African Republic	Equatorial Guinea	Iceland	Lithuania	North Macedonia	Singapore	Ukraine
Bangladesh	Chad	Estonia	India	Luxembourg	Norway	Slovak Republic	United Arab Emirates
Barbados	Chile	Eswatini	Indonesia	Malawi	Oman	Solomon Islands	United Kingdom
Belarus	China	Fiji	Iran, Islamic Republic	Mali	Pakistan	South Africa	United States
Belgium	Colombia	Finland	Iraq	Malta	Papua New Guinea	Spain	Uruguay
Belize	Comoros	France	Ireland	Mauritania	Paraguay	St. Kitts and Nevis	Vanuatu
Benin	Congo, Dem. Republic	Gabon	Israel	Mauritius	Peru	St. Lucia	Vietnam
Bhutan	Congo, Republic	Gambia, The	Italy	Moldova	Philippines	St. Vincent and the Grenadines	

members of the Eurozone. However, even taking the shortcomings of the data set into account the huge variations in these indications call for a deeper analysis.

Table 2

Summary statistics

	GDP Growth	Claims on central government	Domestic credit to private sector	FDI	Gross capital formation	Domestic credit to private sector by banks	Broad Money
	In %	In % of GDP					
Mean	3,1	7,2	73,6	5,4	25,0	68,8	62,5
Median	3,2	4,8	55,1	3,2	23,8	54,2	53,2
Maximum	8,3	121,1	327,3	58,0	54,4	327,3	340,6
Minimum	−1,4	−39,2	0,3	−0,9	9,6	−0,4	11,2
Standarddeviation	2,1	16,5	61,0	7,8	7,0	58,0	45,4

N = 151.

Source: Own calculations; Database The Worldbank.

In a first step, we take the general linkage between GROWTH and MONEY. Using a descriptive approach, we clearly see that for our data set the economic growth nowadays is negatively linked to monetary development. Thus, the simple assumption that higher real sector growth rates go in line with a larger money supply cannot be found (Figure 1). Furthermore, here we get a negative

Figure 1

Monetization and growth—a negative linkage, 2008–2017

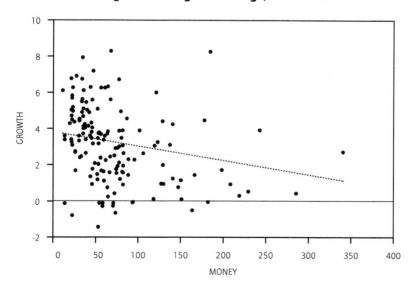

Source: Own calculations; Database The Worldbank.

Figure 2

Credit and growth—a negative linkage, 2008–2017

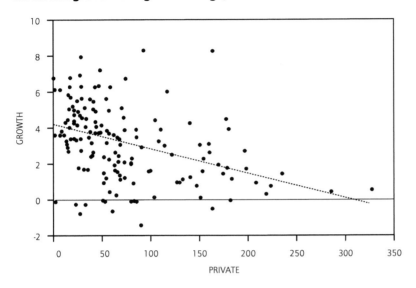

Source: Own calculations; Database The Worldbank.

slope which could be interpreted as a hint for changes in the finance-money-growth nexus after the international financial crisis.

Now we turn to influence of selected financial indicators. In the next we focus on the nexus between claims on private sector in percent of GDP (PRIVATE) and GROWTH. At a glance we see that the positive finance-growth nexus which was reported for many years and different country sets seems to be distorted. After the international financial crisis this nexus seems to get a NEGATIVE sign. The slope of the trend curve in Figure 2 is clearly negative.

3   First results

To analyze the given data set we take a simple cross-country regression approach. In doing so, can address the question whether long-term economic GROWTH is linked to financial development. In a first step we check for the influence of the variables GOVERN and PRIVATE on GROWTH. Table 3 gives the results of the cross-section regression.

The simple regression shows that the variable PRIVATE is negatively linked to long-run economic growth. The variable GOVERN has no statistical influence. In a second step, to check for the robustness of the results we add the variables FDI and check for the influence of capital formation on growth. Both variables turn out to be insignificant (Table 4).

Table 3

Cross-section results I

	Coefficients	Standard Deviation	t-Statistic	P-Value
C	4,124170093	0,246260023	16,747217210	5,54482E-36
Claims on Government	0,016067736	0,010891501	1,475254526	0,142268347
PRIVATE	−0,015362142	0,002939741	−5,2256786	5,80005E-07

N = 151.

Source: Own calculations; Database The Worldbank.

Table 4

Cross-section results II

	Coefficients	Standard Deviation	t-Statistic	P-Value
C	4,562280726	0,630376026	7,237395681	2,40317E-11
Claims on Government	0,016224427	0,010947697	1,481994551	0,140496895
PRIVATE	−0,015495568	0,002960266	−5,234519100	5,6541E-07
FDI	−0,011153675	0,020257771	−0,550587479	0,582757955
Gross capital formation	−0,014748242	0,022507863	−0,655248456	0,513338899

N = 151.

Source: Own calculations; Database The Worldbank.

The main message of the analysis, that after the international financial crisis credits to the private sector and economic growth still seem to be linked—however in a negative way. Higher credits to the private sector go in line with slightly lower growth rates. Why? This we cannot infer from the data. However, it can be assumed that the zero- and low-interest rate policy of many central banks has led to higher liquidity in the enterprise sector. Many enterprises which are realizing profits take them to finance investment. The extreme low interest rates itself did not necessarily lead to investment booms. The future is uncertain especially for investment. Thus, the times seem to be over during which it could be assumed that finance triggers growth easily.

4   Conclusion

In our very simple paper we could show that the finance-growth nexus changed after the international financial crisis. Nevertheless, there still seems to be finance-nexus. From descriptive statistics we get the impression that countries differ widely in terms of economic growth rates and the provision of credit to the private sector. From our results we got the impression that the nexus between finance and growth turned into negative. In more detail: The higher the ratio of credits to the private sector over GDP is the lower is the growth rate or, in other words, the lower the growth rate the higher is the ratio of credits to the private sector.

This finding—even since it results from a very simple analysis—is very interesting. It gives first hints that the time of financial development is over. Development today might go back more to technological changes.

However, this paper gives us only a first and very roughly speaking results. Further research is necessary to address the open questions. Where does growth come from? Therefore, a broader set of data and indicators could be employed. In addition, more sophisticated regression techniques might lead to more sophisticated results.

References

— Beck, T. (2012): Finance and growth: Lessons from the literature and recent crisis. London. Retrieved from http://www.thorstenbeck.com/108089814
— Cecchetti, S. G., and E. Kharroubi (2012): Reassessing the impact of. BIS Working Papers No 381, BIS. Retrieved from https://papers.ssrn.com/sol3/papers.cfm?abstract_id=2117753
— Cecchetti, S. G., and E. Kharroubi (2015): Why does financial sector growth crowd out real economic growth? Retrieved from http://people.brandeis.edu/~cecchett/WPpdf/2015_Cecchetti_Kharroub.pdf
— Eurostat (2019): Your key European Statistics . Retrieved from https://ec.europa.eu/eurostat/web/national-accounts/data/database
— King, R., and R. Levine (1993a): Finance and growth: Schumpeter might be right. The Quarterly Journal of Economics, 108 (3), 717–737. Retrieved from www.jstor.org/stable/2118406
— King, R., and R. Levine (1993b): Finance, entrepreneurship and growth. Journal of Monetary Economics, 3, 513–542.
— Levine, R., N. Loayza, and T. Beck (2000): Financial intermediation and growth: Causality and causes. Journal of Monetary Economics, 46 (1), August, 31–77.
— McKinnon, R. I. (1973): Money and capital in economic development. Washington D. C., Brookings Institution.
— Pagano, M. (1993): Financial markets and growth: an overview. European Economic Review, 37, 13–22.
— Rajan, R. G., and L. Zingales (1998): Financial dependence and growth. American Economic Review, 88, 559–586.
— Robinson, J. (1952): The generalization of the general theory. In the rate of interest and other essays. London, MacMillan.
— The Worldbank (2019): World Bank open data. Retrieved from https://data.worldbank.org/

Why we should embrace institutional diversity in banking

AXEL BERTUCH-SAMUELS*

Axel Bertuch-Samuels, e-mail: axel.be.samuels@verizon.net

Summary: The contribution of institutionally diversified financial sectors to more sustainable growth and financial stability—in particular the role of effective local banking structures—is not always fully appreciated, whether in the context of development cooperation or in policy discussions in the advanced economies. At the same time, a growing number of studies—ranging from analyses of the drivers of financial inclusion in developing countries to assessments of various banking groups' performance during and after the global financial crisis (GFS)—find that financial institutions whose business models focus on local economies, retail and relationship banking do, indeed, have a positive impact on economic development, growth and financial stability. Those findings are also supported by a closer examination of the factors, which contributed to the successful evolution of the German savings banks and cooperative banks over a period of more than 200 years. These factors include: the concentration of their banking activities on a limited geographical region while working as a network of cooperating autonomous institutions; the prioritization of savings mobilization; a mandate to serve the economic and social wellbeing of the local region, while remaining profitable and financially viable over the long run, rather than narrowly focusing on profit maximization. Similar success factors can also be observed in the context of financial institution building and the deliberate promotion of locally oriented and people-focused microfinance and banking institutions in several developing economies.

Zusammenfassung: Der Beitrag von Institutionen-Vielfalt im Finanzsektor zu nachhaltigem Wachstum und Finanzstabilität – insbesondere die Rolle effektiver lokaler Bankstrukturen – wird nicht selten unterschätzt, sei es im Rahmen der Entwicklungszusammenarbeit oder in der strukturpolitischen Diskussion in den hochentwi-

→ JEL classification: G00 G01 G21 G28
→ Keywords: Financial crisis, diversified financial sectors, savings banks, cooperative banks, commercial banks

* Former Deputy Director, Monetary and Capital Markets Department, IMF; former IMF Special Representative to the United Nations

ckelten Volkswirtschaften. Dabei kommen in jüngster Zeit mehr und mehr Untersuchungen zu dem Ergebnis, dass Finanzinstitute mit einem Geschäftsmodell, welches die Pflege langfristig angelegter Geschäftsbeziehungen zu breiten Bevölkerungsschichten und zu mittelständischen Unternehmen vor Ort in den Mittelpunkt stellt, in der Tat einen positiven Einfluss auf Wirtschaftsentwicklung und Stabilität ausüben. Diese Untersuchungen reichen von Studien über Faktoren, die inklusive Finanzstrukturen in Entwicklungsländern vorantreiben helfen, bis hin zu vergleichenden Analysen der Geschäftsergebnisse unterschiedlicher Bankengruppen in Folge der globalen Finanzkrise. Diese Forschungsergebnisse werden überdies auch bestätigt, wenn man die spezifischen Erfolgsfaktoren hinter der mehr als 200-jährigen Geschichte des deutschen Sparkassen- und Genossenschaftsbankwesens einmal genauer unter die Lupe nimmt. Zu solchen Faktoren gehören unter anderem: Die Konzentration ihrer Aktivitäten auf eine geographisch begrenzte Region bei gleichzeitiger Zusammenarbeit in einem „Verbund" (das heißt in einem Netzwerk autonomer Institute); die Förderung des Sparens und eine Fokussierung auf das Einlagengeschäft, und last but not least, ein Mandat, sich für das wirtschaftliche und soziale Wohl der Region einzusetzen, und zwar auf der Basis von nachhaltiger Ertragskraft und finanzieller Solidität anstatt enger Ausrichtung auf kurzfristige Profitmaximierung. Ähnliche Erfolgsfaktoren finden sich auch in einer Reihe von Entwicklungsländern im Zusammenhang mit dem Aufbau eines heimischen Finanzinstitutionengefüges und damit einhergehenden dezidierten Anstrengungen zur Förderung von Mikrofinanzinstituten und lokal verankerten Banken, deren Angebot an Finanzdienstleistungen nicht zuletzt auf die Bedürfnisse der ärmeren Bevölkerungsschichten ausgerichtet ist.

1   Introduction

It would appear obvious that assessments of the performance of financial institutions in advanced economies over different periods of time—including more recent analyses following the GFC—should provide important inputs for policy makers in *all* countries around the world, and *not only* for the more exclusive membership of the G20, the FSB and the "Basel community" of regulators and supervisors. However, what seems less well understood is that studies focused on issues of financial inclusion and improving the effectiveness of financial sectors in developing economies, which are mainly intended to assist development partners, *also* yield very relevant lessons for advanced economies' financial sector policy. This article, therefore, gathers findings from a cross-section of pertinent studies (section 2) and brings them together with a number of stylized facts that explain the long-lasting success of the German savings and cooperative banks (section 3). The objective of this exercise is to demonstrate that there is a well-founded case to be made in defense of diversity in banking models, regardless of country group or stages of economic development, as summarized in the concluding section IV.

2   The role of access to financial services and effective banking institutions in the process of saving & borrowing and fostering growth & stability

2.1   Macroeconomic effects of financial inclusion

Recent studies based on ex-post project assessments in countries with multi-year microfinance support programs show that the promotion of financial inclusion benefits poverty reduction and development (Demirgüç-Kunt, Klapper and Singer 2017). This complements findings in earlier literature on the nexus of finance and growth, which describes the positive effects of financial deepening on economic development, including its welfare-enhancing influence on previously marginalized segments of the population (for example Levine 2005). Even those who later have argued that microfinance has promised more than it could deliver agree that it has made a significant contribution to a more inclusive financial system by building robust, durable financial institutions to bring useful services to millions of people in need (Roodman 2012, 2014).[1] Indeed, and more specifically, the micro-level evidence on the benefits of access to basic payments and savings, especially among poor households, is quite supportive. At the same time, the micro-level evidence of the experience with increased access to credit shows somewhat more mixed results (World Bank 2014). However, until a few years ago a more rigorous analysis of the macroeconomic effects of financial inclusion was lacking because consistent macro-level data over sufficiently long time periods was either unavailable or not systematically put together. This changed once the IMF started to devote more resources toward assembling better and more granular financial sector data—including cross-country data on access to and use of financial services—and began to incorporate these into the analysis of macroeconomic issues of income inequality and inclusive growth.

This analysis confirms that financial inclusion can indeed have positive macroeconomic effects, both in terms of growth and stability (Sahay et al. 2015a). The findings can be summarized as follows:

- *Financial sectors that are not only deep but also more diverse in providing broader access to finance appear to be more conducive to economic growth* although, at high levels of financial development, the marginal benefits to growth of increasing financial inclusion begin to decline.

- *Sectors that are more dependent on external finance grow more rapidly in countries with greater financial depth, and even more so with greater financial inclusion;* also, financial inclusion is especially beneficial in sectors where pledging collateral is more problematic.

- *Financial inclusion can also enhance stability, through direct and indirect channels.* Directly, if more people use bank deposits, banks could have a more solid funding base, especially in periods of stress.[2] Indirectly, financial inclusion can provide clients of financial firms with better risk management tools, boosting their resilience. However, the impact on banking stability of broadening access to credit depends on the quality of supervision. In countries with weaker bank supervision, the negative effect of broadening credit access on bank buffers is more pronounced. Conversely, at sufficiently high levels of supervisory quality, credit inclusion is positively associated with higher bank buffers.

- *Closing gender gaps in account usage and promoting diversity in the depositor base would help to improve growth without impairing financial stability.* More inclusive financial sec-

---

1   Roodman also has commented positively on the 'German school of institution building', which shines through in much of the development of Germany's savings and cooperative banks described in section III. Below (see Roodman's Blog of October 17, 2012. www.cgdev.org/blog/german-school-institution-building-microfinance).

2   This finding is in line with studies cited below that banks, which have always relied on a strong retail deposit base, turned out to be more resilient during the GFC than banks that were very dependent on wholesale funding (for example Ayadi et al. 2015, Kotz and Schmidt 2016).

tor governance can also be important for financial stability (see also Sahay and Čihák 2018).

2.2 The fundamental role of savings

Thrift lies at the heart of savings and capital accumulation, and when savings are effectively transformed into enterprise financing and put to productive use, this will generate economic growth and development. The promotion of saving is critical not only at the macroeconomic level, but also at the individual level, including among the poor. Savings also help low-income households and the poor to smooth consumption and provide a degree of 'self-insurance' to cope with unforeseen problems, including illness and temporary inability to earn a living. As individual or family income grows, savings can help finance investments in education or with starting a micro or family businesses. For example, according to the World Bank's Global Findex Database 2017, saving for a business was especially common in Sub-Saharan African economies: In Ethiopia, Kenya, Liberia, Nigeria, Uganda and Zambia, 29 percent or more of the adults surveyed reported having done so. This is twice the global average. Hence, at the aggregate level, an increasing accumulation of savings is strongly predictive of future economic growth (Karlan et al. 2104). Yet, despite the progress over the past decade in improving access to finance, many people with bank accounts do not necessarily use a banking institution for their savings. As shown in the Global Findex Database, only 31 percent of account holders in developing countries reported in 2017 that they have saved at a financial institution during the past 12 months. A considerable share of people saves semi-informally, for example through a village savings club or simply by holding cash at home and in the form of jewelry. Informal saving still meets consumption smoothing and self-insurance needs. But money "parked" outside the financial system is not available for the professional intermediation of savings into credit. This is where effective local banking with its ability to reach communities and generate trust comes into the equation.

2.3 Credit and its importance for small business

Individuals as well as firms depend on reliable access to credit no matter how advanced an economy's stage of development, and studies find that bank credit is generally associated with higher growth rates if one controls for other factors (Ayyagari, Demirgüç-Kunt and Maksimovic 2011). But often there is a mismatch between demand for and supply of credit, which is especially problematic when it comes to small firms and start-ups. According to a 2010 expert group report to the G20, formal SMEs contribute up to 45 percent of employment and up to 33 percent of GDP in developing economies and these numbers are significantly higher when taking into account the estimated contributions of SMEs operating in the informal sector. Research also shows that the availability of external finance is associated with greater innovation by MSMEs, and business start-ups. However, market information asymmetries, high transaction costs, lack of movable collateral frameworks and credit information systems as well as other weaknesses of the financial sector infrastructure and legal environment often constrain access to finance for these firms, in particular in developing economies (World Bank 2014).

According to World Bank surveys, more than one third of small firms in developing countries cite access to finance as a major constraint. Even among large firms, that number is significant (25 percent). And lack of access for SMEs is also still a significant issue in the developed economies (World Bank 2014, Sahay et al. 2015a). These numbers are based on a sample of 137 countries from 2005-2011. More recent country-by-country data from the 2017 Global Findex Database report show that as much as 40–50 percent of small firms, in particular in Sub-Saharan African economies, still report lack of access to be a major constraint.

Credit is not always the most suitable instrument to finance a business, but for many firms it may be the only available external source of finance. Start-ups as well as micro and small firms often have hardly any other options but to rely on banks in order to add external capital to leverage internally generated finance. And it is often only at the local level, where they can overcome their financing challenges. This is because, if anywhere, it is at this level that the age-old 'know your customer' banking rule tends to work to the mutual benefit of both the lender and the borrower.

Small firms have more of a chance to establish trust and build sound relationships for the longer term with a local banking partner that is familiar with the local business environment. From the perspective of the lender, relationship banking that is focused on local clients affords the lending institution a superior risk assessment, based on local, soft information (Petersen and Rajan 1994). Such a 'commonality of interest' between local banks and local businesses becomes even more obvious for banks with a business model that specializes in MSME financing and/or includes a mission to support the local/regional economy (Behr, Foos and Norden 2013). This type of local business financing by banks has been shown to be effective and sustainable, and certainly more so than government-directed lending.[3]

2.4 Financial sector structure in the context of development and growth

Market finance and bank finance play different and complementary roles in the growth and development process. The highly positive correlation between financial depth and economic growth is uncontroversial, although there is some disagreement in the literature about the direction of causality. Some studies have shown evidence of a positive effect of financial development on growth, while others argue that financial development advances when economic growth leads to greater profits for financial institutions.[4] However, while the pros and cons of bank finance versus market finance have been the subject of much analysis and debate for a long time, there has been a relative dearth of literature on the relative benefits of different types of banking institutions or banking models. Of particular interest here is the question of whether some financial institutions or certain banking business models are better suited than others to improve access to finance for businesses, especially for MSMEs and start-ups.

A useful, albeit partial answer to the question can be found in a chapter of the World Bank's Global Financial Development Report 2014, which analyses the drivers of financial inclusion. In that chapter, the World Bank staff undertakes a valuable review of the role of different types of financial institutions (World Bank 2014). This review also presents data about regional variations in the relative importance of financial institutions other than commercial banks. For example, in Latin America and East Asia and the Pacific, there is a high ratio of cooperative banks, whereas in Sub-Saharan Africa—at a ratio of MFIs to bank branches of almost 1 : 2—MFIs are much more prevalent than anywhere else. Interestingly, the ratio of cooperatives to commercial bank branches

---

3 Directed lending often has been associated with market distortions and financial stability concerns. The risk of such problems materializing is even greater in countries suffering from poor governance and weak institutions.

4 For an overview of the arguments see Levine (1997, 2005), who concludes that the preponderance of evidence suggests that both financial intermediaries and markets matter for growth and that reverse causality alone is not driving this relationship.

is highest in the advanced economies of Western Europe; Germany and Austria actually have more cooperative than commercial bank branches. However, while a literature review finds that a higher share of savings and credit cooperatives, credit unions, and MFIs may result in improved access to finance in low-income countries, it does not produce evidence that smaller institutions more generally perform better than larger ones in providing access to finance more generally (Beck, Demirgüç-Kunt and Singer 2013). In fact, the World Bank report cites several examples of larger banks that have profitably managed to provide greater access to finance, such as Banco Azteca in Mexico (see also Ruiz 2013). What appears to matter more than the size or governance structure of banks in improving access to finance in a commercially successful manner is the special lending technique that such banks have developed and/or the business model of relationship banking. Research also confirms that competition in the financial sector is a key factor in enhancing firms' access to finance (Love and Martinez Peira 2012). The World Bank report then concludes that a financially diverse landscape, featuring a variety of financial institutions and improved competition in the financial sector, can be associated with improved access to finance and provide a better basis for growth.

With regard to the European banking system, a series of innovative studies assesses the performance of various groups of banks and their lending behavior through the economic cycle. The 'Banking Business Models Monitor' emphasizes the ownership structures and assesses the financial and economic performance, resilience and robustness, across retail, investment, and wholesale oriented banks (Ayadi et al. 2014). The analysis finds, *inter alia*, that the contribution to the real economy of the locally focused retail bank model has been significantly higher than other business models, and banks that engage more in traditional retail banking activities with a mix of funding sources fared well during the different phases of the GFS compared to other bank models. In a similar vein, studies by Butzbach and von Mettenheim (2012, 2014) find that "alternative banks" (including cooperative, savings, and special purpose banks) often equal or outperform joint-stock banks. These types of banks have business models that are based on sustainable returns with longer time horizons and include social and public policy goals. Kotz and Schmidt (2016) draw similar conclusions from their analysis of the development of German banks' corporate governance since the 1950s.

2.5 Financial sector diversity and financial stability

History is rife with banking crises that caused major economic turmoil, followed by national and supra-national efforts of lawmakers, supervisors and regulators to design stronger tools for crisis resolution and prevention. However, such well-intentioned efforts to reduce systemic risk eventually tend to get watered down in the face of heavy lobbying by vested interests. The new regulations then can turn out to be insufficient to prevent the recurrence of excessive risk taking at the systemically important large banks. Yet they cause disproportionate burdens for local banks, which did not cause the crisis in the first place. In fact, it could be argued that the latter are more resilient, while investment and wholesale banks tend to accelerate the accumulation of risk at system level and to be less resilient to shocks (Ayadi 2015). This argument is also shared by Kotz and Schmidt (2016), who observe: "Experience bears witness to the fact that banking systems including boring banks, i. e. those with a broader stakeholder orientation and less of a focus on short-term profits, appear to be more resilient." [5]

Indeed, the stability and growth benefits of an institutionally diversified banking sector can be illustrated rather well with the experience in Germany. Here, the decentralized system of local banks, which has always focused on retail (deposits and lending) and SME business, has been much more resilient during the GFS than the large, internationally active commercial and investment banks. The financial stability of the decentralized banking groups, coupled with their ability to maintain strong "house bank" relationships with SMEs and trades and crafts people, has prevented an economy-wide credit crunch. This also explains at least partially why the crisis-induced recession was shorter lived in Germany, and its economy has managed to come out of it much stronger than that of other comparable countries. Incidentally, a study published by the ILO makes similar points for cooperatives in other countries (Birchall 2013). Figure 1 shows the divergent trend in lending between the large commercial banks on the one hand and the savings and cooperative banking groups on the other between 2000 and 2018: The lending behavior of the former is rather volatile, and total credit outstanding declines during and following the financial crisis and the subsequent economic downturn, whereas the total credit extended by either the savings banks or the credit cooperatives shows a steady increase during the same period.

Unfortunately, safer banking structures and business models that favor stable long-term bank-client relationships were increasingly considered to be outdated or "boring" (Kotz and Schmidt 2016) during the final decades of the 20th century. As a result, the privatization of state and public banks, the restructuring of decentralized banking groups into larger banks, or mergers with large commercial banks became the norm across many member countries of the OECD and beyond, in particular during the investment banking hype of the 1990s.[6] All the while, the ascent of investment banking and financial engineering, combined with the revolution in IT, ushered in an era of "financialization", i. e. an increasing disconnect of global banks and financial markets from the real economy. Shareholder value orientation became a standard for most and pushed profitability benchmarks in banking to unsustainable levels. In fact, it was unrealistic for banks with a business model focused on relationship banking and the financing of SMEs to achieve the strongly elevated targets for returns on assets (ROA) propagated by large investment banks and the capital markets. As a consequence, a number of those, mostly mid-size regional banks sought to boost their results by investing in the high-yielding complex structured products engineered from US mortgages, but eventually ran into huge problems.[7] With hindsight, therefore, the GFS has also served as a stark reminder of what happens when banks depart from traditional business models with familiar risks and take new risks that can easily become excessive.[8]

---

5   This pattern has led to increased calls in Europe, for example, to stop pursuing one-size-fits-all regulation and introduce proportionality to better align regulation with business models: i. e. set more stringent rules for those bank business models which tend to accelerate systemic risks than for those which are more resilient to extreme shocks and have stronger links to the real economy.

6   As one of the few exceptions in Europe, the German government resisted pressures to privatize its decentralized networks of savings banks.

7   One such bank—the first to fall in Germany in the wake of the GFC—was Industrie Kreditbank (IKB) in Düsseldorf. Landesbanken, too, suffered losses on their investments in "toxic assets", were subject to bailouts by their owners (regional savings banks associations and Länder) and were forced to undergo management changes and major restructuring.

8   The renowned Asian regulator and scholar, Andrew Sheng remarked with hindsight: "I used to think that we should build Wall Street in Asia. I now think that is exactly what we should not do. I am still a firm believer that finance must be at the service of the real economy, not the other way around. I still believe that finance must look after the interests of the public first and foremost before its own interests.

Figure 1

Total credit outstanding to domestic enterprises & self-employed

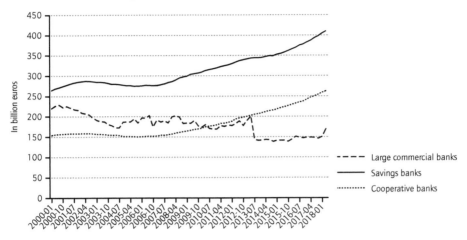

Source: Banking statistics of the Deutsche Bundesbank and calculations by the DSGV (German Association of Savings Banks).

3 The example of the savings and cooperative banks in Germany's "3-Pillar System of Banks": Longevity of diversity in banking demonstrated

Both the savings banks (Sparkassen) and the cooperative banks (Volks- und Raiffeisenbanken) in Germany have successfully followed a self-sustaining business model over more than two centuries.[9] The savings banks group and the cooperative banking sector form two of the so-called "three pillars" in the German banking system, with the commercial banks (publicly listed or private) constituting the third pillar (Schmidt, Bülbül and Schüwer 2013). Together, both of these two decentralized locally anchored banking groups have by far the largest market share in retail deposits and small business lending in modern day Germany (Tables 1 and 2). Savings banks have emphasized the virtue of saving across all generations until the present day, which may explain at least in part their long-lasting leading market share in savings deposits as well as deposits overall.

The institutional model of the German savings banks is rather unique today, not least due to its particular legal, governance and ownership structure (see, *inter alia*, Clarke 2010, Simpson 2013, Schmidt, Seibel and Thomes 2016). Cooperative financial institutions can be found today in many parts of the world, and the cooperative movement that started in the 19th century in Europe has inspired MFIs in many developing countries. By contrast, while savings banks were also founded in many other European countries in the 18th and 19th centuries, many have disappeared, were

We change these beliefs at our peril." Quoted from: Annual Ngee Ann Kongsi Distinguished Lecture, Singapore Management University, 28 October 2010 "Global financial reforms and its implications for Asia and its financial systems".

9   See also Schmidt, Seibel and Thomes (2016), Deutsche Bundesbank (ed.) (1976), Pohl, Rudolph and Schulz (2005), Faust (1977).

Table 1

Deposits – market shares 2018 by type and banking group	Total deposits (exclusive term deposits of over two years duration)	Savings bonds	Savings deposits	Term deposits (up to two years)	Sight deposits
Savings banks	35,4	43,4	51,3	17,4	33,8
Cooperative banks	21,9	12,3	31,8	11,3	21,0
Large banks	20,8	8,4	14,1	37,0	20,4
Regional banks	21,9	35,9	2,8	34,3	24,8

Source: Deutsche Bundesbank Banking Statistics and calculations by DSGV.

Table 2

Credit market shares 2018 by type and banking group	Total loans to domestic non-banks	Loans to domestic public authorities	Consumer loans	Residential real estate loans*	Loans to the craft and trade sector	Loans to enterprises and self-employed**
Savings banks	37,8	39,3	21,2	38,1	72,4	40,6
Cooperative banks	20,4	1,5	19,1	26,1	14,3	18,4
Large banks	13,8	7,8	11,3	17,3	2,7	11,9
Regional banks	28,0	51,4	48,4	18,5	10,6	29,1

* Private and commercial housing construction loans. ** Excluding commercial construction loans.
Source: Deutsche Bundesbank Banking Statistics and calculations by DSGV.

restructured into supra-regional banks or merged with other banks and lost much of their initial mission along the way (von Mettenheim and Butzbach 2012). German savings banks, too, have consolidated over time, but did not abandon their local and regional focus. And they have adhered to the key tenets of their structure, governance and business model: savings banks continue to have close ties to local governments, pursue social as well as business objectives and a bottom line of profitability but not profit maximization. They are authorized to operate only in their local region. That creates commonalities of interests between the savings banks and the municipalities or counties as well as with the local communities and economies they serve. To secure economies of scale, they formed associations, which allowed them to coordinate back-office functions and operate as a network of cooperating autonomous institutions. To help manage liquidity in the network and larger scale operations, including wholesale, international and capital market-related business, which would overwhelm an individual municipal savings bank, they also created apex banks, i. e. central institutions, organized along state lines (hence their name "Landesbanken", i. e. banks of the states).[10]

---

10   The cooperative banks organized similar networks and central institutions for the same reasons which have by now been consolidated at the national level.

The geographical constraint serves as an incentive to provide high quality financial services. Savings banks cannot move into other or more lucrative regions to expand their earnings potential; they have to try harder to retain customer loyalty. They also tend to maintain good banking relations with their local SMEs, the crafts and the trades people through the economic cycle, because the future commercial viability of the savings bank hinges on the economic success of the local business community. The cultivation of strong local ties also ensures greater familiarity by loan officers and bank management with the local firms and their businesses environment, which makes them better judges of the longer-term prospects of loan applicants. This facilitates risk management and gives the local savings bank an edge over branches of large commercial banks, which are more constrained by conditions imposed from far-away headquarters.

This model of banking is more crisis resilient and beneficial for the stabilization of local/regional economic development. For example, according to surveys conducted among German businesses during the global financial crisis (quoted in Ayadi et al. 2009), businesses that rely on the larger banks suffered during that period because of a reduction in lending by those banks (see also Figure 1 in section 2.5 above). By contrast, the businesses that relied on the savings banks and the credit cooperatives did not witness similar restrictions in availability of credit. Hence, the savings banks have behaved counter cyclically during the economic downturn (Behr, Foos and Norden 2013 and 2015). The principle "local deposits into local loans" provides resilient financing opportunities for economically weaker regions and counteracts potentially larger capital outflow from these areas. This can also be observed with credit cooperatives in other countries (see Birchall 2013).

The traditional partnership between savings banks and their trustees, the municipalities and counties, has also contributed significantly to local and economic development across all regions. This link has helped finance communal investment into utilities, infrastructure and education during the industrialization and modernization of the late 19th and early 20th centuries. And in recent decades, this partnership has assisted in the process of adjustment to structural change, as savings banks have sponsored innovative local start-ups and business parks in cooperation with local authorities in the old mining and steel areas of the West or, after reunification, in structurally weak regions of the East.

Both the German savings bank and the cooperative bank models have proven to be successful in a highly competitive banking sector. The German economy has always benefitted from the secure and stable provision of financial services across all regions by these decentralized banking groups. Looking beyond Germany, one can identify several important constitutive elements of this banking business model, which have been adopted successfully in developing economies' financial sector institution building, namely: the mandate to serve the local economy and community; an emphasis on the importance of both saving and lending; a special focus on the financing of SMEs and start-ups;[11] the pursuit of economic viability rather than profit maximization; and a dedication to financial inclusion, i.e. making skilled and professional financial banking services and advice available to everyone (Schmidt, Seibel and Thomes 2016).

---

11   A 2010 report by the G-20 Financial Inclusion Experts Group's (FIEG) SME Finance Sub-Group notes that the German savings banks model presents particularly high levels of scale, sustainability and track record and has been replicated successfully in other countries, such as Peru.

4   Conclusion

- Promoting savings is indispensible for sustained investment and growth, regardless of the development stage of an economy. Greater access to financial services for all segments of the population and economic sectors contributes both to the mobilization of savings and the availability of sustainable financing, especially in rural and economically weaker areas.

- Whether in urban or rural areas, improved access to credit, especially for start-ups and MSMEs, is a key factor in broadening the basis for economic growth and development at the local level, as well as—in the aggregate—at the macroeconomic level.

- But credit alone is not sufficient. Not only must the provision of more credit opportunities be managed prudently with good oversight & supervision; the increased supply of credit also requires an adequate legal framework, good governance and, more generally, a strong, sound financial infrastructure together with effective banking institutions.

- Particular types of financial institutions, such as savings and cooperative banks, as well as associated business models, tend to be more effective than others at achieving financial access for all, including in rural and structurally weaker regions, and can serve as safer and more reliable banking partners to start-ups, MSMEs and SMEs than large commercial, investment or wholesale banks.

- A competitive financial sector with an institutionally diversified financial landscape helps improve financial inclusion and fosters more inclusive growth. Decentralized and locally anchored banking structures can also be more resilient in the face of economic shocks and financial crises and mitigate their negative economic impact through countercyclical behavior.

References

— Ayadi, Rym and Willem Pieter De Groen (2014): Banking Business Models Monitor 2014: Europe. CEPS Paperbacks, 2014. Available at SSRN. https://ssrn.com/abstract=2510323
— Ayadi, Rym, Reinhard H. Schmidt, Santiago C. Valverde, Emrah Arbak and Francisco R. Fernandez (2009): Investigating Diversity in the Banking Sector in Europe: The Performance and Role of Savings Banks. Centre for European Policy Studies, Brussels.
— Ayyagari, Meghana, Asli Demirgüç-Kunt and Vojislav Maksimovic (2011): Small vs. Young Firms across the World: Contribution to Job Creation, Employment and Growth. World Bank Policy Research Working Paper 5631. World Bank, Washington, D.C.
— Beck, Thorsten, Asli Demirgüç-Kunt and Dorothe Singer (2011): Is Small Beautiful? Financial Structure, Size, and Access to Finance. Policy Research Working Paper No. 5806. World Bank, Washington, D.C. https://openknowledge.worldbank.org/handle/10986/3569
— Behr, Patrick, Daniel Foos and Lars Norden (2013): Financial constraints of private firms and bank lending behavior. Journal of Banking & Finance, 2013/37, 3472–3485.
— Behr, Patrick, Daniel Foos and Lars Norden (2015): Cyclicality of SME lending and government involvement in banks. Deutsche Bundesbank Discussion Paper 39/2015. Frankfurt a.M.

— Berger, Allen N., and Gregory F. Udell (2006): A More Complete Conceptual Framework for SME Financing. Journal of Banking and Finance, 30 (11), 2945–2966.
— Bertuch-Samuels, Axel (2018): Financial Sector Development—The role of effective local banking structures. Background paper for the 2019 UN Inter-Agency Task Force Report on Financing for Sustainable Development. https://developmentfinance.un.org/sites/developmentfinance.un.org/files/Background%20Paper_Financial%20Sector%20Development.pdf
— Birchall, Johnston (2013): Resilience in a downturn: The power of financial cooperatives. International Labour Office (ILO), Geneva.
— Bruhn, Miriam, and Inessa Love (2009): The economic impact of banking the unbanked: evidence from Mexico. Policy Research Working Paper Series 4981. World Bank, Washington, D. C.
— Butzbach, Olivier, and Kurt von Mettenheim (2014) Alternative Banking and Theory. Accounting Economics and Law, 5 (2), December 2014.
— Clarke, Stephen L. (2010): German Savings Banks and Swiss Cantonal Banks, lessons for the UK. Civitas, The Institute for the Study of Civil Society. London.
— Demirgüç-Kunt, Asli, Leora Klapper and Dorothe Singer (2017): Financial inclusion and inclusive growth: a review of recent empirical evidence. Policy Research Working Paper 8040. World Bank. Washington, D. C.
— Demirgüç-Kunt, Asli, Leora Klapper, Dorothe Singer, Saniya Ansar and Jake Hess (2018): The Global Findex Database 2017: Measuring Financial Inclusion and the Fintech Revolution. World Bank, Washington, D. C.
— Deutsche Bundesbank (ed.) (1976): Währung und Wirtschaft in Deutschland 1876–1975. Frankfurt a. M.
— Faust, Helmut (1977): Geschichte der Genossenschaftsbewegung. Ursprung und Aufbruch der Genossenschaftsbewegung in England, Frankreich, und Deutschland sowie ihre weitere Entwicklung im deutschen Sprachraum. 3rd ed. Frankfurt a. M.
— Financial Inclusion Experts Group (FIEG) – SME Finance Sub-Group (2010): Scaling-Up SME Access to Financial Services in the Developing World. Report to the G20.
— IMF (2017): Financial Access Survey (FAS) Trends. Washington, D. C.
— Karlan, Dean, Aishwara Ratan and Jonathan Zinman (2014): Savings by and for the Poor: A Research Review and Agenda. Review of Income and Wealth. International Association for Research in Income and Wealth, 60 (1), 36–78.
— Kotz, Hans-Helmut, and Reinhard H. Schmidt (2016): Corporate Governance of Banks—A German Alternative to the Standard Model. Zeitschrift für Bankrecht und Bankwirtschaft (ZBB)/Journal of Banking Law and Banking (JBB), 28 (6), 427–444.
— Levine, Ross (1997): Financial development and economic growth: Views and agenda. Journal of Economic Literature, 35 (2), 688–726.
— Levine, Ross (2005): Finance and Growth: Theory and Evidence. Handbook of Economic Growth. In: Philippe Aghion and Steven Durlauf (eds.): Handbook of Economic Growth. Elsevier, 865–934.
— Levine, Ross, and Sara Zervos (1998): Stock Markets, Banks, and Economic Growth. American Economic Review, 88 (3), 537–558.
— Love, I., and M. S. Martínez Pería (2012): How Bank Competition Affects Firms' Access to Finance. Policy Research Working Paper 6163. World Bank, Washington, D. C.
— Mettenheim, Kurt von, and Oliver Butzbach (2012): Alternative banking: Theory and evidence from Europe. Revista de Economia Política, 32, 580–596.

— Petersen, Mitchell, and Raghuram Rajan (1994): The Benefits of Lending Relationships: Evidence from Small Business Data. The Journal of Finance, XLIX (1).
— Pohl, Hans, Bernd Rudolph and Günter Schulz (2005): Sparkassen in der Geschichte. Stuttgart.
— Rajan, Raghuram G., and Luigi Zingales (1998): Financial Dependence and Growth. American Economic Review, American Economic Association, 88 (3), 559–586, June.
— Roodman, David (2012): Due Diligence: An Impertinent Inquiry into Microfinance. Center for Global Development, Washington, D. C.
— Roodman, David (2014): Armageddon or Adolescence? Making Sense of Microfinance's Recent Travails. CGD Policy Paper 035. Center for Global Development. Washington, D. C.
— Ruiz, Claudia (2013): From Pawn Shops to Banks: The Impact of Formal Credit on Informal Households. Policy Research Working Paper 6634. World Bank, Washington, D. C.
— Sahay, Ratna, Martin Čihák, Papa N'Diaye, Adolfo Barajas, Srobona Mitra, Annette Kyobe, Yen Nian Mooi, and Seyed Reza Yousefi (2015a): Financial Inclusion: Can It Meet Multiple Macroeconomic Goals? IMF Staff Discussion Note 15/17. International Monetary Fund, Washington, D. C.
— Sahay, Ratna, Martin Čihák, Papa N'Diaye, Adolfo Barajas, Ran Bi, Diana Ayala, Yuan Gao, Annette Kyobe, Lam Nguyen, Christian Saborowski, Katsiaryna Svirydzenka and Seyed Reza Yousefi (2015b): Rethinking Financial Deepening: Stability and Growth in Emerging Markets. IMF Staff Discussion Note 15/08. International Monetary Fund, Washington, D. C.
— Sahay, Ratna, Martin Čihák and other IMF Staff (2018): Women in Finance: A Case for Closing Gaps. IMF Staff Discussion Note SDN 18/05. International Monetary Fund, Washington, D.C.
— Schmidt, Reinhard H., Dilek Bülbül and Ulrich Schüwer (2013): The Persistence of the Three-Pillar Banking System in Germany. In Oliver Butzbach and Kurt von Mettenheim (eds.): Alternative Banking and Financial Crisis. Pickering & Chatto, 101–122.
— Schmidt, Reinhard H., Hans Dieter Seibel and Paul Thomes (2016): From Microfinance to Inclusive Banking—Why local banking works. Edited by Sparkassenstiftung für internationale Kooperation. Weinheim.
— Sheng, Andrew (2009): From Asian to Global Financial Crisis: An Asian Regulator's View of Unfettered Finance in the 1990s and 2000s. Cambridge, Cambridge University Press.
— Sheng, Andrew, and Xiao Geng (2017): Putting Asia's Savings to Work in Asia. www.business-standard.com. February 27, 2017.
— Simpson, Christopher V.J., Simpson Associates (2013): The German Sparkassen (Savings Banks)—A commentary and case study. Civitas: The Institute for the Study of Civil Society. London.
— World Bank (2014): Global Financial Development Report 2014: Financial Inclusion. World Bank, Washington, D. C.
— World Bank (2018): Global Financial Development Report 2017/2018: Bankers without Borders. World Bank, Washington, D. C.

What future for the European banking system?

LORENZO BINI SMAGHI*

Lorenzo Bini Smaghi, Société Générale, e-mail: Lorenzo.binismaghi@gmail.com

Summary: The paper assesses the main factors underlying the decreasing profitability in the European banking sector, in comparison with the US. It underscores in particular the role of low interest rates, lower concentration, tighter regulation and the absence of a deep and liquid capital market. A stronger European banking system requires true pan-European banks and a true capital market union.

Zusammenfassung: Das Papier beleuchtet die Hauptgründe, die der sinkenden Rentabilität des europäischen Bankensektors im Vergleich zum US-amerikanischen zugrunde liegen. Sie unterstreicht insbesondere die Rolle niedriger Zinsen, geringerer Konzentration, strengerer Regulierung und des Fehlens eines tiefen und liquiden Kapitalmarktes. Ein stärkeres europäisches Bankensystem erfordert echte gesamteuropäische Banken und eine echte Kapitalmarktunion.

→ JEL classification: G00 G01 G21 G28
→ Keywords: Banks, Banking union, bank profitability

* The views expressed in this note reflect only those of the author.

The evolution of the banking sector since the collapse of Lehman brothers, ten years ago, seems quite paradoxical. Although the crisis started on the other side of the Atlantic, as a result of an under-regulated and over-sized US financial system, and although regulation and supervision have been tightened since then, with a view to reduce the so-called too-big-to-fail problem, US banks have grown even bigger. In Europe, instead, the baking system has shrunk. Just to take a simple indicator, the combined balance sheet of US banks nearly doubled in the last decade, while that of the Eurozone remained broadly unchanged (Figure 1).

Figure 1

Banks' total assets

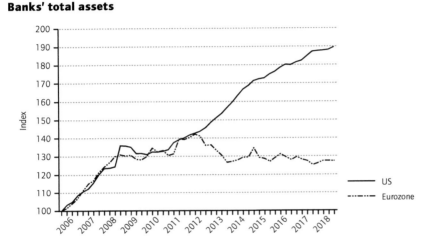

Source: Bloomberg, Société Générale.

This has been reflected in market valuation. Between 2007 and 2018, the overall market cap of the eleven largest US banks[1] increased from 915 to 1365 billion dollars, with a 50 percent gain. In the same time span the combined market cap of the 19 largest Eurozone banks dropped from 713 to 438 billion euro, with a 40 percent loss (Figure 2). In ten years, the market value of the largest US bank, JP Morgan Chase, doubled and is now worth more than the ten largest European banks combined. Before the crisis it capitalized slightly more than one and a half times the largest European bank, Santander; it is now 5 times larger.

The divergence is reflected in the different support that the two systems have provided to the economy. Over the last ten years bank credit to the private non-financial sector increased by 40 percent in the US, against only 10 percent in the Eurozone (Figure 3). Given the importance of bank credit in the European economy, the slower pace in Europe represents an obstacle to growth and job creation.

---

[1]   Bank of America, Citigroup, Goldman Sachs, Morgan Stanley, PNV Fin Serv, State Street, Capital One Financial Corp, BB&T Corp, Wells Fargo, JPMorgan Chase, SunTrust Bank.

Figure 2

Banks' market cap

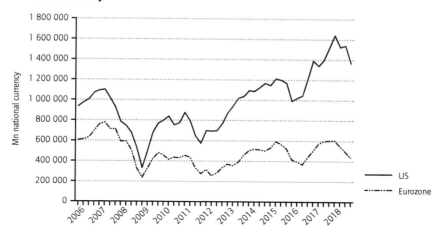

Source: Bloomberg, Société Générale.

The slower pace of bank credit in the Eurozone might be due either to a weakness in supply, determined by a fragility of the banking system, or in the demand for credit, due to a less buoyant economic activity resulting from the double recession experienced in Europe. Disentangling the demand and supply effects is not easy. However, the issuance of market debt by the non-financial private sector increased strongly both in the US and Europe after the crisis (Figure 4). This sug-

Figure 3

Bank credit to the private sector

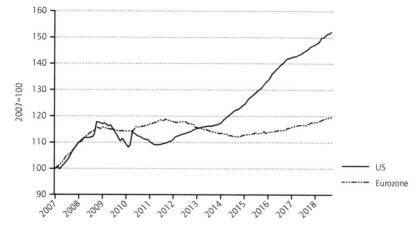

Source: Fed, ECB.

Figure 4

Private sector market financing

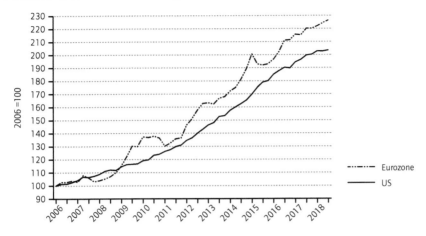

Source: ECB, Fed, Société Générale.

gests that the slow pace of bank credit experienced in Europe is due mainly to the supply side, i. e. the state of the banking system.

It is thus key to understand what might explain the different performance of the US and European banking system over the last decade, and how it can evolve with a view to support economic growth.

Considering first the capital position of the two banking systems, it has substantially strengthened after the crisis. The average CoreTier1 ratio of US and European banks, which was around 7 percent at the end of 2007, raised above 13.5 percent, nearly twice as much, ten years later (Figure 5). The US system was recapitalized much more rapidly, as a result of the TARP package, while in Europe the adjustment differed across countries. However, as from 2015 the two systems are broadly aligned.

This is the result of the regulatory measures implemented after the crisis and the tougher stance taken by supervisory authorities, and by banks themselves, towards risk management. This has pushed the system towards higher and better-quality capital buffers. The same applies to liquidity.

Overall, the banking system has become more robust and better equipped to absorb shocks arising from the financial system or the real economy. The increased stability does not explain however the very different performance across the two areas.

A factor that may explain the different bank performance, both in terms of valuation and credit growth, is profitability. Banks that are more profitable are better valued by the markets and are better positioned to generate new capital and thus provide credit to the real economy. This has been a major discriminating factor between the US and Europe.

Figure 5

Bank capitalization (Cet1)

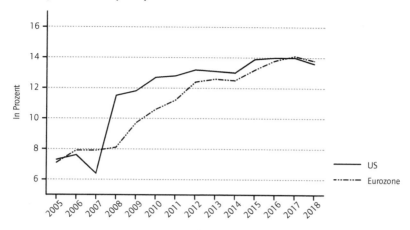

Source: Bloomberg, Société Générale.

Banks' return on capital fell in both areas to close to zero in 2009–2010, as a result of the crisis. However, it rose back towards 10 percent in the US, as the economy recovered, but remained low in Europe until 2016 (Figure 6). In countries like Germany and Italy profitability was negative for several years, as a result of the cyclical downturn and the slow pace in balance-sheet restructuring.

Banks' profitability depends not only on the return but also on the cost of capital, which is generally estimated on the basis of capital asset pricing models. Estimates are based on several parameters, such as the risk-free rate of return, the cost of debt, the risk premium and price volatility. If the return is higher than the cost, investors will be led to increase the holding of the asset, with respect to other alternatives, and valuations will tend to rise, and vice versa.

It is interesting to note that both in the US and Europe the cost of capital has benefitted neither from the reduction of interest rates on risk-free assets nor the strengthening of regulation and banks' capital position. Although yields on both US Treasuries and German bunds fell sharply, especially after the implementation of quantitative easing by the Federal reserve and the ECB and the above-mentioned strengthening of banks' capital position, the cost of capital has remained elevated, higher than pre-crisis levels.

In the US, the cost of capital increased after the crisis but gradually came back to slightly above 10 percent. In Europe instead, the cost of capital remained high, over 15 percent, for a prolonged period of time (Figure 7). In Italy the cost has been affected by the rise in Government bond yield in 2011–2012 and in the most recent period.

What is the reason for such a high cost? Contrarily to what some academics like to think, the banking sector cannot be simply assimilated to a utility, which is highly regulated activity characterized by a combination of low rates of return and low volatility. Banks' profitability is correlated with macroeconomic developments, since revenues are not determined by regulated tariffs but rather

Figure 6

Banks' return on capital

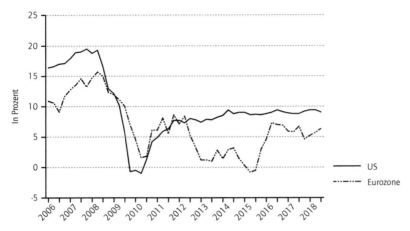

Source: Bloomberg, Société Générale.

subject to strong competition within the sector. The increase in capital requirements have not reduced the perceived cost of capital but have compressed profitability.

Comparing the cost and the return on capital helps explaining the different performance of US and European banks. For the former, the return on capital has basically caught up with costs, while in Europe there is still a substantial gap, with costs remaining higher than returns, especially in Germany and Italy.

There are seven factors that explain the difference between US and European banks' profitability.

The first is the level of interest rates and the yield curve, which basically reflect the different stage of the cycle across the Atlantic. The higher the interest rate and the steeper the yield curve, the higher is profitability, especially when banks' assets have longer maturities than liabilities. The profitability of the traditional banking business, based on the holding of short-term deposits and the supply of longer terms loans to the private sector, depends on the steepness of the yield curve. The sharp reduction of short-term rates after the crisis, in line with the policy rate cuts, and the fall in long term rates, especially after the implementation of quantitative easing, compressed the profitability on both sides of the Atlantic. The US have nevertheless benefitted from a quicker exit from the low interest rate policy, which instead persists in Europe. In the Eurozone, the banking system is also penalized by negative rates (−0.4 percent) on bank deposits with the central bank, which cannot be easily passed to the customers. This represents a tax on the amounts of deposits banks hold with the central bank, while in the US banks are remunerated at positive rates on their excess reserves.

Looking ahead, the difference is likely to last for some time if the European cyclical position continues to lag behind that of the US. Any new announcement by the ECB to prolong the zero

Figure 7

Banks' cost of capital

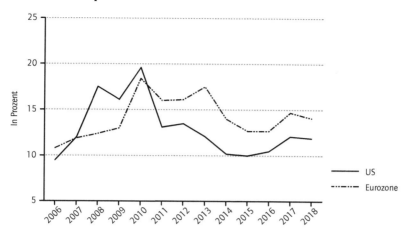

Source: Bloomberg, Société Générale.

interest rates forward guidance contributes to depress bank valuation. The ECB may at some stage consider alleviating the burden created by negative interest rates on deposits, adopting for instance a tiered system like in Japan, exempting certain deposits from the penalty. This could in fact have a positive impact on credit conditions, by providing banks with greater room for maneuver in their capital position.

The second factor influencing bank profitability is taxation. In recent years the US banking system benefitted from the reforms implemented by the Trump administration, which has substantially reduced the fiscal burden. Taxation has instead increased in Europe, with specific measures such as the recent ones implemented in Italy and Spain. In the Eurozone, banks must also contribute to the creation of the 50 billion euro Single Resolution Fund, which represents an implicit taxation. In some countries banks also contributed "voluntarily" to the resolution of smaller banks, like in the case of the Atlante Fund in Italy.

Looking forward, it doesn't seem that the more favorable fiscal position for US banks will change over the coming years.

The third factor is related to the cleaning up of banks' balance sheet after the crisis. Indeed, the higher is the ratio of non-performing loans, the lower is banks' profitability, especially if the value of the collateral is not adequately accounted for. In the US, the overall NPL ratio reached a peak around 6 percent in 2009, but fell rapidly thereafter, getting back to the pre-crisis level by 2015 (Figure 8). In the Eurozone the rise in NPL was initially slower but accelerated after the second recession of 2012–2013. The reduction was also slower, and the pre-crisis levels have not yet been reached.

The difference between the US and Europe is due to several factors, including the different bankruptcy legislation and accounting rules. The US legislation is more flexible and easier to apply,

Figure 8

Banks' Non-performing Loans

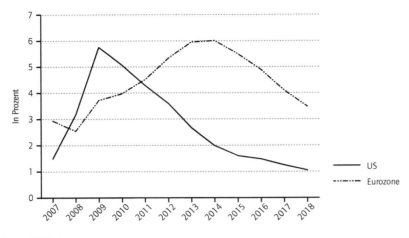

Source: ECB, Fed.

while accounting rules are stricter. The US capital market is also deeper and better equipped to absorb securitized NPLs, while it took some time in Europe to develop a market for this type of asset. The ECB recently adopted measures aimed at aligning the speed of NPL reduction in banks' balance sheets to that of the US.

Overall, US banks have cleaned up their balance sheets much more quickly, also as a result of the forced capitalization implemented in the context of the TARP. In Europe the fear to destroy value through an excessively rapid reduction of NPLs in banks' balance sheets produced the opposite result. Banks which did not dispose sufficiently quickly of their NPLs experienced a sharp reduction of profitability and a rise in the cost of capital. The destruction of value has been even larger.

Going forward the situation is expected to improve in the Eurozone. The reduction of NPLs should continue in the coming years, bringing the ratio back to pre-crisis levels. Profitability should thus rise again, unless the economy slows down sharply, producing a new jump in NPLs.

The fourth factor which explains the higher profitability of the US banking sector is its degree of market concentration. The Gini coefficient of the US system is around 50 percent, higher than in European countries and in the Eurozone as a whole. The five largest banks cover over 50 percent of the market. Concentration is even higher in the capital market. This means that US banks have greater pricing power and more degrees of freedom in setting rates and commissions. They can benefit from economies of scale, due to their larger size, and have the critical mass to produce services in-house that they then sell to their customers, rather than having to distribute other banks' products, which obviously lowers profitability. The larger size better enables them to face the challenge of new entrants and eventually buy them out.

In Europe concentration progressed differently across countries. It has advanced in Nordic countries, Benelux, France and even Spain, as a result of the crisis. In Germany and Italy, instead, the system remains fragmented. In several countries the strong presence of cooperative institutions, which have a much lower cost of equity and thus lower requirements in terms of return on equity, puts pressure on the profitability of listed banks.

Looking ahead, there will be strong pressure for consolidation within borders, especially in Germany and Italy. However, the fear of having banks that are too big tends to discourage aggregations, even between weak banks, under the false assumption that the sum of weaknesses does not create a strength. This ignores the fact that synergies and efficiencies can be generated through mergers between institutions that have a strong overlapping business. Aggregations are also discouraged by conflicts of powers within and between boards, where political considerations may play a substantial role. In the US, bank mergers continue to take place, as the issue of being too-big-to-fail seems to have been reconsidered.

At the European level, the pressure for greater cross-border concentration should emerge as a consequence of low profitability and the need to compete on a similar scale with US and Asian banks. However, it is unlikely that the existing obstacles to concentration will rapidly fade away. The difference between legal systems make it difficult to extract synergies, especially in retail banking, that would make mergers attractive. Furthermore, national political authorities have become increasingly sensitive to the risk of having their banks merge with or being acquired by banks from different countries. The system of exemptions to the EU regulation, which allows national regulators to restrict capital and liquidity mobility within cross border banking groups, is unlikely to be changed in the near future. The fear, especially in smaller countries where branches are located, that the burden of adjustment would be borne by the latter, explains the reluctance of some national authorities to move towards a full implementation of the banking union.

Another obstacle for progressing towards a complete banking union, in particular a common deposit insurance scheme, derives from the still high level of Government bonds held by some banking systems, which produces a high correlation between bank and sovereign risk, the so-called doom-loop. This issue is however not easy to solve, as Europe would be penalized if it was the only area in the world to adopt a system which would limit the extent to which banks can hold Government bonds in their balance sheets. Ideally, the Eurozone should adopt a safe asset, that banks can easily invest in, especially to satisfy their liquidity ratios, but this solution appears politically premature.

The fifth factor, which is linked to the previous one, concerns the different state of development of the capital market in the US and Europe. The US capital market has developed over the last 30 years in line with the process of bank concentration that took place after the Savings and loan crisis and the removal of the prohibition of inter-state banking. Major US banks are active in the capital market, as originators, market makers and advisors. They can extract fees and commissions on a broad range of products, both on the buy and sell side. The strong degree of market concentration ensures high profitability of the so-called universal bank model, which combines retail and capital market activities. The crisis accelerated such a development. The largest banks strengthened their market position, contributing to bail out smaller or more specialized banks, such as Bear Sterns or Washington Mutual.

In Europe the capital market is smaller and fragmented. Bank financing represents still around 70 percent of the total financing to the economy, against less than 30 percent in the US. This means that a large part of the loans provided by banks remains on their balance sheet and cannot be securitized and sold in the capital market. One of the major obstacles is the different nature of national markets and banking practices in different European countries. Since a French mortgage is different from an Italian or Dutch mortgage, they cannot be bundled together and traded and is the case of the US. There is no such a thing as a Fanny May or Freddie Mac in Europe.

The European Commission launched a European Capital market union project, but progress has been slow. Time will be needed before legal and tax barriers are removed. Furthermore, in order to function properly, a capital market requires participants, which are typically banks, that have the size and capability to perform various tasks such as origination, securitization, dealership, advisory, analysis. As European banks shrink their investment banking activity, the likelihood of a capital market diminishes.

In principle, all countries are in favor of creating a capital market union, especially after Brexit. The new European Commission is expected to launch an initiative with new concrete proposals. In practice, there is still strong national resistance, in particular with respect to giving stronger regulatory powers to ESMA, the European market supervisory authority.

The sixth factor concerns regulation. New rules have been defined after the crisis, in the context of the cooperative framework underlying the Basle Committee. However, these rules tend to penalize the European banking system in several respects. In particular, the desired incentive for standardization, in particular in the use of models to assess risk, can be fully captured only in the presence of a deep and liquid capital market. In the fragmented banco-centric European system the benefits of standardization cannot be fully reaped. As a result, the new rules tend to discourage credit, and make it more expensive. Another example is the additional capital buffer which is charged on large banks, which is based on the absolute value of the balance sheet, which tends to penalize a banco-centric financial system like the European one.

Furthermore, the implementation of the new regulation differs between the US, where supervisory authorities enjoy substantial discretion, and Europe where regulation is comprehensive and rule-based. The new US Administration has clearly inverted the regulatory trend of the previous decade. In Europe, instead, the late creation of the single supervisor, in 2014, forced a process of harmonization and standardization of rules and procedures which on the whole have become stricter. There is still some degree of uncertainty on how some of the new Basel rules will be implemented in the European context. In spite of all the regulatory effort, the remaining uncertainties have contributed to raise the cost of capital.

The last factor explaining the different profitability between the US and European banking system is played by the different flexibility of the labor markets. The financial crisis and the emergence of new technologies in financial transactions has put pressure on the traditional banking models, especially in the simpler activities like deposit taking, credit and payment. There is less need for an intensive interaction between customers and bank employees and for a diffused network of bank branches. Data has become the key resource for financial institutions. The higher the number of clients, and the more information banks have on their clients, the greater the ability to design efficient products and services at the desired price. Having more clients is less costly and more profitable than in the past. In short, size matters.

The change in the business model requires strong investments in new technologies and a high flexibility of labor, both to attract new talent and to ease the exit of excess labor. The US have certainly benefitted from a more favorable environment to implement these changes, compared to European countries, where the reduction in costs has been slower and more complex.

To sum up, the combination of the above-mentioned factors explains the divergence between the profitability of the US and European banking systems, and within Europe between that of different countries. Over the last decade, US banks have grown in terms of size and activity, while European banks have reduced the scope of their activities. US banks have taken the lead in capital markets, including the European ones, leveraging on their stronger and more profitable domestic market. Even in the non-banking sector, such as wealth management, US players count amongst the largest.

European supervisory authorities understood, with some delay, that a banking system that is not sufficiently profitable can become a source of fragility over time. One of the potential problems is the ability to generate sufficient resources to continue investing, especially in technology, including for cyber-security, which is key to increase revenues and safeguard profitability. Furthermore, a system that is not sufficiently profitable is not able to attract investors, which may be needed especially at times of crisis.

More important, a banking system which is not sufficiently profitable is not able to adequately support economic growth, especially in a banco-centric financial system like the European one. Furthermore, a capital market union cannot be created in Europe without a strong and profitable banking system. A well-functioning capital market, capable of financing the real economy and absorbing asymmetric shocks within the monetary union, cannot rely on US investment banks alone. Without a strong European banking system there can be no banking union, capable of supporting the growth of European companies in the global competition.

While the problem may start to be understood, no concrete solution is being foreseen. Regulation continues to be tightened; negative interest rates continue to prevail; no euro safe asset is being developed; cross-border capital and liquidity mobility continues to be restricted by national regulators; taxes on banks continue to be raised; the willingness to move towards banking union is still constrained by national political considerations and mutual distrust. The result is that the profitability of the banking system remains impaired. European banks are losing grounds in the global competition, in particular to US banks. As a consequence, banks' ability to grow and to support economic growth in Europe is much more limited than in the US.

What ultimately seems to be missing in Europe, both at the Union level and within its member states, is a strategic view of the role that the banking system can and should play in the process of economic development. Ten years after the crisis, the banking system continues to be viewed in Europe as the main cause of the crisis and, at most, as a potential source for raising taxes. In the US and in China, instead, there is a shared awareness among policy-circles that a strong and profitable banking system, based on large international institutions that have the means of supporting their clients in the global competition, is a strategic priority.

It may be time for Europe to learn from experience. And possibly change its policy.

Diversity across EU banking sectors: Poorly researched and underappreciated

HANS-HELMUT KOTZ AND DOROTHEA SCHÄFER

Hans-Helmut Kotz, Center for European Studies, Harvard University, Cambridge, MA, SAFE Policy Center, Goethe-Universität, Frankfurt a. M., e-mail: kotz@fas.harvard.edu
Dorothea Schäfer, German Institute for Economic Research DIW Berlin, CeFEO at Jönköping International Business School and CERBE Center for Relationship Banking and Economics, Rom, e-mail: dschaefer@diw.de

Summary: Interest in the role of diversity in banking sectors has increased substantially since the financial crisis (and the subsequent sovereign debt crises) have hit European countries differentially. The purpose of this note is to hint at crucial research gaps in terms of appreciating consequences of this variety. In preparation for this, we take stock of the across country diversity of banking sectors in the European Union before and after the financial crisis. Key issues in a future research agenda for evaluating diversity in the banking sector (and the financial sector more generally) have to do with: (a) defining the concept's empirical meaning and hence its measurable properties, (b) the relationship between diversity and the level of competition (market power) in the banking sector, (c) the link between diversity and banking sector stability, (d) the pertinence of banking sector diversity for mitigating access to finance problems, in particular for SMEs and (e) the interlinkages between diversity in the banking (financial) sector and non-financial, "real" economy diversity ("goodness of fit"-issue, institutional embeddedness). Filling the indicated research gaps would be an important contribution to both the debate on deeper integration of Europe's financial markets (Banking Union, Capital Markets Union) as well as the debate on a sustainable financial architecture, being at the same time conducive to innovation and growth whilst protecting society effectively from large-scale financial crises.

Zusammenfassung: Das Interesse an der Rolle der Vielfalt im Bankensektor hat erheblich zugenommen, seit die Finanzkrise (und die anschließenden Staatsschuldenkrisen) die europäischen Länder in unterschiedlicher Weise getroffen haben. In diesem Überblicksartikel werden entscheidende Forschungslücken im Bereich der Vielfalt im Bankensektor herausgearbeitet. Vorbereitend dazu bilanzieren wir die Vielfalt der Bankensektoren in der Europäischen Union und beleuchten die Unterschiede vor und nach der Finanzkrise. Kernpunkte einer künftigen Forschungsagenda zur Bewertung der Diversität im Bankensektor (und im Finanzsektor im Allgemeinen) sind: (a) die Definition der empirischen Bedeutung des Konzepts und damit seiner messbaren Eigenschaften, (b) die Beziehung zwischen Diversität und Wettbewerbsniveau (Marktmacht) im Bankensektor, (c) die Verbindung zwischen Diversität und Stabilität des Bankensektors, (d) die Relevanz der Diversität im Bankensektor

→ JEL classification: G01, G20, G21, G28
→ Keywords: Diversity, banking sector structure, sector stability, SME, financial constraints

für einen erleichterten Zugang zu Finanzierung, insbesondere für KMU, und (e) die Verknüpfungen zwischen Diversität im Bankensektor (Finanzsektor) und nichtfinanzieller, „realer" wirtschaftlicher Diversität („Goodness of fit"-Problematik, institutionelle Einbettung). Die aufgezeigten Forschungslücken zu schließen, wäre ein wichtiger Beitrag sowohl zur Debatte über eine tiefere Integration der europäischen Finanzmärkte (Bankenunion, Kapitalmarktunion) als auch zur Debatte über eine nachhaltige Finanzarchitektur, die gleichzeitig Innovation und Wachstum fördert und die Gesellschaft wirksam vor großen Finanzkrisen schützt.

I   Diversity within and across banking sectors—what does it mean?

Diversity over functional characteristics often comes with positive connotations. Ecologists, for example, were convinced for a long time that variety, allowing for a richer set of responses to shocks or new challenges, implies stability: *"Simple communities are more easily upset than [...] richer ones; that is, more subject to destructive oscillations in populations, and more vulnerable to invasions"* (Elton 1958). What regards financial assets, we are well-advised not to put all our eggs into one basket, i. e. instead increase our exposure to a variety of income streams, at least up to a point. This is, of course, a staple of the literature on portfolio management. As Markovitz, Tobin, Sharpe and others have demonstrated, portfolio robustness comes from diversification. Exploiting less than perfect correlation across financial claims allows investors to reduce shortfall risks, given an expected return (efficiency frontier). Investors following this approach do not pretend to know, they just choose the market portfolio. And they express their "behavior towards risk" in the share of the portfolio which is allocated to the risk-free asset. Obviously, exposing oneself to a specific risk could be more profitable. But this would come with substantially higher uncertainty, in particular increasing the probability of really bad outcomes. On average, taking idiosyncratic risk is not rewarded (Markovitz 1952, Tobin 1957).

Of course, diversity is not necessarily beneficial. It can contribute positively to goal achievement, as just illustrated. At the same time, heterogeneity can also be the source of problems, for example, contribute to social tensions and undermine societal capital (Alesina, Guiliano 2015, Putnam 1993). Thus, diversity can be positive, allow for better problem solving, as well as negative, i. e. undermine trust (e. g. Page 2014).

To be brief: In ecology, bio-diversity seemingly promises resilience (see also Schmidt in this issue). Seemingly only, since the claim of a positive association between diversity and dynamic stability is contested (see McCann 2000 and Tilmann 1999). Of course, this is reasoning by analogy (or in metaphors). Still, it can hint at essential features, being usefuly in a 'transdisciplinary' way (Page 2014). Closer to home, in finance, the Markovitz-Tobin-Sharpe diversification paradigm promises insurance against idiosyncratic (as opposed to systematic) risks. Providing insurance against substantial losses and the capacity to absorb shocks are also essential characteristics of a sound banking system. Given the enormous societal costs emanating from banking—or financial institution—crises, it is therefore worth pursuing the question whether a more diverse set of financial institutions rhymes with "sound banking", contributing to the resilience of the European banking landscape.

This is clearly not a moot issue: Up until the Great Financial Crisis, somehow along the lines of the Hansmann-Kraakman (2000) "end of history" argument (concerning corporate governance, Kotz 2007), a view became dominant according to which only privately owned, publicly traded and shareholder-value maximizing banks could deliver. Conversely, cooperative and in particular public sector savings banks were diagnosed as fraught with incentive conflictsand are, as a consequence, structurally underperforming and hence doomed. They could not muster the capacities to run large-scale, (ex-ante seemingly) highly profitable structured credit business lines. Of course, the GFC has led to a reappraisal: Meanwhile, "boring banking", i. e. more risk-averse and with much less ambitious RoE-targets, did measure up rather positively with the former champions. In fact, evidence was brought to bear documenting that banks with the 'best' corporate governance (according to the formerly dominant template) performed worst (Beltratti and Stultz 2011, Kotz and Schmidt 2017)

In this line of reasoning—which, of course, has a longstanding pedigree—, the European Parliament stated that *"the diversity of legal models and business objectives of the financial entities in the retail banking sector (banks, savings banks, cooperatives, etc.) is a fundamental asset to the EU's economy which enriches the sector, corresponds to the pluralist structure of the market and helps to increase competition in the internal market [...]"*. This was not, to be sure, a dominating position (including in the EP) before the GFC. Nonetheless, against this backdrop one could have expected that research on the costs and benefits of banking sector diversity would have been intensified. Surprisingly, however, this was not the case. Still, Ayadi, Llewellyn, Schmidt, Arbak and de Groen (2009) and (2010) published, shortly after the Lehman-AIG etc. debacle, are two pioneering studies on the importance of banking sector diversity for economic stability (and allocational efficiency). However, by and large, the research about which institutional structure of the financial system serves the economy best kept focusing on the simple dichotomy between market- and bank-based financial systems (e. g. Langfield and Pagano 2016).

Yet, this binary perspective has been too simplistic for a long time. In fact, links—the deep interconnectedness—between banks and (anonymous) capital, money and derivatives markets have been too close to ignore for at least since the mid-1980s. To give just two examples: Banks, in particular the large ones, have been "buying" deposits in interbank wholesale markets for decades (instead of collecting retail deposits). Hence, at the margin, their funding costs were determined by demand and supply. Moreover, pricing of loans, that is, the assessment of credit risks, at least as what concerns corporate loans, was also closely following market-determined swap rates plus a risk premium.

Debates in the policy domain where much more in line with contemporaneous developments in the financial sphere: There, industrial diversity in general and banking sector diversity in particular gained in salience in particular in the wake of the GFC. Arnout W. Boot, for example, emphasized the pertinence of diversity when commenting upon the performance of Dutch banks in the 2014 stress test of the European Banking Authority: *"The Netherlands offers a perfect example of how not to do it. Before the crisis, the large financial institutions were becoming to look like each other and were taking comparable risks, and when the crisis hit, they were damaged in the same way. [...] Greater diversity is desirable to prevent one bank from exacerbating the problems of another [...]"* (cited in De Nederlandsche Bank (2015: 22).[1] Very recently, the EU commission also emphasized the importance of diversity in the economy in general. Margrethe Vestager, at the time commissioner for

---

1   The original article is written in Dutch (Boot 2014).

competition, argued "that diverse collection of businesses like a healthy, varied ecosystem in the natural world—can help to keep our economy strong and resilient" (Vestager 2018).[2]

Despite such statements, ten years after Lehman's bankruptcy, empirical work on how banking (and financial) sector diversity affects competition, bank stability, the financing of the real economy, and, in particular, the funding of small and medium-sized enterprises (SMEs) is still rather scarce. However, filling this research gap is crucial. On the one hand, important regulatory initiatives that do impact sector diversity have already been implemented (think of the series of directives and regulations for financial markets conceived as response to the two crises) or are waiting for realization and implementation. First, also based on the observation that European firms and households are (compared to the U.S.) too bank-dependent, the European Commission launched in 2014 the Capital Markets Union initiative. However, the CMU program, striving for de-segmentation through more homogeneity and standardization, largely disregards effects of banking sector diversity for, inter alia, regional economic prospects. Second, it has long been ignored that EU-bank regulation, introduced to protect society from the devastating consequences from a failure of a systemically-important, large bank, may have unintended side effects on banking sector diversity and, via this channel, on particular social and political goals (see also Ferri and Neuberger in this issue).

To reiterate: Banking sector diversity is under-researched. At the same time, the issue of whether institutional diversity is a societal asset or a public good has become more topical. A number of European banking systems, and here the plural is apposite, still struggle to gain stability. In some (national) markets a significant roster of banks, not earning their cost of capital, are palpably not viable on current trajectories. At the same time, some (national) markets, with only a few, dominant players, are doing better. Taking these cases as a template therefore leads some to conclude that consolidation should be pursued (see Bini Smaghi in this issue), if feasible, on a European scale. Should one expect a more robust financial system from such a development?

In the remainder of this note we ponder two issues. First, we take stock of developments in European banking sectors in the post-Lehman years, sketching the trajectory of key aggregate indicators. Here we try to assess whether EU banking sectors have become more diverse or whether, conversely, homogeneity has risen. Subsequently, we explore how to capture (measure) banking sector diversity and we also briefly review the most important research areas revolving around institutional diversity in the EU banking sectors.

2   Banking sector diversity within the EU: Increasing in the wake of the crises?

What do key country-level (macro) indicators tell us about diversity between EU banking sectors, that is: across the different national banking markets? Can we uncover differences over time, between pre- and post the financial crisis? To throw some light on this, we use the World Bank's Global Financial Development Database (GFDD). As indicators (or dimensions) of diversity we

---

2   Dimon (2016) emphasizes the complementarity of large and small banks.

take differences in size (relative to GDP), concentration, competition and stability across national markets as well as compare their pre- and post-crisis levels.

2.1 The relative size of banking sectors has decreased in many EU countries

Table 1 reports commercial banks' (i.e. deposit-taking and lending institutions') assets relative to GDP in 2007 and 2016. In the wake of the GFC, banking sectors in Cyprus, Ireland, United Kingdom, Spain and Germany shrank the most in relative terms. In contrast, Italy and Greece and Poland even experienced increases relative to their GDPs. The unweighted mean across the banking markets included went down between 2007 and 2016. Banks shrank their balance sheets, i.e. deleveraged, also to meet higher capital requirements (relative to their risk-weighted assets). Thus, when accounting for the standard deviation of intermediation ratios between 2016 and 2007, national banking systems have become more similar. At the same time, in 2016 aggregated bank assets were higher than the GDP in 13 EU countries.

Table 1

Deposit banks' assets relative to GDP

Country	2007	2016	Change	Country	2007	2016	Change
Denmark	194.1	179.0	−15.1	Croatia	69.2	88.8	19.6
Spain	166.1	139.8	−26.3	Belgium	87.3	81.9	−5.4
Portugal	139.8	134.5	−5.3	Estonia	74.8	72.5	−2.4
Sweden	115.7	132.4	16.7	Poland	44.9	70.4	25.6
United Kingdom	158.3	130.5	−27.8	Slovak Republic	47.4	67.7	20.3
Netherlands	121.4	127.0	5.6	Slovenia	70.3	65.3	−4.9
Italy	96.0	124.7	28.7	Czech Republic	51.1	63.7	12.5
Greece	93.8	122.4	28.6	Bulgaria	52.0	62.9	11.0
France	100.3	112.5	12.1	Ireland	148.7	56.1	−92.6
Luxembourg	81.6	105.3	23.7	Hungary	69.7	55.1	−14.6
Malta	125.7	102.8	−22.9	Latvia	73.7	51.6	−22.2
Finland	76.1	101.8	25.7	Lithuania	53.0	46.9	−6.2
Austria	102.8	100.4	−2.4	Romania	28.4	39.8	11.4
Germany	117.6	93.4	−24.2	Cyprus	187.0	18.0	−169.0
Country average	98.1	91.0					
Standard deviation	44.2	37.2					

Source: Global Financial Development Database (GFDD), Worldbank (2017). Own calculations, the minus sign indicates a decrease in the country's deposit banks' assets relative to GDP.

2.2 Concentration has increased in most EU banking sectors subsequently to the GFC

Table 2 shows, for each EU member state, the concentration of bank assets, measured by the share of the five and three largest banks (CR5 and CR3-bank asset concentration). In 2016, Greece

Table 2

Asset share of the five largest banks in the domestic bank sector

Country	Asset share of the five largest banks in the domestic banking sector (5-bank asset concentration) (%)			Asset share of the three largest banks in the domestic banking sector (3-bank asset concentration) (%)		
	2007	2016	Change 2007–2016	2007	2016	Change 2007–2016
	(2)	(3)	(4)	(5)	(6)	(7)
Greece	81	100	19	60	77	17
Lithuania	88	99	11	73	88	15
Malta	100	98	-2	91	91	1
Estonia	99	96	-3	93	75	-18
Sweden	98	95	-4	97	92	-5
Denmark	88	94	7	81	87	6
Netherlands	94	91	-3	90	85	-5
Slovak Republic	80	90	9	63	75	12
Cyprus	90	89	-1	70	75	5
Portugal	88	87	-1	83	81	-2
Ireland	83	86	3	65	66	2
Hungary	69	86	17	48	67	18
Belgium	96	86	-10	83	64	-19
Finland	100	83	-16	98	70	-28
Spain	79	81	2	67	62	-5
Czech Republic	79	79	0	66	60	-6
Slovenia	69	78	9	57	60	2
Latvia	74	78	4	58	53	-5
Bulgaria	69	77	9	49	56	7
Germany	85	77	-8	72	67	-5
Romania	68	76	8	56	59	4
Croatia	73	75	3	53	60	7
France	74	74	0	61	58	-3
Austria	84	72	-12	78	55	-23
Italy	55	71	16	45	59	14
United Kingdom	77	70	-6	60	51	-9
Poland	57	57	1	42	40	-1
Luxembourg	42	43	1	31	32	1
Country average	80	82		67.5	66.6	
Standard deviation	14	13		17	15	

Source: Global Financial Development Database (GFDD), Worldbank (2017). Own calculations, in column (4) and (7) the minus sign indicates a decrease in the degree of concentration.

(CR5) and Sweden (CR3) had the highest concentration levels of all EU countries. During the crisis years, on this metric, EU banking sectors obviously moved into different directions. In some countries, banking sectors have become more concentrated, while in others concentration has strongly decreased (Column (4) and (7)). Particularly substantial changes are observable in Finland (decrease of 16 percent and 28 percent, respectively) and in Greece (increase of 19 and 17 percent, respectively). On average, CR5-bank asset concentration has grown while CR3-bank asset concentration has remained constant since the start of the crisis.

However, cross-country differences in concentration have become smaller over the crisis period. More specifically, the standard deviation of asset concentration across countries has decreased by 1 percentage point (CR5) and 2 percentage points (CR3), respectively. In other words, on this metric EU-banking sectors have become (slightly) more similar.

2.3   Competitive environment: Banks gained market power

Table 3, documenting the evolution of the Lerner index, gauges the aggregate price setting (market) power in European Union banking sectors. The Lerner index is defined as markup divided by the price of the product:[3]

$$Lerner\ index = \frac{\text{Price} - \text{Marginal Cost}}{\text{Price}}.$$

Capturing the proportional difference between monopoly and competitive prices, higher values indicate a higher average price setting power in the respective country, possibly as a result of a lower degree of competition (Beck, Jonghe and Schepens 2013), from other banks or from non-bank banks ('shadow banks') or other financial service providers such as Fintechs. On average, Banks in Latvia enjoyed the highest market power in 2014, followed by Sweden and the Czech Republic. Germany and Finland rank at the bottom, implying that in those countries competition among banks is high and markups are commensurately small. Latvian banks experienced the highest increase in market power over the crisis years (Column 4). On average, the price setting power in banking sectors has risen by 17 percent between 2007 and 2014. Even in the lowest ranking countries, Germany and Finland, the Lerner Index is meanwhile higher than it was in 2007. Surprisingly, at the country level, UK banks lost the most market power in this period. The standard deviation of the country-level Lerner Index has only slightly increased, indicating that the across-country diversity remained broadly unchanged.

Boone (2008) developed an indicator to capture competitive intensity by measuring the response of profits to a change in marginal costs (Table 4). The underlying drivers could be lower barriers to entry or a more aggressive conduct of competitors. Regressing the log of profits on marginal costs one obtains a coefficient for the profit elasticity:[4] The Boone-coefficient measures the percentage fall in profits in response to an increase in marginal costs. A negative value indicates that a decrease in marginal costs, obtained by more efficient banks, causes a redistribution of profits

---

3   The price is usually proxied by the total bank revenue over assets and the marginal costs are obtained from an estimated translog cost function with respect to output (e.g. Beck et al 2013). In the GFDD the individual banks' Lerner values, calculated from underlying bank-by-bank data from Bankscope, are aggregated to obtain the country-level Lerner Index (Demirgüç-Kunt and Martínez Pería 2010), www.worldbank.org/en/publication/gfdr/data/global-financial-development-database.

4   The Boone Indicator in the GFDD is calculated from underlying bank-by-bank data from Bankscope: "To obtain the elasticity, the log of profits (measured by return on assets) is regressed on the log of marginal costs. The estimated coefficient (computed from the first derivative of a trans-log cost function) is the elasticity. Estimations of the Boone indicator in the GFDD database follow the methodology used by Schaeck and Cihák (2010)."

Table 3

Lerner Index—country level

Country Name	2007	2014	Difference	Country Name	2007	2014	Difference
	(2)	(3)	(4)		(5)	(6)	(7)
Latvia	0,265	0,445	0,181	United Kingdom	0,439	0,276	−0,163
Sweden	0,279	0,412	0,133	Ireland*	0,223	0,268	0,045
Czech Republic	0,317	0,400	0,083	Luxembourg	0,114	0,261	0,147
Lithuania	0,324	0,377	0,052	Estonia*	0,289	0,236	−0,053
Malta*	0,227	0,371	0,144	Slovenia	0,215	0,234	0,019
Bulgaria	0,341	0,368	0,028	Belgium	0,075	0,211	0,136
Cyprus	0,295	0,355	0,060	Greece*	0,231	0,209	−0,022
Poland	0,295	0,348	0,052	Hungary	0,256	0,192	−0,064
Slovak Republic	0,247	0,345	0,099	Netherlands	0,218	0,174	−0,044
Denmark	0,196	0,326	0,131	Italy	0,059	0,136	0,077
Spain	0,273	0,322	0,050	France	0,058	0,132	0,074
Portugal*	0,368	0,307	−0,061	Romania	0,236	0,122	−0,114
Croatia	0,262	0,292	0,030	Finland*	0,078	0,092	0,015
Austria	0,241	0,288	0,048	Germany	0,047	0,085	0,038
Country average	0.231	0.277					
Standard deviation	0.099	0.104					

*The most recent Lerner Index of Estonia, Greece, Finland, Ireland and Malta is from 2010, that of Portugal from 2013.
Source: Global Financial Development Database (GFDD), Worldbank (2017), own calculations. Most recent data are from 2014. In column (4) and (7) the minus sign indicates a decrease in the Lerner index between 2007 and 2014.

from less to more efficient banks and hence an increase in their profits. Since competition forces banks to increase efficiency, the Boone Indicator is an alternative to the Lerner Index.[5] The more negative the Boone Indicator is, the stronger is the reallocation effect, and hence the higher is the inferred level of competition.

Table 4 shows that the Boone Indicator has increased on average over the crisis years. The mean is higher in 2014 than it was in 2007, also the differences between 2007 and 2014 values are often positive. In 2014, Slovenia, Ireland, Bulgaria, Netherlands, Finland, Greece and Italy had the highest Boone Indicators, implying comparatively low levels of competition in their banking sectors. In contrast, Luxembourg, Portugal, Spain, Latvia and Malta have the most competitive banking sectors (the lowest value of the Boone indicator). Interestingly, the standard deviation substantially decreased, indicating that banking sectors emerged from the acute crisis more similar than they were at the start. This result contrasts with the findings from the Lerner Index. Although both

---

5   Whereas the Lerner Index relies on market structure in representing the degree of competition, the Boone Index also accounts for the degree of market contestability or barriers to entry. Of course, metrics of market structure (concentration ratios) are only indirect proxies of competition, claiming a one-way causality between structure and performance. Hence, they do not allow for the fact that concentration ratios are the upshot of competitive behavior. The Boone Index (and similar approaches like the Panzar Rosse metric) are not vulnerable to this critique (see Degryse, Kim and Ongena 2009).

Table 4

Boone Indicator

Country	2007	2014	Difference	Country	2007	2014	Difference
Luxembourg	-70.892	-50.060	20.831	Austria	-0.023	-0.023	0.000
Portugal	-0.663	-1.028	-0.365	Belgium	-0.078	-0.021	0.057
Spain	-0.751	-0.606	0.145	Slovak Republic	-0.019	-0.006	0.013
Latvia	-0.208	-0.155	0.054	Cyprus	-0.084	-0.005	0.080
Malta	-0.192	-0.127	0.066	Romania	-0.126	-0.003	0.123
Hungary	-0.165	-0.096	0.069	France	-0.035	-0.001	0.034
Estonia	-0.171	-0.095	0.075	Lithuania	-0.054	0.000	0.054
Poland	-0.114	-0.079	0.035	Italy	-0.048	0.002	0.050
Denmark	-0.159	-0.070	0.089	Greece	-0.108	0.003	0.110
Czech Republic	-0.110	-0.069	0.042	Finland	0.117	0.090	-0.027
Croatia	-0.142	-0.050	0.092	Netherlands	-0.080	0.132	0.212
Sweden	-0.086	-0.048	0.037	Bulgaria	-0.096	0.214	0.310
United Kingdom	-0.111	-0.047	0.064	Ireland	2.814	0.654	-2.159
Germany	-0.043	-0.028	0.016	Slovenia	5.007	11.345	6.338
Country average	-2.38	-1.43					
Standard deviation	13.47	9.77					

Source: Global Financial Development Database (GFDD), Worldbank (2017), own calculations. Most recent data are from 2014.

competition indicators reveal on average a decrease of competitive intensity over the crisis years, Table 2 and 3 tell quite different messages. For example, considering the Lerner Index, The Netherlands rank in the last quarter of countries, indicating a high competition intensity. In contrast, the Boone Indicator value of the country is the 4th highest among all EU countries, indicating very low competition intensity. Similarly, according to the Boone Indicator the level of competition in Finland's banking sector is rather low (high value of the Boone indicator) but is rather high if the Lerner Index is used (low level of the Lerner Index).

What might explain the contrasting evidence between the two indicators? Both, the Lerner Index and the Boone Indicator, measure competition only indirectly. The Lerner Index focusses on the banks' market power to set high prices for their products. In contrast, the Boone Indicator emphasizes banks' capacity to lower marginal costs. Competition is a training program for the latter but has a negative influence on the first. Accordingly, the assessment of the level of competition in a country can vary quite substantially depending on what indicator is considered.

2.4 Capital to assets ratios have increased in most EU banking sectors

The ratio of bank capital to total assets captures capital buffers available for covering potential losses, and is, therefore, an indicator of stability (Table 5).[6] According to this ratio, Sweden, Italy, Finland, Netherland and France had the lowest capacity to cushion shocks to their banking sectors in 2016. Their *capital to assets ratios*, aggregated over all domestic banks, were below 6 percent. On the other end of the scale are Irish and Croatian banks, they held the highest capital buffers. The Irish banking sector has experienced the largest growth of the capital buffer since the crisis (adding 8.9 percentage points). Decreases of capital buffers in the wake of the crisis are very rare. Only the banking sectors of Italy, Sweden, Finland, Hungary and Slovenia had a lower *capital to assets*

Table 5

Bank capital to total assets

Country	2007	2016	Difference	Country	2007	2016	Difference
	(1)	(2)	(3)		(4)	(5)	(6)
Sweden	4.8	4.4	-0.4	Hungary	10.7	8,2	-2.5
Italy	7,9	5,5	-2,4	Slovenia	8,4	8,2	-0,2
Finland	8,0	5,6	-2,4	Portugal	6,5	8,4	1,9
Netherlands	3,3	5,7	2,4	Romania	n.a.	8,9	--
France	4,1	5,7	1,6	Poland	8,0	9,5	1,5
Germany	4,3	6,0	1,7	Latvia	7,9	10,0	2,1
Belgium	4,1	6,9	2,8	Lithuania	7,9	10,4	2,5
United Kingdom	5,5	7,0	1,5	Cyprus	n.a.	10,4	--
Czech Republic	5,7	7,3	1,6	Greece	6,8	10,7	3,9
Austria	6,5	7,3	0,8	Estonia	8,6	10,8	2,2
Luxembourg	5,0	7,4	2,4	Slovak Republic	8,0	11,0	3,0
Denmark	6,2	7,4	1,2	Bulgaria	7,7	11,6	3,9
Malta	6,0	7,5	1,5	Ireland	4,6	13,5	8,9
Spain	6,7	7,8	1,1	Croatia	12,4	14,0	1,6
Country average	6,6	8,7					
Standard deviation	2	2,4					

Source: Global Financial Development Database (GFDD) of the Worldbank. Own calculations. Most recent data are from 2016.

---

6   Capital is defined very broadly and goes beyond the Common Equity Tier 1 and Retained Earnings which is used in the EBA stress tests for indicating a bank's capability for loss absorption. In the GFDD data, the "Ratio of bank capital and reserves to total assets" has the following ingredients: "Capital and reserves include funds contributed by owners, retained earnings, general and special reserves, provisions, and valuation adjustments. Capital includes tier 1 capital (paid-up shares and common stock), which is a common feature in all countries' banking systems, and total regulatory capital, which includes several specified types of subordinated debt instruments that need not be repaid if the funds are required to maintain minimum capital levels (these comprise tier 2 and tier 3 capital). Total assets include all nonfinancial and financial assets. Reported by IMF staff. Note that due to differences in national accounting, taxation, and supervisory regimes, these data are not strictly comparable across countries." https://data.worldbank.org/indicator/FB.BNK.CAPA.ZS.

ratio in 2016 than in 2007. Among those with lower capital buffers, Italian and Swedish banks lost over two percentage points in the aggregate. According to this metric, banking sectors differ slightly more in 2016 than in 2007. The standard deviation of *capital to assets ratios* has grown from around 2 percent in 2007 to 2.4 percent in 2016.

2.5 *Z-scores* have increased in most EU banking sectors over the crisis years

The *Z-score* is a standard measure of distance to default, i. e. for gauging bank soundness (Schaeck and Chihák 2010). It reflects how many standard deviations the return on assets (ROA) has to fall until a bank's equity buffers are depleted:

$$Z - score = \frac{\text{Return on Assets} + \text{Equity over Assets}}{\text{Standard Deviation of Return on Assets}}.$$

Accordingly, a higher *Z-score* is associated with higher resilience.[7] The GFDD presents a country-level variant of the Z-score. Table 6 indicates that the average Z-score has increased substantially between 2007 and 2016. Also, the variation in the resilience levels of EU banking sectors, mea-

Table 6

Z-score

Country	2007	2016	Difference	Country	2007	2016	Difference
	(1)	(2)	(3)		(4)	(5)	(6)
Luxembourg	25.63	46.95	21.32	Ireland	3.40	12.34	8.94
Austria	27.92	25.67	-2.24	Cyprus	9.24	11.89	2.65
Germany	15.99	24.17	8.18	Netherlands	11.68	11.30	-0.38
Spain	17.57	22.83	5.27	Italy	15.43	10.03	-5.40
Denmark	15.45	21.88	6.44	Poland	8.67	8.47	-0.19
France	13.52	21.24	7.72	Bulgaria	7.48	8.38	0.90
Malta	27.01	20.84	-6.17	Hungary	5.87	8.04	2.17
Belgium	10.54	17.45	6.91	Latvia	5.76	7.33	1.57
Slovak Republic	13.87	17.38	3.51	Greece	4.99	6.96	1.97
Portugal*	14.43	15.54	1.10	Lithuania	5.40	6.50	1.10
Finland	16.45	15.11	-1.33	Estonia	4.25	6.46	2.21
Sweden	9.05	14.63	5.58	Romania	5.30	6.46	1.16
Czech Republic	9.97	13.93	3.96	Croatia	4.76	5.30	0.55
United Kingdom	6.32	12.53	6.21	Slovenia	2.61	4.06	1.45
Country average	11. 4	14.4					
Standard deviation	7.02	9.10					

Source: Global Financial Development Database (GFDD) of the Worldbank, own calculations. Most recent data are from 2016. Portugal's most recent data is from 2014.

---

7   *"It captures the probability of default of a country's banking system. Z-score compares the buffer of a country's banking system (capitalization and returns) with the volatility of those returns. [...] ROA, equity, and assets are country-level aggregate figures calculated from underlying bank-by-bank unconsolidated data from Bankscope."* https://datacatalog.worldbank.org/bank-z-score.

sured by the Z-score's standard deviation, has increased. In the vast majority of countries, the level of the Z-score implies that resilience is higher in 2016 than it was in 2007. However, as the negative differences in Column (3) and (6) show, in six countries the country-level Z-score has decreased. Among them, Maltese and Italian banks experienced the highest reduction of the Z-score over the crisis years.

2.6 But: Non-performing loans have also increased

By and large, both country-level indicators, the capital to assets ratio and the Z-score, signal improved resilience. Still, banking sectors in the European Union differ more widely than they did at the advent of the crisis. However, during the European financial and sovereign debt crisis, neither the capital to assets ratio nor the Z-score received much attention. In contrast, non-performing loans became a synonym for the substantial threats to banking sector stability at the level of the respective (national) market (Mesnard, Margerit, Power and Magnus 2015). Therefore, it is somewhat surprising that Euro area banking sectors' diversity levels and their relation to a country's share of non-performing loans have received little attention in the financial stability research, so far.

Thus, if resilience or vulnerability of banking sectors is gauged by the ratio of non-performing loans to all loans (*NPL ratio*),

$$NPL \; ratio = \frac{\text{Non} - \text{performing loans}}{\text{All loans}}$$

a different picture than for Z-score or capital to assets *ratio* arises. Table 7 shows the statistic of the country-level *NPL ratio* for EU member states. The country average of the *NPL ratio* is substantially higher in 2016 than in 2007. On average, over all member states, more than 8 percent of gross loans show distortions in payment, an increase of more than five percentage points between 2007 and 2016.[8] Here, given nationally differentiated macroeconomic as well as legal contexts, obviously, dispersion across EU member states is of the essence. In Cyprus, in 2016, almost half of all loans were categorized as non-performing followed by Greece with around one-third, and Italy with more than 17 percent. On the other end of the scale are the Netherlands, Germany, Luxembourg, Sweden, United Kingdom, Estonia and Finland with percentages equal or below 2.5 percent. The EU banking sectors are much more diverse in terms of NPL ratios in 2016 than in 2007. The standard deviation across countries has increased starkly, from less than two to more than ten percentage points.

A high ratio of non-performing loans may indicate that credit assessment—screening and monitoring—has been flawed, at least from an ex post vantage point. High NPL ratios, however, can also reflect a mediocre macroeconomic environment (substantial and lasting output-gaps). The consequence could be an unhealthy and stability-threatening increase in the ratio of non-performing loans. One may surmise that in banking sectors with low concentration ratios as well as (possibly) intense competition, banks face particularly high pressure on costs, and have therefore been

---

8   The ECB classifies a loan as non-performing when past due for 90 days, i.e. when the agreed payment schedule was not met, that is no repayment was made and no interest were paid. The definition of the World Bank is broader. Regularly operated loans where the debtholder has defaulted on other loans are classified as non-performing, as well as loans that have not been served for less than 90 days (Mesnard et al. 2015).

Table 7

NPL ratio

Country	2007	2016	Difference	Country	2007	2016	Difference
Cyprus	–	48,7	–				
Greece	4,6	36,3	31,7	Poland	5,2	4,0	–1,2
Italy	5,8	17,1	11,3	France	2,7	3,9	1,2
Ireland	0,8	13,6	12,8	Latvia	0,8	3,7	2,9
Croatia	4,8	13,6	8,8	Belgium	1,4	3,5	2,1
Bulgaria	2,1	13,2	11,1	Denmark	0,6	3,2	2,6
Portugal	2,8	11,8	9,0	Austria	2,2	2,7	0,5
Romania	–	9,6	–	Netherlands	5.4	2,5	–2.9
Hungary	2,3	7,4	5,1	Germany	2,7	2,3	–0,4
Spain	0,9	5,6	4,7	Luxembourg	0,4	1,7	1,3
Malta	5,9	5,4	–0,5	Sweden	0,1	1,0	0,9
Slovenia	2,5	5,1	2,6	United Kingdom	0,9	0,9	0,0
Lithuania	1,0	4,9	3,9	Estonia	0,5	0,9	0,4
Czech Republic	2,4	4,6	2,2	Finland	0,3	0,6	0,3
Country average	2,2	8,8					
Standard deviation	1,8	11,0					

Source: Global Financial Development Database (GFDD) of the Worldbank, own calculations. Most recent data are from 2016.

tempted to save on screening and monitoring devices. However, a closer look at concentration ratios (Table 2) or competition measures (e. g. Table 3) on the one hand and *NPL ratios* on the other hand (Table 7) hardly confirms this claim. The (too) simple equation according to which high concentration in the respective national banking sector means a low rate of defaulting loans does not work. In the EU, similar concentration levels are associated with very different levels of non-performing loans. For example, Greece has a very high *NPL ratio* with more than 35 percent in 2016, notwithstanding the fact that Greece has a highly concentrated banking sector. By contrast, the *NPL* ratio was only one percent in the similarly highly concentrated Swedish banking system. In the highly competitive German banking sector, the ratio of non-performing loans remained with two percent very low. There are, clearly, additional (confounding) variables which would have to be accounted for. This is where the national macroeconomic context comes in.

Of course, over most of the crisis years, economic growth in Germany was comparably high and, in line with this, employment rose, and unemployment decreased steadily. Thus, in contrast to many other European countries, German banks benefited from a very positive economic environment. But still, the low ratio of non-performing loans in Germany suggests that a competitive environment does not necessarily endanger banking sector stability. These observations raise two crucial questions: What role plays the real economy's structure for the performance of the banking sector? Are concentration and competition measures good proxies for institutional diversity in the banking sector?

2.7   Does it fit? Diversity in the real economy

The fit (or lack thereof) between structural features of the "real" economy and the financial sector, deemed to serve those needs, has been a controversial issue, obviously for a long time (Allen and Gale 2000, Kotz 1993). Answers found, varied across time and region. For instance, in the 1990s, a substantial part of the underperformance of the US economy was laid at the door of its under-performing financial system, geared towards short-termism (Dertouzos, Lester and Solow 1989). Different national specializations potentially come with different financial sector requirements (Chandler 1990). Firms thriving on intangible capital (IP) have different financing needs than capital-intensive industries (automotive, steel, chemical etc.). To illustrate across-country diversity in the real economy, we here focus on the capital-intensive manufacturing industry.

To account for structural differences of the real economy across EU member states, measurement is obviously key. Given the bulkiness of their capital expenditures, manufacturing firms are more likely to have large external funding needs and access to finance is crucial. Therefore, the struc-ture of the banking sector may matter for this sector more than for other, less capital-intensive industries. For example, if a country's manufacturing sector consists only of a few large firms, the appropriate structure of the banking sector to serve those firms' financial needs may be a different one than if the firms are spread rather evenly across all size classes. Accordingly, we describe the structure of the sector using firm size classes. The most common method for aggregating size classes into a country-level index value capturing diversity is the Gini-Simpson Index (Michie and Oughton 2013),

$$GSI_M = 1 - HHI_M = 1 - \sum_{k=1}^{K} s_k^2.$$

is the share of a specific size class in the economy. This share can be based on total assets, turn-over, employees, number of firms or other key indicators. To illustrate how different the manufac-turing sectors are across EU member states, we focus on two indicators, the number of employees and the number of firms in a particular size classes.

Eurostat differentiates between five size classes $k = \{1,2,3,4,5\}$ with $k=1$ (from 0 to 9 persons em-ployed), $k=2$ (from 10 to 19 persons employed), $k=3$ (from 20 to 49 persons employed), $k=4$ (from 50 to 249 persons employed) and $k=5$ (250 persons employed or more). The employment share $s_k = \frac{e_k}{E}$ of size class k equals the number of employees e in this size class divided by the total work force in the manufacturing industry. The more equal the number of employees is distributed across size classes the higher is the GSI_M, and the lower is the concentration of the workforce among firm types. If the number of employees is equal in each size class, the index has the high-est possible value,

$$GSI_M = 1 - \sum_{k=1}^{5} \left(\frac{1}{5}\right)^2 = 0,8.$$

If all employees are concentrated only in one size class, the HHI_M is at its maximum and equals one. Accordingly, the GSI_M equals zero. Table 8 presents the distribution of the GSI_M of firm size classes across the EU. The manufacturing industry's diversity index, based on the number of employees, is the highest in Italy, Cyprus and Greece. The lowest values are observed for Slovakia, Czech Republic and Germany.

Table 8

GSI$_M$ based on number of employees in five classes of firm size

Country	2008	2016	Difference	Country	2008	2016	Difference
Italy	0,7877	0,7859	−0,0018	United Kingdom	0,7074	0,6949	−0,0125
Cyprus	0,7871	0,7853	−0,0017	Denmark	0,6759	0,6847	0,0088
Greece	0,7559	0,7812	0,0253	Sweden	0,6727	0,6822	0,0095
Portugal	0,7795	0,7732	−0,0063	Belgium	0,6772	0,6792	0,0021
Spain	0,7826	0,7662	−0,0164	Finland	0,6496	0,6783	0,0287
Latvia	0,7455	0,7473	0,0019	Ireland	0,7086	0,6712	−0,0375
Estonia	0,7310	0,7385	0,0075	Romania	0,6860	0,6702	−0,0158
Netherlands	0,7405	0,7358	−0,0047	Poland	0,6780	0,6678	−0,0102
Croatia	0,7148	0,7337	0,0189	Hungary	0,6908	0,6666	−0,0241
Bulgaria	0,7244	0,7280	0,0036	Austria	0,6696	0,6537	−0,0159
Lithuania	0,7223	0,7257	0,0034	Slovakia	0,6140	0,6461	0,0321
Slovenia	0,6826	0,7051	0,0225	Czechia	0,6605	0,6432	−0,0172
France*	0,7029	0,6986	−0,0043	Germany	0,6263	0,6165	−0,0098
Country average	0,7067	0,7061					
Standard deviation	0,0469	0,0473					

Source: Eurostat. Own calculations. The value for France is based on data from 2009.

Another way to proxy across-country diversity is to use the share $s_k = \frac{n_k}{N}$ where equals the number of firms n in the size classes k. With the number of firms being equal in each size class, the index would be at its maximum of 0.8. If all firms belong to only one size class the GSI_M equals zero. Table 9 shows the distribution of the GSI_M, based on the number of firms in the different size classes across the EU. The manufacturing sector in the Czech Republic, Slovakia and Greece show a particularly low Gini-Simpson Index. The highest values are observed for Luxembourg, Germany and Austria.

It should be noted, however, that diversity and concentration do not necessarily coincide. For example, if the GSI_M based on the number of firms in distinct size classes is zero because all firms in the economy belong to only the largest size class, one would obviously label the sector as highly concentrated. In contrast, if this is zero since all firms belong to the smallest size class, each of the small firms has only a small market share. In this case, the sector is highly dispersed.

Table 9

GSI based on number of firms in five classes of firm size

Country	2008	2016	Difference	Country	2008	2016	Difference
Luxembourg	0.564	0.593	0.029	Latvia	0.504	0.300	−0.205
Germany	0.571	0.568	−0.003	Hungary	0.271	0.282	0.010
Austria	0.457	0.453	−0.004	Lithuania	0.377	0.268	−0.109
Romania	0.458	0.451	−0.007	Ireland	0.327	0.266	−0.061
Bulgaria	0.486	0.409	−0.077	France*	0.285	0.247	−0.038
Denmark	0.457	0.403	−0.054	Netherlands	0.378	0.230	−0.148
Estonia	0.539	0.396	−0.142	Poland	0.228	0.218	−0.010
United Kingdom	0.421	0.374	−0.046	Sweden	0.235	0.214	−0.021
Finland	0.323	0.335	0.012	Slovenia	0.251	0.213	−0.038
Portugal	0.313	0.322	0.008	Cyprus	0.230	0.198	−0.032
Croatia	0.286	0.312	0.026	Czechia	0.176	0.134	−0.041
Italy	0.323	0.310	−0.013	Greece	0.085	0.132	0.047
Spain	0.355	0.309	−0.046	Slovakia	0.702	0.113	−0.589
Belgium	0.327	0.300	−0.027				
Country average	0.3678	0.3093					
Standard deviation	0.0185	0.0138					

Source: Eurostat. Own calculations. *France pre-crisis value is calculated using the 2009 value as the 2008 data are not available. Malta is removed from the sample because of too many missing values.

3 How to measure banking sector diversity?

In the 1980s and 90s financial development was considered as major determinant of economic growth and productivity (see Schrooten in this issue). However, the 2007/8 international financial crisis clearly revealed the shortcomings of neglecting the institutional structure of the financial sector. All of the above documents that gauging the institutional diversity of a banking sector raises a number of pertinent questions. They, first of all, refer to the characteristics or properties over which banks might differ. The most pertinent indicators of difference have to do with a bank's size and scope (of activities, its business model (activities emphasized), its funding structure (interacting with the structure of assets) as well as ownership structures and objectives (maximizing profits, or performance objectives: for example, serving membership needs, as cooperatives strive for, Kotz et al. 2007).

As seen before, in terms of size of institutions, indicators of concentration and competition may serve as proxies. Therefore, market shares can be a good starting point for building a diversity indicator. However, given that banks are multi-product firms, one would also have to account for various business lines or activities, such as taking deposits, lending, structure of assets and liabilities or employment. Given this variety, the research question at hand should determine what market share is the relevant one to be used in the diversity indicator. For example, assume that one wants to assess the impact of diversity on bank stability. Large banks are more globally connected than small or local banks. Therefore, size-related risk plays an important role in financial stability regulation. The Basel Committee on Banking Supervision (BCBS) accounts for size-related risks by defining "buckets requiring corresponding to higher capital buffers that they are required to hold by national authorities".[9] Size is an important criterion for being assigned to a particular bucket. The higher a bank's bucket the larger is the capital surcharge.[10] Size is also an important criterium within the European Single Supervisory Mechanism (ESM). The ECB is charged with directly supervising a bank if the size of its balance sheet is larger than 30 million euros.[11] Accordingly, for assessing the impact of diversity on bank stability, the distribution of total assets across a banking industry can serve as a suitable indicator.

There are as many ways to group banks as defining characteristics—attributes—are assessed as pertinent. These properties can serve to break out—cluster—banks into fairly homogenous groups (using specific metrics—e.g. Euclidian distance—to capture similarity). A common grouping criteria in banking is according to business models or missions, either as commercial banks (profit-seeking), saving banks (serving a public purpose) or credit unions (serving their members). In most countries, more than 80 percent of banks fall under these three headings. Accordingly, different missions are at the center of the discussion revolving around banking sector diversity.

Thus, dividing criteria are selected to create groups with rather homogenous banks. The degree of homogeneity within commercial banks, saving banks and credit unions may be considered as a case in point. Ayadi et al (2009, 2010) employ a different taxonomy. They define five distinct business model and group banks along those business models. In line with Ayadi et al (2009, 2010), Bley (in this issue) and Gischer and Ilmann (in this issue) also use the distinctness of business models to distinguish bank types (see also Gärtner and Flögel in this issue for an alternative concept to identify distinct banking groups).

Another way of grouping banks would be to start from pre-defined size classes. Grouping into size classes requires defining the number of classes, which is obviously arbitrary. Alternatively, each bank could be treated as distinct type. Then, grouping is unnecessary. Each bank's market share would be used in the diversity indicator without aggregation over groups.

Finally, for each country's banking sector the market share of the selected group in the selected dimension needs to be aggregated into one single indicator of diversity for the country. As already mentioned, the most common method of aggregation is the Gini-Simpson Index,

$$GSI = 1 - \sum_{n=1}^{N} s_n^2.$$

The index increases with the number of banks or banking groups and decreases with the degree of inequality in the market shares of each bank or banking group. For example, in case of 3 banking groups, say commercial banks, savings banks and cooperative banks, the GSI would be the highest if each banking group possesses an equal market share of one-third of total assets (or deposits or gross loans, etc.) in the domestic banking sector. The country-specific indicator would

---

9   www.fsb.org/wp-content/uploads/P161118-1.pdf

10   www.bis.org/publ/bcbs255.pdf

11   www.bankingsupervision.europa.eu/banking/list/criteria/html/index.en.html

be minimal if only one group exists, $GSI = 1 - 1 = 0$. Note that GSI increases in the degree of equality in market shares but also in the number of distinct banking groups.

Another standard measure for aggregation is the Shannon index:

$$SI = -\sum_{n=1}^{N} s_n \ln s_n,$$

SI is also known as entropy measure of industrial diversification (see e. g. Brown and Greenbaum 2017, Attaran and Zwick 1987). The entropy is the average ln probability of belonging to a specific group where N is the number of groups (size classes, specialization groups etc.). With equal shares $1/N$ in total assets/deposits/gross loans the Shannon index is at its maximal value of $ln\ N$.

4   Banking sector diversity and stability

Previous research proposes that banking sector diversity basically affects financial stability through two channels. One channel is diversification. In the literature two concepts of diversification are used, diversification across bank types and bank-internal diversification. Although both rely on diversification, the expected relation to bank stability is quite different.

Bank-internal diversification refers to diversification at the level of an individual bank: meaning for example expanding into new business fields, establishing new branches, or catering to new geographies (e. g. Baele, Jonghe and Vennet, 2007). This within-diversification is often about economies of scale and scope, hence advantages pursued arise from conglomeration and size. As a corollary, the more comprehensive the lines of business pursued and the wider the reach of markets, the larger bank balance sheets will be. This could raise efficiency, depending on activity lines (Berger and Humphrey 1997), though only up to a point: Given the higher number of diverse, weakly-linked business activities, bank-internal diversification poses substantial challenges to bank management, potentially reducing monitoring efficiency (e. g. Acharya, Hasan and Saunders 2006, Stiroh and Rumble 2006). Regularly, the strive for scale at the level of individual banks (often through mergers), increases concentration ratios in national banking markets. Moreover, strategies pursued by bank managements are often quite similar. Under the scrutiny of markets (and peers), it is too costly to deviate. In the aggregate, this creates homogeneity. And it builds systemic vulnerability when a shock hits (see again Boot 2014), which can of course also arise internally, within the banking (or financial) system. Accordingly, from a societal perspective, risks (potential societal costs) arising from bank-internal diversification, beyond a certain level, could over-compensate the alleged benefits of size and scope.

At a sectoral level, diversity captures differences in bank types, i. e. between individual intermediaries, differentiated along a number of defining characteristics (mentioned above). Of course, this is a longstanding debate, always rehearsed in the immediate wake of financial sector troubles. In the early 2000s, when the EU launched its Financial Services Action Plan, the consensus view was that capital markets should be emphasized. This had already been the policy pursued in France in the mid-1980s (Melitz 1999). Concurrently, a somehow opposite view was taken in the US. There, in order to rein in short-termism, a re-orientation towards universal banking (and less of stock-market reliance) was strongly recommend (see again Dertouzos et al. 1989). This led to the demise of Glass-Steagall (separation of commercial and investment banking) and McFadden (prohibition of interstate banking). In this line of reasoning, quite unsurprisingly, the most recent Great Financial Crisis has spawned a new interest in financial architecture with a renewed emphasis on less innovative and more boring banking (Schackmann-Fallis and Weiss, in this issue). Given the almost prohibitive costs of the GFC (going far beyond its financial fallout), this is too easy to understand. In a few pioneering studies it is argued that a diverse banking sector (i. e. diverse in terms of individual institutions) will enhance financial stability when the system is shocked (among them Ayadi et al 2009, Ayadi et al 2010, Haldane and May 2011). Banking crises regularly come with access to funds problems, especially for credit-dependent clients. These are, for reasons of their information-impactedness, mainly SMEs. With the access to capital markets practically infeasible (for reasons of information asymmetries, agency problems and ensuing prohibitive transaction costs, see Stiglitz and Weiss 1981)), they are mostly affected when credit crunches hit. Hence, the argument goes, banks (or intermediaries) less exposed to problematic assets (non-performing loans or exposures) could substitute in their funding function for the 'real' economy institutions which are in trouble. The search for the one (and only) optimal financial system is probably vain (Allen and Gale 2000). Financial systems come with strong national traits, also in the EU. They are embedded (and influenced) by other societal systems (e. g., insolvency mechanisms, retirement funding etc.). Still, getting a better understanding of how diversification impacts on efficiency as well as stability is crucial.

5   Banking sector diversity and competition

The second channel through which diversity could affect financial stability is competition, the contestability of markets. Again, this is obviously an old, pertinent policy issue. And, over time, different solutions have been found. The US, for example, for a long time upheld (and practically implemented) the idea banking at its core should be driven by community banks. There is an underlying political economics to that (Roe 2003). In any case, politics is important to understand activity (Glass-Steagall Act) as well as regional restrictions (McFadden Act), in place until the late 1990s. In Europe, up until the 2000s, it was not so much size but differences in business models which defined diversity. The German banking industry, with its three-pillar structure, is a particular pertinent case. However, it seems to be less an issue of missions or governance, than the structure of balance sheets (and what is going on off balance) that has been the defining characteristic of diversity. Balance politics speaks louder than mission words (Kotz and Schmidt 2017). Still, the relationship is under-researched: For example, what aspect of diversity is important with regard to competition? Does diversity necessarily spell a higher level of competition? One could, for instance, argue that a diverse landscape of banks, in terms of size and business models, could increase the choice set of clients and hence sharpen competition. (It would show in lower returns on equity—and seems to be borne out by the German case.) If this were true, diversity and competition were complementary, almost two sides of the same coin. Hence, possible trade-offs between competition/diversity and stability would be the same.

Starting from here, one strand of the competition literature proposes that a more competitive and less concentrated banking system is more fragile and less stable (Beck, Demirguc-Kunt and Levine 2005, Berger, Klapper and Turk-Ariss 2008, Beck, Jonghe and Schepens 2013, Smaghi in this issue). Banks are less profitable, can build lower capital buffers and therefore are more vulnerable. As concerns developments post-GFC, Canada, Australia or Sweden and France are often rendered as cases in point. At the same time, though not speaking to the financial stability issue, based on micro data of banks in different regions of Kazakhstan from 2004, Schäfer, Siliverstovs and Terberger (2010) show that more competition can affect SME-lending positively in an emerging economy. Schaeck, Wolfe and Cihàk (2009), confirming standard priors, report that competition could stimulate firms' innovativeness and encourage banks' efficiency by keeping loan rates low. Both results would imply beneficial effects for financial stability. On the other hand, markets with high concentration ratios and inevitably "too big to fail"-banks, hence with implicit government guarantees, are prone to take excessive risk, thus potentially endangering stability. That is why those institutions call for more rigorous regulations (capital and liquidity ratios).

Schaeck and Cihák (2010) use a panel dataset for European banks from Austria, Belgium, Denmark, France, Italy, Germany, Luxembourg, the Netherlands, Switzerland, and the United Kingdom, covering the period 1995–2005 and a cross-sectional sample of banks operating in rural counties in the U.S. in 2005. They reveal that competition increases banks' efficiency. Akins, Li, Ng and Rusticus (2016) uses data of banks from all US States during the period 2000–2010. They find that higher competition has a disciplining effect in the sense that it is associated with lower risk-taking by banks and higher mortgage rejection rates. Such behavior should make banks less likely to suffer from non-performing loans. Most recently, Götz (2017) found that an increase in market contestability in the US significantly increases bank stability, lowers the share of non-performing exposures and improves bank profitability.

6   Banking sector diversity and structure of financial system

The most recent debate on the optimal structure of the financial system leaves the issue of banking sector diversity largely aside. Instead, it focusses on the question of whether banks are too dominant vis-a-vis other financial intermediaries. Langfield and Pagano (2015) document that an increase in the size of the banking system relative to equity and private bond markets is associated with more systemic risk and lower economic growth, particularly during housing market crises. Gambacorta, Yang and Tsatsaronis (2014) report that if an economic downturn coincides with a financial crisis, the effect of the crisis on GDP-growth is three times more severe for bank-oriented economies then it is for market-oriented ones. Hoffmann and Sorensen (2015) argue, *"that domestic bank dependence made countries, regions, and sectors* [of the European Union] *with many SMEs more vulnerable to global banking sector shocks and, at the same time, provided little risk sharing."* While this might hold on average, Germany and Austria are quite significant outliers.

Based on the diagnosis that European firms and households are too bank-dependent, the European Commission launched the Capital Markets Union (CMU) proposal, which promotes a stronger emphasis on non-bank funding channels in order to improve SME financing (European Commission 2015, Fouche, Neugebauer and Uthemann 2016). The policy strategy thus does not suggest dis-intermediation but dis-banking. The CMU-proposal builds heavily on the market- versus bank-based paradigm but, astonishingly enough, the European Commission left the issue of banking sector diversity aside (Kotz and Schäfer 2017 (editors), Kotz and Schäfer 2017).

However, while the dichotomy between market-oriented versus bank-oriented economies does serve a pedagogical purpose, it has long been inappropriate to understand the closely knit interaction between markets and intermediaries: Much of what seemingly is at the discretion of bank management is obviously largely driven by market prices. The binary view hence cannot account for a much more complex reality. For example, Gambacorta et al.'s (2014) findings, i. e. that market-based systems are (on average) better able to absorb shocks than bank-based systems, may suffer from an omitted variable problem as they do not control for the heterogeneity of diversity in banking sectors. They also disregard differences in macroeconomic environment, in particular the interaction between fiscal and monetary policy. Thus, the explanation for their findings may well be found beyond the dichotomy of market-oriented versus bank-oriented economies.

7 What role does institutional diversity play in financing SMEs?

Stein (2002) finds that large banks focus primarily on transaction-based lending and lending to large businesses. Hardie and Howarth (2013) suggest that the dominance of large banks goes hand in hand with the rise of transaction-based financing and the decline of relationship lending. Previous research proposes that relationship lending is especially important for small and medium sized firms (SMEs, see e. g. Boot 2000). These firms are often opaque and information asymmetries are particularly pertinent (Petersen and Rajan 1994 and Berger and Udell 1995). Consequently, they are more likely to be subject to financial constraints and severe funding gaps than large firms. Moreover, if SMEs are innovative the difficulties of receiving funds may even be more pronounced (see e. g. Schäfer, Stephan and Solórzano Mosquera 2016). Using US data, Berger, Miller, Petersen, Rajan and Stein (2005) reveal that smaller banks have a comparative advantage in relationship lending. Small banks are supposed to face less severe contracting problems and organizational dis-economies than larger institutions with multiple layers. They are closer to their clients, foster long-term relationships (see also the excellent survey by Hellwig 1991). De Haas, Ferreira and Taci (2010) find that small banks in transition countries lend a higher share of their loan volume to SMEs than do large banks. Behr, Norden and Noth (2013) report that local publically-owned banks in Germany reduce firms' financial constraints and have a less cyclical lending behavior. Hakenes, Hasan and Molyneux (2015) construct a theoretical model proposing that in regions with substantial hurdles in terms of access to finance, small, local banks can spur local economic growth better than larger banks, acting on an inter-regional scale. They produce confirming evidence by using German data.

Economies of specialization in relationship lending would imply that the disappearance of smaller banks is non-neutral in terms of innovation and growth. Financial access for small, opaque businesses may become more difficult (e. g. Lehmann and Neuberger 2001). Consequently, SMEs' innovation potential and growth as well as their survival chances could be hampered (Schäfer und Talavera 2009). Relationship lenders are also more likely to invest in restructuring know-how (Schäfer 2002, Brunner and Krahnen 2008) and also to stay with their clients during difficult times (D'Aurizio, Oliviero and Romano 2015).

Gambacorta and Marques-Ibanez (2011) find that during crisis periods banks with greater dependence on funding through markets and more volatile non-interest income activities restrict loan supply more than other banks do (see also Dwenger, Fossen and Simmler 2015). Bartoli, Ferri, Murro and Rotondi (2012) support the notion of complementarity between both lending technologies—transaction-based and relationship-based lending—but reject substitutability. In addition, Bolton, Freixas and Gambacorta (2016) propose that only comparatively safe firms prefer transaction-based funding while normal (risky) firms opt for a combination of transaction and relationship borrowing.

Given that the coexistence of different bank types increases the likelihood of some banks staying solvent when others are existentially hit by a crisis, the above mentioned literature implies that SMEs' resilience and growth would benefit from institutional diversity in the banking sector. Considered from these perspectives, the coexistence of large (international) and small, locally oriented, banks in a country's banking sector should be conducive for SMEs, lowering barriers to financial access and enhancing resilience.

Despite the immense importance of SME financing for innovation and growth, previous research focusing on the Eurozone member states has not yet provided conclusive evidence about the role of banking sector diversity for availability and stability of SME funding. Country-specific case studies (see Flögel in this issue), more comprehensive individual firm data in combination with country-level measures of institutional diversity in the banking sector and key indicators representing the structure of the "real" (i. e. non-financial) economy may help to make considerable progress in this respect.

8   Conclusions

Policies—as well as changes in the basic conditions of banking (e. g. technological innovations)— do have structural impacts. This, clearly holds true for the major reform initiatives the EU Commission has launched over the recent decades, including the FSAP of the early 2000s, as well as the banking regulations (leading to the CRRD IV or MiFiDII and MIFIR) and recent initiatives around the Capital Markets Union. They have a bearing on industry structure (size and number of competitors) as well as the diversity of institutions along a number of dimensions. Essentially, they often reduce diversity, increase homogeneity. Diversity, of course, comes with costs and benefits. It creates segmentation and produces gaps between markets. But it also seems to allow for improving problem solving capacities and resilience (e. g. Page 2014).

In the recent financial crisis, all else equal, those banking systems which had institutions with distinct differences in activity profiles seemed to have fared better (e. g. see Bertuch-Samuels and Schackmann-Fallis and Weiß in this issue). Interestingly, most of these banks, given their ownership structures, were less demanding in terms of their profitability objectives. Also, they were not exclusively concerned about shareholder value. Instead, they often pursued finding a balance between a more comprehensive set of objectives, including debtholders as well as employees. This showed, in particular, in differences in asset structures as well as leverage. A more diverse banking industry also seems to improve problems of access to funds, obviously for the most bank-dependent firms, i. e. SMEs. Through this channel, diversity could support innovative SMEs and thus nurture growth, coming with overall societal benefits.

Clearly, more research would be practically useful here. Financial intermediaries and markets are continuously responding to contextual changes. Thinking about a healthy—sustainable—architecture for finance is thus a lasting challenge. In light of its inevitable reverberations—there's a substantial complementarity between finance and other societal sub-systems, not touched upon here (see especially Hall and Soskice 2001 and Amable 2005)—far beyond finance, this is also a debate with high pertinence for a general public.

References

— Acharya, V. V., I. Hasan and A. Saunders (2006): Should banks be diversified? Evidence from individual bank loan portfolios. The Journal of Business, 79 (3), 1355–1412. https://ideas.repec.org/a/ucp/jnlbus/v79y2006i3p1355-1412.html

— Akins, B., L. Li, J. Ng and T.O. Rusticus (2016): Bank competition and financial stability: Evidence from the financial crisis. Journal of Financial and Quantitative Analysis, 51 (01), 1–28.

— Alesina, A. and P. Giuliano (2015): Culture and Institutions. Journal of Economic Literature, 53 (4), 898–944.

— Allen, F., and D. Gale (2000): Comparing financial systems. Cambridge, MIT Press.

— Amable, B. (2005): Les Cinq Capitalismes. Diversité des Systèmes Économiques et Sociaux dans la Modernisation. Paris, Seuil.

— Attaran, M. and M. Zwick (1987): An information theory approach to measuring industrial diversification. Journal of Economic Studies, 16 (1), 19–30.

— Ayadi, R., D. Llewellyn, R. Schmidt, E. Arbak and W. de Groen (2009): Investigating diversity in the banking sector in Europe: The performance and role of savings banks. Centre for European Policy Studies (CEPS), Brussels.

— Ayadi, R., D. Llewellyn, R. Schmidt, E. Arbak and W. de Groen (2010): Investigating diversity in the banking sector in Europe: Key developments, performance and role of cooperative banks. Centre for European Policy Studies (CEPS), Brussels.

— Baele, L., O. D. Jonghe and R. V. Vennet (2007): Does the stock market value bank diversification? Journal of Banking and Finance, 31 (7), 1999–2023. www.sciencedirect.com/science/article/pii/S0378426607000118

— Bartoli, F., G. Ferri, P. Murro and Z. Rotondi (2013): SME financing and the choice of lending technology in Italy: Complementarity or substitutability? Journal of Banking & Finance, 37 (12), 5476–5485.

— Beck, T., A. Demirguc-Kunt and R. Levine (2005): Bank concentration and fragility: Impact and mechanics. NBER Working Paper No. w11500. https://ideas.repec.org/p/nbr/nberwo/11500.html

— Beck, T., A. Demirgüc-Kunt and D. Singer (2013): Is small beautiful? Financial structure, size and access to finance. World Development, 52 (C), 19–33. https://ideas.repec.org/a/eee/wdevel/v52y2013icp19-33.html

— Beck, T., O. D. Jonghe and G. Schepens (2013): Bank competition and stability: Cross-country heterogeneity. Journal of Financial Intermediation, 22 (2), 218–244. www.sciencedirect.com/science/article/pii/S1042957312000344

— Behr, P., l. Norden and F. Noth (2013): Financial constraints of private firms and bank lending behavior. Journal of Banking & Finance, 37 (9), 3472–3485. www.sciencedirect.com/science/article/pii/S0378426613002379

— Berger, A. N. and G. F. Udell (1995): Relationship lending and lines of credit in small firm finance. The Journal of Business, 51 (01), 351–381. https://ideas.repec.org/a/ucp/jnlbus/v68y1995i3p351-81.html

— Berger, A. N., and G. F. Udell (2002): Small business credit availability and relationship lending: The importance of bank organisational structure. Economic Journal, 112 (477), F32–F53. https://ideas.repec.org/a/ecj/econjl/v112y2002i477pf32-f53.html

— Berger, A. N., and D. B. Humphrey (1997): Efficiency of financial institutions: International survey and directions for future research. European Journal of Operational Research, 98, 175–212.

— Berger, A. N., L. F. Klapper and R. Turk-Ariss (2008): Bank competition and financial stability. Policy Research Working Paper Series 4696, The World Bank. https://ideas.repec.org/p/wbk/wbrwps/4696.html

— Berger, A. N., L. F. Klapper and G. F. Udell (2001): The ability of banks to lend to informationally opaque small businesses. Journal of Banking & Finance, 25 (12), 2127–2167. www.sciencedirect.com/science/article/pii/S0378426601001893

— Berger, A. N., N. H. Miller, M. Petersen, R. Rajan, G. Raghuram and J. C. Stein (2005): Does function follow organizational form? Evidence from the lending practices of large and small banks. Journal of Financial Economics, 76 (2), 237–269.

— Bolton, P., X. Freixas and L. Gambacorta (2016): Relationship and transaction lending in a crisis. Review of Financial Studies. http://rfs.oxfordjournals.org/content/early/2016/06/06/rfs.hhw041.abstract

— Boone, J. (2008): A new way to measure competition. Economic Journal, 118, 1245–1261.

— Boot, A. W. (2000): Relationship banking: what do we know? Journal of Financial Intermediation, 9, 3–25.

— Boot, A. W. (2014): Banken echt niet gezond na deze stresstest. NRC Handelsblad (Opinie) (28 October).

— Brown, L., and R. T. Greenbaum (2017): The role of industrial diversity in economic resilience: An empirical examination across 35 years. Urban Studies, 54 (6), 1347–1366. https://doi.org/10.1177/0042098015624870

— Brunner A., and J. P. Krahnen (2008): Multiple Lenders and Corporate Distress: Evidence on Debt Restructuring. The Review of Economic Studies, 75 (2), 415–442. https://doi.org/10.1111/j.1467-937X.2008.00483.x

— Chandler, A. (1990): Scale and scope. The dynamics of industrial capitalism. Cambridge, MA, Harvard UP.

— Cihak, M., and K. Schaeck (2010): Banking competition and capital ratios. European Financial Management, 18 (5), 836–866.

— D'Aurizio, L., T. Oliviero and L. Romano (2015): Family firms, soft information and bank lending in a financial crisis. Journal of Corporate Finance, 33, 279–292. www.sciencedirect.com/science/article/pii/S0929119915000036

— De Haas, R. D., D. Ferreira and A. Taci (2010): What determines the composition of banks loan portfolios? Evidence from transition countries. Journal of Banking & Finance, 34 (2), 388–398. www.sciencedirect.com/science/article/pii/S0378426609002015

— De Nederlandsche Bank N. V. (2015): Perspective on the structure of the Dutch banking sector. DNB Study. www.dnb.nl/en/news/news-and-archive/dnbulletin-2015/dnb323320.jsp

— Degryse, H., M. Kim and S. Ongena (2009): Microeconometrics of banking. Methods, applications and results. Oxford, OUP.

— Demirgüç-Kunt, A., and M. S. Martinez Peria (2010): A framework for analyzing competition in the banking sector: An application to the case of Jordan, December 1. World Bank Policy Research Working Paper No. 5499. Available at SSRN: https://ssrn.com/abstract=1726248.

— Dertouzos, M., R. Lester and R. Solow (1989): Made in America. Regaining the productive edge. Cambridge, MIT Press.
— Dimon, J. (2016): Large banks and small banks are allies, not enemies. Wall Street Journal, April 5.
— Dwenger, N., F. M. Fossen and M. Simmler (2015): From financial to real economic crisis: Evidence from individual firm-bank relationships in Germany. Discussion Papers 150/2015. German Institute for Economic Research. https://ideas.repec.org/p/diw/diwwpp/dp1510.html
— Elton, C. S. (1958): Ecology of Invasions by Animals and Plants. London, Chapman & Hall.
— European Commission (2015): Building a capital markets union. Green Paper COM (2015). European Commission. http://eur-lex.europa.eu/legal-content/DE/TXT/?uri=CELEX:52015DC0063
— Fouche, M., K. Neugebauer and A. Uthemann (2016): SME financing in a capital markets union. Policy Research Working Paper Series. Swedish Institute for European Policy Studies.
— Gambacorta, L., and D. Marques-Ibanez (2011): The bank lending channel: Lessons from the crisis. Economic Policy, 26 (66), 135–182. https://ideas.repec.org/a/bla/ecpoli/v26y-2011i66p135-182.html
— Gambacorta, L., J. Yang and K. Tsatsaronis (2014): Financial structure and growth. BIS Quarterly Review. https://ideas.repec.org/a/bis/bisqtr/1403e.html
— Goetz, M. R. (2018): Competition and bank stability. Journal of Financial Intermediation, 35, 57–69. www.sciencedirect.com/science/article/pii/S1042957317300426
— Hakenes, H., I. Hasan, P. Molyneux and R. Xie (2015): Small banks and local economic development. Review of Finance, 19 (2), 653–683. https://ideas.repec.org/a/oup/revfin/v19y2015i2p653-683.html
— Haldane, A. G., and R. M. May (2011): Systemic risk in banking ecosystems. Nature, 469 (7330), 351–355. www.nature.com/nature/journal/v469/n7330/full/nature09659.html
— Hall, P. and D. Soskice (2001): An Introduction to Varieties of Capitalism. In: P. Hall and D. Soskice (eds.): Varieties of Capitalism: The Institutional Foundations of Comparative Advantage, Oxford, OUP.
— Hansmann, H. and R. Kraakman (2000): The end of history for corporate law. Havard Law School DP, no. 280.
— Hardie, I., and D. Howarth (eds.) (2013): Market-based banking and the international financial crisis. Oxford, Oxford University Press. http://EconPapers.repec.org/RePEc:oxp:obooks:9780199662289
— Hellwig, M. (1990): Banking, financial intermediation and corporate finance. In: A. Giovannini and C. Mayer (eds.): European financial integration. London, 35–63.
— Hoffmann, M., and B. Sorensen (2015): Small firms and domestic bank dependence in Europes great recession. Discussion Papers 2015 012. Directorate General Economic and Financial Affairs (DG ECFIN), European Commission. http://EconPapers.repec.org/RePEc:euf:dispap:012
— Kotz, H-H. (1993): Banque universelle: un avantage capital? Revue Banque 538 (June 1993), 32–36.
— Kotz, H.-H. (2004): Finanzmarktmoden. Wirtschaftsdienst, 07/2004, 32–37.
— Kotz, H.-H. (2007): Europeanization of financial market regulation: Conceiving a new model by default? Droit et Société, no. 65, 75–89. www.cairn.info/revue-droit-et-societe1-2007-1-page-75.html

— Kotz, H.-H., A. Hackethal and M. Tyrell (2007): Les banques coopératives en Allemagne: performance et défis. Association d'Économie Financière. Rapport Morale, no. 7, Paris. www.aef.asso.fr/publications/rapport-moral-sur-l-argent-dans-le-monde/rapport-moral-2007/les-banques-coop-eacute-ratives-en-allemagne-performance-et-d-eacute-fis.

— Kotz, H.-H., and D. Schäfer (2017): Can the Capital Markets Union deliver? Vierteljahrshefte zur Wirtschaftsforschung, 2/2017, 89–98.

— Kotz, H.-H., and D. Schäfer (2017) (eds.): EU Capital Markets Union: An alluring opportunity or a blind alley? The macro-perspective: CMU and risk-sharing. Vierteljahrshefte zur Wirtschaftsforschung, 2/2017, 5–7.

— Langfield, S., and M. Pagano (2016): Bank bias in Europe: Effects on systemic risk and growth. Economic Policy, 31 (85), 51–106.

— Lehmann, E., and D. Neuberger (2001): Do lending relationships matter? Evidence from bank survey data in Germany. Journal of Economic Behavior & Organization, 45 (4), 339–359. www.sciencedirect.com/science/article/pii/S0167268101001512

— Markowitz, H. (1959): Portfolio selection efficient diversification of investment. New York, John Wiley & Sons.

— McCann, K. (2000): The diversity-stability debate. Nature, 405, May, 228–233.

— Melitz, J. (1990): Financial Deregulation in France. European Economic Review, no. 2/3, 394–402.

— Mesnard, B., A. Margerit, C. Power and M. Magnus (2015): Non-performing loans in the Banking Union: Stocktaking and challenges. Briefing Directorate-General for Internal Policies, Economic Governance Support Unit, 2015.

— Michie, J., C. Oughton (2013): Measuring diversity in financial services markets: A diversity index. Discussion paper series. Centre for Financial and Management Studies CeFiMS, University of London. www.cefims.ac.uk/cgi-bin/research.cgi

— Page, S. E. (2014): Where diversity comes from and why it matters? European Journal of Social Psychology, 44, 267–279.

— Petersen, M. A., and R. G. Rajan (1994): The benefits of lending relationships: Evidence from small business data. Journal of Finance, 49 (1), 3–37. https://ideas.repec.org/a/bla/jfinan/v49y1994i1p3-37.html

— Putnam, R. D. (1993): Making democracy work: Civic traditions in modern Italy. Princeton, Princeton University Press.

— Roe, M. (2003): Political determinants of corporate governance. Political context, corporate impact, OUP, Oxford.

— Schaeck, K., and M. Cihák (2010): Competition, efficiency, and soundness in banking: An industrial organization perspective. Discussion Paper 2010-68S. Tilburg University, Center for Economic Research. https://ideas.repec.org/p/tiu/tiucen/35600d21-0ec7-40be-9a18-55b0bbd7af5d.html

— Schaeck, K., S. Wolfe and M. Cihàk (2009): Are competitive banking systems more stable? Journal of Money, Credit and Banking, 41 (4), 711–734. http://dx.doi.org/10.1111/j.1538-4616.2009.00228.x

— Schäfer, D. (2002): Restructuring know how and collateral. Kredit und Kapital, 35 (4), 572–597. www.econstor.eu/handle/10419/127479

— Schäfer, D., B. Siliverstovs and E. Terberger (2010): Banking competition, good or bad? The case of promoting micro and small enterprise finance in Kazakhstan. Applied Economics, 42 (6), 701–716. http://dx.doi.org/10.1080/00036840701720820

— Schäfer, D., A. Stephan and J. Solórzano Mosquera (2017). Family ownership: Does it matter for funding and success of corporate innovations? Small Business Economics, 48 (4), 931–951.
— Schäfer, D., and O. Talavera (2009): Small business survival and inheritance: Evidence from Germany. Small Business Economics, 32 (1), 95–109. https://ideas.repec.org/a/kap/sbusec/v32y2009i1p95-109.html
— Stein, J.C. (2002): Information production and capital allocation: Decentralized versus hierarchical firms. The Journal of Finance, 57 (5), 1891–1921. http://dx.doi.org/10.1111/0022-1082.00483
— Stiglitz, J., and A. Weiss (1990): Banks as social accountants and screening devices for the allocation of credit. Greek Economic Review, 12, Supplement, Autumn, 85–118.
— Stiroh, K.J. and A. Rumble (2006): The dark side of diversification: The case of US financial holding companies. Journal of Banking & Finance, 30 (8), 2131–2161. www.sciencedirect.com/science/article/pii/S0378426605001342
— Tilman, D. (1999): The ecological consequences of changes in biodiversity: A search for general principles. Ecology, 80, 1455–1474.
— Vestager, M. (2018): Strength in diversity. Speech, 20 November 2018. https://ec.europa.eu/commission/commissioners/2014-2019/vestager/announcements/strength-diversity_en

AUTHORS

Axel Bertuch-Samuels most recently served as the IMF's Special Representative to the United Nations from 2012–2016. He previously held the positions of Deputy Director in the Monetary and Capital Markets Department and of Special Advisor to the IMF's Managing Director. Prior to joining the Fund, he served as Director of the President's Office at the European Bank for Reconstruction and Development (EBRD) in London and, before that, he was Chief Economist of the Association of German Savings Banks (DSGV). His career as an economist began at the German Federal Ministry of Finance, where he rose to become the Deputy Minister's Personal Advisor. He graduated in economics from the University of Cologne, Germany, in 1984, and subsequently participated in the Summer Internship Program at the IMF.

Andreas Bley, Dr. rer. pol., was born in 1965 in Bonn. He studied economics at the Free University of Berlin and then worked as a scientific assistant at the Institute for Economic Theory there from 1993 to 1997. After completing his doctorate on a labor market theory topic, he worked at Landeszentralbank Berlin-Brandenburg in the Department for Economics from 1997 to 2001. In 2001, he joined the National Association of German Cooperative Banks (BVR) in Berlin, where he was a senior economist until 2008. He is currently head of the Department for Economic Research, where the core task areas are business cycle analysis, economic forecasts, financing, monetary policy, and SME policy (Mittelstandspolitik).

Giovanni Ferri, Ph.D., full professor of Economics at LUMSA, Rome, where he directs the Master in Management of Sustainable Development Goals (http://mastermsdg.lumsa.it). Prior to that he worked at the University of Bari, the World Bank and the Banca d'Italia. He visited: Hong Kong Monetary Authority, University of Tokyo, Asian Development Bank Institute (Tokyo), Princeton University, NBER. He is editor-in-chief of Economic Notes and of the Journal of Entrepreneurial and Organizational Diversity. He has led (or participated in) research and policy projects in Europe, the Middle East and East Asia. He conducts research on: money, banking and finance, rating agencies, corporate governance, finance-growth links, family business, migration, company internationalization, Chinese economy, inequality, sustainability.

Franz Flögel, Dr., has been a research associate at the Institute for Work and Technology (Westfälischen Hochschule Gelsenkirchen) since 2010. He works in the Spatial Capital research department. He studied human geography, economics, and political science at the University of Potsdam, Humboldt University of Berlin, and the University of Nottingham. In 2017, he completed his PhD at the professorship of Economic Geography at the Catholic University of Eichstätt-Ingolstadt. In his PhD thesis he compared the lending processes of regional and large banks in SME finance. His key research interest lies in finance and regional development.

Stefan Gärtner, Dr., (banker, Dipl.-Ing. in spatial planning, urban planner) is the head of the Space Capital research department at the Institute for Work and Technology (Westfälischen Hochschule Gelsenkirchen). He studied spatial planning at the Technical University of Dortmund and the University of Liverpool. He received his PhD in spatial planning at TU Dortmund, focusing on the importance of savings banks for balanced regional development in Germany. His research focuses on regional development and regional structural policy, sustainable economies, and space and banking.

Horst Gischer, Prof. Dr., is Professor for Monetary Economics and Public Financial Institu-tions at Otto-von-Guericke University Magdeburg and Managing Director of the Research Center for Savings Banks' Development (Forschungszentrum für Sparkassenentwicklung e. V.). He studied economics at the University of Dortmund and holds as well a doctoral and habilitation degree in Economics from the University of Dortmund. He has conducted many national and interna-tional research projects and published extensively in international journals in the relevant fields. His current research focuses on Monetary Macroeconomics, in particular indicator properties of interest rate structures, Industrial Economics, in particular problems in imperfect markets and financial systems together with financial market regulation.

Christian Ilchmann, M. Sc., born 1991, studied economic sciences and economics at Dresden Uni-versity of Tech-nology. After an intern at the ifo Institute, Dresden Branch, he is currently research and teach-ing associate at the Chair of Monetary Economics and Public Financial Institutions at Otto-von-Guericke University Magdeburg. His research focuses on the integration of the financial economy and the real economy, financial systems together with financial market regulation and monetary policy.

Hans-Helmut Kotz is a Program Director at the SAFE Policy Center, Goethe University, Frankfurt as well as a Resident Fellow at Harvard University's Center for European Studies where he is also a visiting professor in the Economics Department. Moreover, Kotz is a member of the Econom-ics Faculty at Freiburg University. In addition, he is a Senior Advisor to McKinsey & Co. as well as the McKinsey Global Institute, mainly involved in macroeconomic, financial markets and risk issues. He serves as well as Non-Executive Director on the Board of Caixa Geral de Depósitos, Lis-bon. Between 2002 and 2010 Prof. Kotz has been a Member of the Executive Board of Deutsche Bundesbank, in charge of Financial Stability, Markets and Statistics. He was also a member of committees of the Bank for International Settlements, the Financial Stability Board as well as the OECD, where he was chair of the Financial Markets Committee. He was also the German Central Bank Deputy for the G7 and the G20 processes. Prior to that, he was President of the Landeszen-tralbank Bremen, Lower Saxony and Saxony Anhalt (1999–2002) and before that Chief Economist of Deutsche Girozentrale (1984–1999).

Doris Neuberger, Dr., full professor of Economics—Money and Credit—at the University of Ros-tock. Research Fellow DIW Berlin, co-director CERBE (Center for Relationship Banking and Eco-nomics) Rome, research director iff Hamburg, founding member of Bürgerbewegung Finanz-wende (Finance Watch Germany). Member of: Bündnis gegen den Wucher (Alliance against Usury), Senate Competition Committee of the Leibniz Association, Committee for Industrial Economics at the German Economic Association (Verein für Socialpolitik). Co-editor of Quarterly Journal of Economic Research and of Economic Notes. Doctorate and habilitation at the Friedrich-Alexander-University Erlangen-Nuremberg. Main areas of research: household finance and con-sumer protection, SME finance, Industrial Economics of banking, financial systems, social role of banks Professorin für Volkswirtschaftslehre—Geld und Kredit—an der Universität Rostock. Research Fellow DIW Berlin, Kodirektorin CERBE (Center for Relationship Banking and Econom-ics) Rom, Forschungsdirektorin iff Hamburg, Gründungsmitglied der Bürgerbewegung Finanz-wende/Finance Watch Deutschland. Mitglied von: Bündnis gegen den Wucher, Senatsausschuss Wettbewerb der Leibniz-Gemeinschaft, Industrieökonomischer Ausschuss des Vereins für So-cialpolitik. Mitherausgeberin der Vierteljahrshefte zur Wirtschaftsforschung und der Economic Notes. Promotion und Habilitation an der Friedrich-Alexander-Universität Erlangen-Nürnberg.

Forschungsschwerpunkte: Household Finance und Verbraucherschutz, Finanzierung von KMU, Industrieökonomik der Bank, Finanzsysteme, Gesellschaftliche Rolle von Banken.

Karl-Peter Schackmann-Fallis, Dr, has been an Executive Member of the Board of the German Savings Banks Association (DSGV) since November 2004, with responsibility for the economics, politics and banking management division. Prior to this, he was Secretary of State for Finance in both Brandenburg and Saxony-Anhalt. After completing his PhD in Economics, he began his career at Germany's Federal Ministry of Economics. As well as his responsibilities on the Board of the DSGV, Dr Schackmann-Fallis holds a number of other posts, including Chairman of the Supervisory Board of S-Rating GmbH, Managing Director of the Savings Banks Protection Scheme and Member of the Board of Administration as well as of the Risk and Credit Committee of the Landesbank Hessen-Thüringen. Since 2004 he has been a Member of the Advisory Board of the German Federal Financial Supervisory Authority (BaFin) and since September 2015 a Member of the European Economic and Social Committee (EESC).

Dorothea Schäfer, Dr., Habilitation in Business Economics, Diploma in Economics, Research Director Financial Markets at the German Institute for Economic Research (DIW Berlin), Adjunct Professor of Jönköping International Business School, Jönköping University; Editor-in-Chief of the Eurasian Economic Review (EAER) and of the Vierteljahrshefte zur Wirtschaftsforschung (Quarterly Journal of Economic Research); Head of various research projects, inter alia, funded by the German Science Foundation (Deutsche Forschungsgemeinschaft DFG), the EU Commission, the Fritz Thyssen Stiftung and the Stiftung Geld und Währung; Evaluator/reviewer of research programs/proposals for the German Science Foundation, EU Commission, the Federal Ministry of Education and Research (BMBF) and the LOEWE (Initiative for the Development of Scientific and Economic Excellence, State of Hesse: Chairwoman of the committees for the evaluation of the LOEWE center SAFE-Sustainable Architecture for Finance in Europe). She has published in The European Journal of Finance, Finance Research Letters, Small Business Economics, the Journal of Financial Stability, the International Journal of Money and Finance, German Economic Review, Economics of Transition, the Journal of Comparative Economics, the Journal of Institutional and Theoretical Economics and many other journals. She is a co-organizer of the DIW Lectures on Money and Finance which brings together representatives of government, legislatures, the financial sector, think tanks, and academia to discuss how policy makers and monetary authorities can create policies and regulations that foster a more sustainable financial system. Schäfer gave expert testimonies for the Finance Committee of the Deutsche Bundestag, for the Committee on Social Affairs, Health and Sustainable Development, Parliamentary Assembly, The Council of Europe and for the Commission on the Financing of the Nuclear Phase-out. She was advisor to the Enquete Committee of Deutsche Bundestag, "Growth—Prosperity—Quality of Life" (Wachstum Wohlstand Lebensqualität) of the German Bundestag, Sub-Committee "Policy for a Sustainable Political and Economic Governance" (Nachhaltige Ordnungspolitik) and gave expert testimony in the preparatory meeting for the European Parliament Committee on Economic and Monetary Affairs ahead of the European Parliament's Monetary Dialogue with the President of the European Central Bank.

Reinhard H. Schmidt has been a senior professor in the Finance Department of the Goethe University in Frankfurt since his retirement in 2013. His research and teaching activities in recent years have focused on the comparison of financial systems and finances in developing countries, countries in transition, and emerging economies. He publishes work regularly on both topics in national and international journals. In the field of development aid, he has worked as a consultant and an expert. Mr. Schmidt is a member of the European Shadow Financial Regulatory Committee (ESFRC).

Mechthild Schrooten holds a professorship in economics with focus on money and international integration at the City University of Applied Sciences Bremen. She is the director of both, International Studies in Global Management (ISGM, B.A) and of the master program in Global Management (MGM; MBA). She is speaker of the „Arbeitsgruppe Alternative Wirtschaftspolitik" (Memogruppe) which offers a heterodox-keynesian analysis of recent economic trends. Her actual research focus liesi n modern forms of money especially in the context of international financial transactions. Until 2007, she worked in DIW Berlin, her last position was deputy head of department "international economics".

Lorenzo Bini Smaghi is currently the Chairman of Société Générale. He is also Project Associate at the Harvard Kennedy School's Belfer Center for Science and International Affairs and Senior Fellow at LUISS School of European Political Economy in Rome. He is also Chairman of Italgas and a member of the Board of Tages Holding, and President of the Italian Alumni of the University of Chicago. From June 2005 to December 2011 he was a Member of the Executive Board of the European Central Bank. He started his career in 1983 as an Economist in the Research Department of the Banca d'Italia. In 1994 he moved to the European Monetary Institute, in Frankfurt, to head the Policy Division, to prepare for the creation of the ECB. In 1998 he became Director General for International Affairs in the Italian Treasury, acting as G7 and G20 Deputy and Vice President of the Economic and Financial Committee of the EU. He was also Chairman of the WP3 of the OECD. He has been Chairman of the Board of SNAM, SACE, and member of the Boards of Finmeccanica, MTS, the European Investment Bank and Morgan Stanley International. He was the first Chairman of Fondazione Palazzo Strozzi, a cultural institution in Florence. He holds a Bachelor's Degree in Economics from the Université Catholique de Louvain (Belgium), a Master's degree from the University of Southern California and a Ph.D from the University of Chicago. He is author of several articles and books on international and European monetary and financial issues (available in www.lorenzobinismaghi.com). He published „Austerity: European Democracies against the Wall" (CEPS, July 2013), „33 false verità sull'Europa" (Il Mulino, April 2014) and "La tentazione di andarsene: fuori dall'Europa c'è un futuro per l'Italia?" (Il Mulino, May 2017).

Mirko Weiß, Dr, studied economics at Otto-von-Guericke-University Magdeburg and Macquarie University Sydney; scholarship holder of the Studienstiftung des deutschen Volkes. 2009 Doctorate (Dr. rer. pol.) at the Faculty of Economics of the Otto-von-Guericke-University Magdeburg (Dissertation: Zur Geldpolitik im Eurowährungsraum – Beschreibung, Auswirkung und Ursachenanalyse von Inflationsunterschieden). Since 2008 advisor at the Deutscher Sparkassen- und Giroverband (DSGV) in the field of "Sparkassen Policy, Banking Regulation, Deposit Insurance". He is also lecturer at the Otto-von-Guericke-University Magdeburg in the economic master programme, a member of the Managerkreises der Friedrich-Ebert-Stiftung and member of the selection committee for the promotion of gifted students at the Studienstiftung des deutschen Volkes. Various German and English publications in the fields of structural issues of banking and financial markets, banking regulation, monetary policy and fiscal federalism.

HINWEISE FÜR AUTORINNEN UND AUTOREN DER VIERTELJAHRSHEFTE

Die Vierteljahrshefte zur Wirtschaftsforschung werden seit 1927 vom DIW Berlin herausgegeben. Sie veröffentlichen Aufsätze zu aktuellen wirtschaftspolitischen Fragestellungen und wenden sich an Wissenschaft, Politik und Wirtschaft.

Alle Beiträge werden begutachtet. Die Themen der nächsten Schwerpunkthefte und ausführliche Hinweise für Autorinnen und Autoren können der DIW-Internetseite entnommen werden (www.diw.de). Beiträge sind an die Redaktion, die Heftverantwortlichen oder zu Händen Ellen Müller-Gödtel einzusenden. Berücksichtigt werden nur Originalbeiträge, die im Falle der Annahme auch tatsächlich zur Veröffentlichung in den Vierteljahrsheften zur Verfügung stehen.

Die Beiträge sind bei deutschsprachigen Heften in deutscher und bei englischsprachigen Heften in englischer Sprache zu verfassen. Bei englischsprachigen Heften sollten die Autorinnen und Autoren ein professionelles Proofreading vor Abgabe ihres Beitrages durchführen lassen. Beiträge von englischsprachigen Autorinnen und Autoren können in deutschsprachige Hefte nur Eingang finden, wenn sie vorher übersetzt wurden. Eine Zusammenfassung des Beitrags ist in deutscher und in englischer Sprache gesondert zu erstellen. Diese soll jeweils nicht mehr als 150 Wörter umfassen. Außerdem müssen dem Manuskript mindestens drei Begriffe der JEL-Klassifikation (www.aeaweb.org/journal/jel_class_system.html) und mindestens drei englischsprachige Keywords beigefügt werden. Neben dem Regelfall des deutschsprachigen Heftes sind auch Vierteljahrshefte in englischer Sprache möglich, wenn die Themenstellung dies nahelegt.

Das Manuskript ist in Schriftgröße 12 pt im Zeilenabstand von 1,5 zu erstellen und mit einem linken und rechten Rand von 2,5 cm zu versehen. Der Umfang des Manuskripts sollte 15 Seiten (circa 30 000 Zeichen, ohne Tabellen und Abbildungen) nicht überschreiten. Die Zitierweise ist den Aufsätzen des Vierteljahrsheftes beziehungsweise der oben genannten Internetseite zu entnehmen.

Der Textteil ist in MS Word zu liefern. Tabellen und Abbildungen sind als separate Dateien (Tabellen in MS Excel, Abbildungen zusammen mit den zugrunde liegenden Daten – entweder ebenfalls in Excel oder einem anderen gängigen Grafikprogramm) zu liefern. Die Stellen, an denen sie im Text erscheinen sollen, müssen im Manuskript markiert werden. Die maximale Breite von Tabellen und Abbildungen beträgt 12,6 cm. Bei Tabellen die Zeilen- und Spaltenmerkmale bitte übersichtlich aufteilen. Anmerkungen und Fußnoten sowie Quellenangabe(n) bitte unter dem Tabellenfeld beziehungsweise der Grafik positionieren.

Wichtiger Hinweis: Falls Sie Abbildungen oder Ähnliches aus dem Internet entnehmen, bitten wir um Mitlieferung einer Kopie der Druckgenehmigung.

Table of contents 2018

Vierteljahrshefte zur Wirtschaftsforschung 3.2018
GELD UND DIE WELT

DANK AN DIE GUTACHTERINNEN UND GUTACHTER

Die Redaktion der „Vierteljahrshefte zur Wirtschaftsforschung" dankt den Heftherausgebern und den weiteren Gutachterinnen und Gutachtern, die im Jahr 2018 die eingereichten Manuskripte beurteilt haben. Ein ergänzendes Gutachten haben erstellt:

A THANK YOU TO THE REFEREES

The Editorial Board of the „Quarterly Journal of Economic Research" wishes to extend its thanks to the editors of the respective journal issues and all other referees who have given their appraisements on manuscripts submitted to the journal in 2018. Additional reports have been written by:

Heft 1/2018

Kornelia Hagen, DIW Berlin – Deutsches Institut für Wirtschaftsforschung

Heft 2/2018

Kornelia Hagen, DIW Berlin – Deutsches Institut für Wirtschaftsforschung

Heft 3/2018

Mechthild Schrooten, Hochschule Bremen

Heft 4/2018

Dorothea Schäfer, DIW Berlin – Deutsches Institut für Wirtschaftsforschung